The Presidency of
GEORGE
WASHINGTON

AMERICAN PRESIDENCY SERIES

Donald R. McCoy, Clifford S. Griffin, Homer E. Socolofsky
General Editors

George Washington, Forrest McDonald
John Adams, Ralph Adams Brown
Thomas Jefferson, Forrest McDonald
James Madison, Robert Allen Rutland
John Quincy Adams, Mary W. M. Hargreaves
Martin Van Buren, Major L. Wilson
William Henry Harrison & John Tyler, Norma Lois Peterson
James K. Polk, Paul H. Bergeron
Zachary Taylor & Millard Fillmore, Elbert B. Smith
James Buchanan, Elbert B. Smith
Andrew Johnson, Albert Castel
Rutherford B. Hayes, Ari Hoogenboom
James A. Garfield & Chester A. Arthur, Justus D. Doenecke
Grover Cleveland, Richard E. Welch, Jr.
Benjamin Harrison, Homer E. Socolofsky & Allan B. Spetter
William McKinley, Lewis L. Gould
William Howard Taft, Paolo E. Coletta
Warren G. Harding, Eugene P. Trani & David L. Wilson
Herbert C. Hoover, Martin L. Fausold
Harry S. Truman, Donald R. McCoy
Dwight D. Eisenhower, Elmo Richardson
Lyndon B. Johnson, Vaughn Davis Bornet

The Presidency of
GEORGE
WASHINGTON

by
Forrest McDonald

UNIVERSITY PRESS OF KANSAS

© Copyright 1974 by the University Press of Kansas
Printed in the United States of America

10 9 8 7 6 5 4

Library of Congress Cataloging in Publication Data

McDonald, Forrest.
The Presidency of George Washington.

(American Presidency series)
Bibliography: p.
1. United States—Politics and government—1789-1797.
2. Washington, George, Pres. U. S., 1732-1799.
I. Title.   II. Series.
E311.M12   973.4′1′0924 [B]   73-11344
ISBN 0-7006-0110-4

To
Sam—the Best Man
I Know

Editors' Preface

The aim of the American Presidency Series is to present historians and the general reading public with interesting, scholarly assessments of the various presidential administrations. These interpretive surveys are intended to cover the broad ground between biographies, specialized monographs, and journalistic accounts. As such, each will be a comprehensive, synthetic work which will draw upon the best in pertinent secondary literature, yet leave room for the author's own analysis and interpretation.

Each volume in the series will deal with a separate presidential administration and will present the data essential to understanding the administration under consideration. Particularly, each book will treat the then current problems facing the United States and its people and how the president and his associates felt about, thought about, and worked to cope with these problems. Attention will be given to how the office developed and operated during the president's tenure. Equally important will be consideration of the vital relationships between the president, his staff, the executive officers, Congress, foreign representatives, the judiciary, state officials, the public, political parties, the press, and influential private citizens. The series will also be concerned with how this unique American institution—the presidency—was viewed by the presidents, and with what results.

All this will be set, insofar as possible, in the context not only of contemporary politics but also of economics, international relations, law, morals, public administration, religion, and thought. Such a broad approach is necessary to understanding, for a presidential administration is more than the elected and appointed officers composing it, since its work so often reflects the major problems, anxieties, and glories of the nation. In short, the authors in the series will strive to recount and evaluate the record of each administration and to identify its distinctiveness and relationships to the past, its own time, and the future.

Donald R. McCoy
Clifford S. Griffin
Homer E. Socolofsky

Preface

The significance of George Washington to the presidency of the United States is somewhat different from what is commonly supposed. He was indispensable to the American experiment in self-government, and the success of his administration made possible the success of the government. And yet, as his actions and the quality of his leadership as president are appraised in the following pages, the reader may wonder just what made Washington himself so special. Among others, his chief justice, two of his cabinet members, and his most trusted adviser in the House of Representatives will appear to have been at least as able as he was—and considerably more important in formulating the programs and policies that insured the perdurance of the federal government.

Yet there is more to the institution of the presidency than what any particular president does: there is a symbolic, ritualistic, almost mystical quality that inheres in the office as well, and it was toward the endowment of the office with that vital if elusive quality that Washington's greatest contribution was directed.

Indeed, it is no exaggeration to say that, but for George Washington, the office of president might well not exist. I do not mean to suggest that his generalship was indispensable in the war that gave birth to the nation; that may or may not be true. Rather, I suggest that the Americans of the Revolutionary generation, given their fear and distrust of executive authority, would not have been willing to make the presidency part of the Constitution at all had not Washington been available to fill the office.

Therein lies a dual mystery about the man: that the American people so trusted him and that historians have paid so little attention to the fact. Eighteenth-century Americans were a contentious lot, and their historians have been even more so; yet neither has found it especially surprising that a nation of independent and cantankerous people could have been unanimous on a question of such moment.

The answer is partly—but only partly—to be found in Washington's career before 1789. He was born into Virginia's lesser gentry in 1732, though his inheritance was meager, for when his father died in 1743 most of the estate went to George's eldest half-brother,

Lawrence. From Lawrence, whom he idolized, George acquired an almost insatiable appetite for land and for military glory. In pursuit of land he was eminently successful. In addition to what he was able to acquire as compensation for services as a surveyor and soldier, he got most of the family acreage when Lawrence died in 1752 and a great deal more when he married the widow Martha Custis six years later. Glory, however, proved elusive: through family connections he obtained high military commissions at a tender age, but in the fighting that led to and took place during the French and Indian War, he showed himself to be considerably more courageous than wise. Ignored by his British superiors once the fighting became serious, he felt compelled to resign, and his disappointment rankled. His hostility toward all things English grew steadily in the sixties and seventies, for British commercial and land policies somewhat hampered his continuing pursuit of wealth—though not enough to prevent him from becoming quite rich. Like most Virginia planters, he saw British policies as a conspiracy to deprive Americans of their life, liberty, and property and was entirely unperturbed by the fact that his own fortune was built upon the labor of slaves and the blood of Indians.

When the Revolution came, the Continental Congress chose Washington as commander in chief, partly because rivals for the post were limited in both numbers and qualifications. Partly, too, he was chosen because, as John Adams candidly admitted, he looked like a general, having a bearing and demeanor that inspired instant and total confidence. (He was cool and aloof, and tall, broad-shouldered, and narrow-hipped; and in a country populated mainly by people who were hot-tempered and overly confidential, and short and fat, such attributes were not to be taken lightly.) As a general, his tactics were mediocre but his strategy was sound: be patient, play the Fabian, never do battle unless the odds are in one's favor, and wait for the enemy to make a fatal mistake. After six long years the British made the fatal mistake, and at the Battle of Yorktown (October 1781), Washington and the United States won their independence. That was the only decisive major military battle he ever won, and afterward he retired. The victory made him a hero, and the retirement made him an even greater one: he was likened to the ancient Roman Cincinnatus, the noble farmer who saved the Republic from the Aequians and then voluntarily laid down the mantle of power.

Washington came out of retirement to serve in the Constitutional Convention of 1787. He was chosen as president of that body, for not even George III would have been comfortable presiding over a man of such splendid bearing; but he added to that convention little more than his august presence.

The pages that follow pick up the story at that point—or rather, just afterward, when Washington became president by the unanimous vote of the electors.

As I have suggested, my account of Washington's presidency may leave the reader mystified by the man's virtual deification in his own times. The solution to the mystery is here, however, if the reader will approach the story in a proper spirit. To be an American in the last decade of the eighteenth century was to be present at the crucial myth-making time in the infancy of the Republic; it was comparable to being a Roman in the age of Romulus and Remus, or a Greek in the age of the Olympians. Thucydides and Herodotus, it is said, invented history by distinguishing what "could be proved to have happened" from that which could not be so proved. The former we call history; the latter we call myth. Here we are dealing with a myth that happens also to have been true, for George Washington, in his own lifetime, was self-consciously both more than a mere man and less than a man: his people craved a myth and a symbol, and he devoted his life to fulfilling that need.

Forrest McDonald

Grosse Pointe, Michigan
April 1973

Contents

1

★★★★★

THE UNITED STATES IN 1789

"The sacred fire of liberty and the destiny of the republican model of government," declared George Washington in 1789, were deeply and finally staked "on the experiment intrusted to the hands of the American people."

That was strong stuff, emanating as it did from the first chief executive of the newest and least civilized member of the Western family of nations. Englishmen, especially, could view Washington's claim as pretentious, for it was from England, after all, that the Americans had derived their very idea of liberty. Moreover, almost every thinking Englishman would have regarded as absurd the new president's coupling of liberty with republicanism. "The greater the share the people have in government," wrote the Methodist theologian John Wesley, "the less liberty, civil or religious, does a nation enjoy." Virtually every Englishman, and no small number of silent Americans, shared that sentiment.

But England, like nearly every other civilized country, was a monarchy, and since 1776 Americans had been irrevocably committed to the proposition that only a republican government could be truly free. Questionable as that commitment was, Americans had stuck with it through trying times, and a recent turn of events had rekindled their faith. It was that turn of events which made Washington's grandiose pronouncement possible.

What had happened was that the Americans had reconstituted their government, so thoroughly as to undo most of the mischief they

1

had created when declaring their independence. In a fit of euphoria they had, on the earlier occasion, cast off the restraints that most of them, in calmer times, would have regarded as essential to good government and indeed to the survival of a political society. Rejecting central authority with excessive enthusiasm, they had lodged power in thirteen virtually unrestrained state governments, under the loose coordination of a general Congress; rejecting monarchy with equal abandon, they had emasculated their several governments by depriving them of viable executive authority. The consequence—as the wisest men everywhere would have predicted, and the more perceptive Americans came to realize—was that the lamp of liberty was very nearly extinguished before the country was a decade old. But then, by writing and adopting the Constitution of 1787, the Americans won a second chance for their grand experiment in self-government.

In one sense there was nothing especially novel about the Constitution, apart from a few details and the fact that it was more or less adopted by popular consent; in the main, it was but a combination of principles and practices evolved through a long period of colonial apprenticeship. Only two things about it were genuinely radical. The first was the means by which Americans now proposed to protect their liberties under a system of self-government. Recent experience had demonstrated (as philosophers had taught) that unrestrained popular government could be as great a menace to freedom as was unchecked monarchy or aristocracy. In England restraint was provided, and therefore liberty was made safe, by a general reverence, felt among high and low, for tradition and for established institutions. In America neither form of reverence was particularly noticeable. What the Constitution proposed as a substitute for social restraint was restraint in government, in an entirely new kind of way: not so much in limiting what government could do, but rather in strictly defining the rules by which publicly sanctioned power could be exercised.

The second radical feature—not radical in the Western world at large, but in the context of the Americans' colonial and recent experience—was that the Constitution provided for a strong and energetic executive authority. Executive power had been the object of distrust in America for a long time: in two colonies the governors had been figureheads, and in most of the others the governor and his sycophants were regarded as alien forces, to be resisted or circumvented when it proved impossible to colonialize them or make them subordinate to local legislative assemblies. As to the Crown, loyalty

2

had been professed and felt in the South only to the extent that the Crown remained an abstract symbol rather than actual authority, and in New England loyalty had been barely professed and felt almost not at all. In the propaganda of the Revolution—and especially in the two most persuasive pieces, Thomas Paine's *Common Sense* and Thomas Jefferson's Declaration of Independence—blame for most of the sufferings of mankind was placed in the lap of the executive branch of government. In the Articles of Confederation and the Revolutionary state constitutions, executive power was all but nonexistent.

Given such a tradition, the creation of the presidency was almost as great an achievement as the creation of the national government itself. Sensitivity on the matter had, in fact, been so marked that the members of the Constitutional Convention of 1787 spent more time debating how the executive branch would be constituted than they spent on any other subject; and in the end they found it expedient (or possible) to sketch the presidency only in broad strokes, in contrast to the careful detail in which they specified the powers, duties, and make-up of the legislative branch.

If Americans could accustom themselves to the central idea that power could be exercised only according to the Constitution's rules of the game, if they could part with accustomed norms enough to permit the development of a viable executive authority, and if certain pressing problems could be resolved within the framework of these innovations, then they stood a fair chance of success in their radical attempt to combine liberty and popular government.

The United States had one vital, if short-lived, advantage in the undertaking, for the Western world was at peace. This was an abnormal condition for the times. During the preceding fifty years Britain, France, Spain, Prussia, and Austria had been at war with one another, in various combinations, almost exactly half the time, and they would be at war again three years out of four in the quarter-century beginning in 1792. Moreover, when war resumed, it would become almost impossible for the United States to remain uninvolved, for dominance of America was one of the bones over which the hungry hounds of Europe contended. But in the meantime, for almost the entirety of Washington's first administration—the crucial formative years—there was peace.

If the Americans were to make the most of this blessing, however, they had to move swiftly and decisively to abate—or better yet, to harness, in the national interest—a number of tensions and difficulties that beset the country. In general terms, these may be viewed

3

under three broad headings—the political, the economic, and the socio-cultural. Each must be understood before sense can be made of the presidency of George Washington.

The best republican political theorists taught, and public figures from Washington down to New England town moderators declared, that the spirit of party and faction was the sorest curse that could infest a republic, but several states had long since evolved rudimentary party systems. The oldest was that in Pennsylvania, where Proprietary and Antiproprietary "parties" had existed at least as early as the 1720s. To be sure, there was not much continuity of personnel, principle, or interest as the Pennsylvania parties were reconstituted during the French and Indian War, during the Revolution, and during the fight over ratification of the Constitution. The habit of organizing political conflict around the differences between two distinct parties, however, was continuous and deep-rooted.

Three other states had two-party systems of more recent origin, but seemed headed toward the kind of institutionalization of habit that prevailed in Pennsylvania. In New York the Delancey-versus-Livingston split in the colonial aristocracy had died when the Delanceyites embraced Loyalism during the Revolution; but a new split had solidified in the 1780s with Governor George Clinton and his adherents, mainly a middling sort of men-on-the-make, combined on one side, and an unlikely coalition of upstate aristocrats and city workers gathered on the other. In Rhode Island the colonial division between factions headed by Samuel Ward and Stephen Hopkins, centered in the rival ports of Newport and Providence, had lately undergone permutations based upon an extremely complex diversity of economic interests; but there, too, the habit of a two-way split in political allegiance was taking firm roots. In New Jersey the colonial division between East Jersey and West Jersey proprietors continued to have popular political appeal, for people in the northeastern and southwestern halves of the state differed sharply in their economic interests and ethnic and religious backgrounds.

Rather more commonly, but no less potently, postwar political alignments within states were based upon allegiance to families or individual leaders. In New Hampshire and Maryland such alignments were relatively simple, revolving in the one around the rivalry between John Langdon and John Sullivan and in the other around the hostility between Samuel Chase and Charles Carroll, though in both these states attachments were tenuous and unstable. In Virginia, Massachusetts, and North Carolina personal followings were considerably more numerous but far more durable.

Otherwise, state politics were dominated by shifting coalitions of factions, as James Madison defined the term—groups brought together by common interests or prejudices, contrary to the needs or desires of the society at large. This was almost unreservedly true of Connecticut, Delaware, and Georgia, somewhat less so of the remaining state, South Carolina. The low-country aristocracy in South Carolina was solid in its domination of the middle- and up-country farmers, whose political voice was minimized by a malapportionment of legislative seats in favor of the low country, anyway; but among themselves the aristocrats squabbled over matters of family pride and differences in ideology, and might on any occasion divide their votes accordingly.

No American concerned with national affairs could afford to be ignorant of these various roots and forms of political divisiveness, but it was more important, just now, to know how local political attachments were related to loyalty to the nation. On one level that question was unanswerable, for it is habitual with man, if indeed not programed into his very genes, to love the people or place he recognizes as "home," and the narrower the definition of home, the more intense the loyalty is likely to be. But to national-minded Americans in 1789, there was a ready touchstone of loyalty: did a person or group support the new Constitution, and, if so, with what reservations?

The answer to even that question, of course, was a matter of degree, and involved two broad sets of considerations—one partisan, the other social, psychological, and geographical. As to the partisan, large and solid majorities in North Carolina and Rhode Island had refused to support the Constitution at all, with the result that neither state had yet ratified the document. Elsewhere, three powerful political coalitions had opposed ratification and continued to harbor misgivings about it, ranging from cautious acquiescence to overt hostility. These were the Constitutionalist Party of Pennsylvania, so called because of its support of the radical state constitution of 1776, not the federal Constitution of 1787; the well-organized followers and supporters of Governor George Clinton of New York; and the collection of factions and groups in Virginia that were under the sway of Patrick Henry. The Pennsylvania anti-Federalists (as all opponents of the federal Constitution were being called) could command 40 percent or more of the popular votes in a given state election, Clinton's party still controlled one branch of the state legis-

5

lature and barely fell short of controlling the other, and Henry so dominated Virginia politics that he was able to name the first two United States senators from his state. Even in these three states, however, "Federalists" were strong and well coordinated; and in the remaining states, organized opposition to the new national government was all but nonexistent.

The other considerations were less immediately tangible but none the less real. Long colonial experience had predisposed most Americans to think of their state as their "country"; the idea of being an American was too new to contain much emotional substance. Various circumstances and events, however, had eroded Americans' localism a great deal by 1789. The most persistent of these was a continuing flood of immigrants, who sought opportunity or sanctuary less in a particular colony than in America, and were slow to break that habit of thinking. Accordingly, people in New England and the older portions of the South, where relatively few European immigrants settled in the eighteenth century, were considerably more intense in their localism than were those in the Middle States and the southern back country, which teemed with newcomers before and after the Revolution.

Second in importance, perhaps, was the trauma of the Revolution itself, especially among those who had actively participated in it. Men who fought and bled together as comrades in the Continental Army were generally apt to be transformed into nationalists by the experience, and many who served the Continental Congress in civilian capacities had likewise shed their provincialism in the doing. So, too, was it with inhabitants of those parts of the United States that were militarily most vulnerable: such ports as Newport, New York, Norfolk, Charleston, and Savannah, occupied or virtually destroyed during the war, and the farm country of New Jersey and that of the Virginia and Carolina tidewater, the main battle areas after 1776.

Related to this last, indeed scarcely distinguishable from it, was an elemental fact of life in preindustrial America. Communication was, for practical purposes, inseparable from transportation, and transportation was primitive. Roads, technology, and the mails being what they were, inhabitants of the interior were so isolated that few would have been able even to *name* more than a half-dozen nonrelatives in other states (after Washington and Franklin the list would quickly have run thin); and many would have been hard pressed to name any outside their home county or town. By contrast, inhabitants of the great port cities had continuous contact with both

6

people and news from all over the Atlantic community. Understandably, the latter thought in broader terms than did the former, and conceived of themselves as Americans in a world populated mainly by non-Americans, rather than as denizens of a Virginiocentric or other province-centered universe.

Finally, there was the influence of peacetime life under the Articles of Confederation. Generally speaking, those states which had been most nearly successful as quasi-sovereign entities (New York, Virginia, North Carolina, Rhode Island) were least enthused about transferring sovereignty, or even a portion of it, to a new national government. Those which had been least successful in pursuing their aims, or had most tenuously hung on to their existence under that condition (Connecticut, New Jersey, Delaware, Maryland), were the most enthused about the transfer. Massachusetts was a special case. The better-established and more prosperous citizens there had been scared out of their wits by Shays' Rebellion in 1786–1787 and had reacted to the rebellion by warmly embracing an appeal for enlarged national authority. The duration of their new-found nationalism would depend on what the new national government did. In Maryland, the slaveholding aristocracy reacted in a similar way to a less violent but equally upsetting challenge from dissident political groups.

These various forces were put to the test in the first congressional elections late in 1788, and the results were gratifying to friends of the new government. Though elections were disputed in New Jersey and one or two districts elsewhere, though Clinton's anti-Federalists held up the elections in New York, and though Henry gerrymandered representative districts even as he chose anti-Federalist senators in Virginia, Federalists still won overwhelming control of the First Congress. Anti-Federalists took only three, or possibly four, of the twenty-two seats in the Senate, and only thirteen of the fifty-nine seats in the House.[1] When North Carolina and Rhode Island at last came under the new roof (November 1789 and May

---

[1] John C. Miller, in *The Federalist Era, 1789–1801* (New York: Harper & Row, 1960), p. 5, says there were eight anti-Federalists in the House; Joseph Charles, in *The Origins of The American Party System* (New York: Harper Torchbooks, 1961), p. 21, says there were no more than a half-dozen. My figure is based upon a comparison of *Biographical Directory of the American Congress* (Washington: Government Printing Office, 1972) with Forrest McDonald, *We the People: The Economic Origins of the Constitution* (Chicago: University of Chicago Press, 1958).

1790), the ranks of the antis increased somewhat, but Federalists remained strong beyond challenge.

There was one more political consideration, however, that could upset all calculations. To a good many Americans the Constitution was appealing only because it was vague or even silent in certain particulars and because its proponents convinced them that it would be fleshed out in a satisfactory manner. For one thing, there was no "bill of rights." For another, the Constitution was ambiguous in the matter of an advisory council for the president. The president could require written opinions from heads of executive departments, and the Senate was to "advise and consent" in matters of appointments and treaties, but it was unclear who, if anybody, was to constitute the regular body of advisers and the extent to which department heads were responsible to the president. For yet another thing, the Constitution was even more sketchy in regard to the judiciary than it was regarding the executive. There was to be a Supreme Court, appointed by the president and approved by the Senate, but it would have original jurisdiction only in cases directly involving state governments and envoys of foreign powers; all other cases would be tried, if at all, only in such courts and on such terms as the Congress should decide. Finally, the Constitution was virtually silent in regard to the details of public finance. Congress could lay and collect taxes, within certain rules and provided that public revenues were collected only for the common defense and the general welfare; and all public debts—government bonds—were to be "as valid" under the Constitution as they were under the Confederation. But Americans owed in public debts, as citizens of states and nation, nearly as much as they owned as private individuals, and the Constitution spelled out nothing about how these debts were to be managed.

Underlying and inextricably bound to politics was the economy, broadly defined—the means of surviving and satisfying material wants. Survival itself, in fact, was never far from conscious thought among eighteenth-century Americans, for death was their constant companion. Death at birth or in early infancy took four children in ten, and smallpox, cholera, and tropical fevers periodically ravaged the adult population. Four of Thomas Jefferson's six children died before reaching maturity, four of Roger Sherman's seven, seven of Benjamin Rush's thirteen; Aaron Burr lost, within a span of eighteen months, every member of a sizable family except a wife and daughter; George Washington came perilously close to death from smallpox as a young man, and again from influenza in the second year of his presidency. The influenza epidemic that almost killed Washington in New York in 1790 took several members of Congress and the administration, and a yellow-fever epidemic in Philadelphia in 1793 killed four thousand, drove thousands more from the city, and all but stopped the workings of the federal government.

Yet in the midst of death was abundance: fish and game were profuse; the soil was rich; and millions of acres of land, stranger to both axe and plow, lay waiting exploitation. Most Americans responded to the profusion, in accordance with the dictates of English or Celtic or German ancestry, by viewing it as an invitation to grow rich, and most spent their lives trying to do just that.

That was what America was all about—the pursuit of wealth. And yet, as Henry Adams long ago pointed out, materialism and idealism were inseparable in America, and on fair comparison the American was the most idealistic man on earth. The European saw the world as a vale of misery, and resigned himself to it; the American looked at a savage wilderness and saw boundless acres of grain and magnificent cities, in a future world that he and his would make. Impelled by this vision, even the humblest immigrant was caught up in the American spirit, "for every stroke of the axe and the hoe made him a capitalist, and made gentlemen of his children."[2]

But there were rules and conventions in the pursuit of wealth, and problems as well. For example, the profits to be reaped from hard labor were so great that few men wanted to work for others, merely for the sake of wages, and so labor was chronically scarce and dear. This shortage had long since given rise to a practice of awarding preferment and prestige to any who devised labor-saving inventions, and the Constitution expressly provided for the continuation of that practice. The same shortage had made it profitable to exploit slave labor in some parts of English America for more than a hundred years, and the Constitution sanctioned that, too. Scores of thousands of Africans had been imported as slaves before the Revolution; and though republican idealism as well as economic circumstance all but stopped the slave trade after the war—only about 8,000 slaves had been imported since 1776, almost all into South Carolina—natural increase brought the slave population, by 1790, to 697,000, or almost one American in five.

In some parts of the United States, notably New England, Calvinist theology had interacted with a hostile soil and harsh cli-

---

[2] The sources of this and other direct quotations in this book are indicated by asterisks in the Note on the Sources, pp. 187–192 below.

mate to produce a hardy breed that could be patient in the pursuit of wealth; but for the most part, Americans were in a hurry. Several ways of getting rich fast were regarded as legitimate, though the most widespread form of fever for quick wealth, infecting Americans like an endemic disease, was land speculation. It could scarcely have been otherwise, for it had long been obvious that early comers could become wealthy by claiming and selling land to latecomers. One worked or connived to obtain a stake, then worked or connived to obtain legal title to a tract of wilderness, then sold the wilderness by the acre to the hordes of immigrants, and thereby lived and died a wealthy man. Appropriately, the most successful practitioner of this craft was George Washington, who had acquired several hundred thousand acres and was reckoned by many as the wealthiest man in America.

It was considerably less legitimate, in the estimation of most Americans, to obtain wealth through means of pure finance—or, as Americans often described it, through "stock jobbing" and "paper shuffling." There was, in fact, abundant reason for promoting the development of financial institutions in the United States, for the shortage of money and other liquid capital was second only to the shortage of labor as a deterrent to the nation's economic development. And, to be sure, the wheels of colonial business enterprise had often been oiled by "land-bank" paper money, and colonial wars had been financed by "bills of credit"; but neither of these forms of public finance was especially stable or satisfactory, and there existed at the time of Washington's inauguration only three commercial banks— Philadelphia's Bank of North America, Boston's Bank of Massachusetts, and the Bank of New York. Despite the shortage and the need, however, most Americans viewed paper transactions and wealth derived therefrom as inherently dishonest, tinged with trickery and bordering on witchcraft, and certainly not "real," like ownership of a portion of the earth.

Besides pursuing main-chance routes to wealth, what Americans did with their time, most of the time, was grow crops and sell them wherever they could. Agriculture and its "handmaiden" commerce, however, had gradually evolved into regional economic patterns, and these want some notice.

Ironically, the richest part of the country by far was the only part where most people were less interested in the main chance than in the glamourless business of growing crops for market. This was the rice-producing low country of South Carolina and Georgia, where slaves outnumbered freemen five to one, where plantation owners also grew indigo and invested surplus wealth in middle-country tobacco lands, where less than 2 percent of the nation's white families sold more than a fifth of the nation's exports and bought nearly a fifth of its imports.

The economy of that area worked simply, and despite dislocations during the first three years after the Peace of Paris, it worked effectively. Rice and indigo plantations were entirely commercialized operations, extremely profitable but no more self-sufficient than a modern factory. World markets were favorable, and slave labor, because of the mortality rate in the swamps, was expensive; and so the South Carolina and Georgia planters wasted neither land nor labor on the production of food for themselves and their slaves. They sold about 40 percent of their rice in England, and the rest in southern Europe and the West Indies. With the proceeds they bought beef and pork and other provisions from Yankees and from up-country drovers and farmers and bought wines, clothing, and luxuries from Europe. In direct exchange with the outside world, Charleston and Savannah regularly showed favorable trade balances and were the only American ports to do so.

More complex was the tobacco-growing segment of the economy, which extended from the South Carolina middle country through North Carolina, Virginia, and much of Maryland and accounted for perhaps a third of the exports from the United States. Tobacco planters had been in and out of trouble for the better part of four decades. The roots of their problems lay in overproduction and—especially in Virginia and Maryland—in the tandem effects of slipshod management and lavish consumption. Tobacco planters had long since learned to attribute their difficulties to sinister outside forces and to try to extricate themselves by speculating in land.

Both their diagnosis and their cure had a measure of merit. Clearly, the monopoly imposed by the Navigation Acts had impaired the profitability of growing tobacco during the colonial period, and so had British and French commercial restrictions imposed since 1783. As to getting well through land speculation, Washington and others had shown it was possible, and thousands more were attempting to emulate their example. But the analysis and the proposed remedy were superficial, and the problems ran deep. Tobacco prices, reflecting production, had soared in the period from 1783 to 1785, sagged during the next two years, and collapsed in 1788. They would not return to profitable levels for as long a period as two consecutive years during the next half-century. Speculative titles to

11

western lands, involved in a political maze since the 1770s, were about to take a turn into an even more tangled legal maze.

Meanwhile, planters did what they could to keep afloat and to protect their sizable investments. Many had taken advantage of the Revolutionary crisis to renege on their debts to British creditors: planters in Virginia and Maryland alone had wiped out an estimated £2 million sterling in such debts through state legislative action during the war. The Constitution jeopardized them anew, for it opened (or seemed to open) the federal courts to suits by foreign creditors, depending on how the judicial branch was organized by the upcoming Congress. Doubtless many a planter took such considerations into account when weighing the merits of the proposed new system.

The more honorable and more prudent tobacco planters had taken other courses. Diversification was one way: in the northern portions of the tobacco belt, wheat, flax, and hemp were extensively cultivated; and in all parts of the area, slaves were kept busy in the off-season felling trees, sawing lumber, and manufacturing crude lumber products for export to the sugar plantations of the West Indies. Another, and socially more important, way was to make the tobacco plantation as nearly self-sufficient as possible: to produce as much as the plantation could be made to produce of the food, clothing, and shelter required on it.

The plantations of Virginia, Maryland, and North Carolina thus became nearly polar opposites of the plantations in South Carolina and Georgia. The first resembled the villages and manors of England; the second its factories.

West of the tobacco belt and extending northward to central Pennsylvania lay the frontier country, with an economy based upon trapping, cattle droving, land speculation, semisubsistence farming, and the raising of corn for feeding hogs and distilling whisky. Economic development in this area depended upon relations with the Indians and upon the improvement of facilities for river transportation. These, in turn, hinged largely upon the doings of Europeans.

In what the Americans styled their Northwest Territory—the area bounded by the Ohio and Mississippi rivers and the Great Lakes and nominally owned by the United States government—a few thousand Yankees had recently settled. Pervading this vast domain, however, and western New York State as well, were scores of tribes of Indians; and most of these were under the influence of the British government in Canada. His Britannic Majesty, in turn, was represented by Lord Dorchester (formerly Sir Guy Carleton), who had not forgiven the traitorous Americans for their success in the late war, and by a dozen military outposts, which, in defiance of the Treaty of Paris, doubled as lucrative trading posts inside the legally defined United States.

South of the Ohio the alien influence was that of Spain. Into what would become Kentucky (then part of Virginia) and Tennessee (then part of North Carolina), more than one hundred thousand Americans had poured since the peace, and so both Indians and Europeans were on the run. But Spain remained dominant, through quirks of technology and geography. From the area, only the lightest goods could be moved over the mountains to eastern markets; all else had to be flat-boated downstream, and every stream led to the Gulf Coast, which for practical purposes meant New Orleans. If New Orleans were open, goods could be reloaded there onto ocean-going vessels; but New Orleans belonged to Spain, and Spain was no more enthused about American expansion than was Lord Dorchester.

The Spanish presence and the Spanish attitude posed more problems than one. The few-score thousand American settlers west of the Appalachian chain of mountains could well be ignored by those to the east, and those in the northern east were disposed to do so. But those in the southern east, and especially tobacco planters who had staked their all in purchases of western land titles, were in a different situation entirely: if Spain closed New Orleans and thereby effectively closed navigation of the Mississippi, they stood to be ruined.

A preview of what this problem held in store for the future of the American Union was shown in 1786. A Spanish minister plenipotentiary, Don Diego de Gardoqui, had offered the United States valuable trading concessions in Spanish America in exchange for American renunciation of navigation rights on the Mississippi. Every member of Congress from states north of Maryland had seen the advantages and leaped at the offer: every congressman from south of Mason and Dixon's line had rallied to defeat the proposal.

In the East, north of the tobacco belt, extending from Mount Vernon to the middle reaches of the Hudson Valley, lay the wheat belt. Farmers in that area raised livestock and garden crops for home consumption and for sale in the cities, but their products that counted in international markets were wheat and flour. Three ports in the area had, by 1789, reached preeminence as grain export centers and had, as well, moved far toward becoming the principal centers for the entire importing trade of America: Philadelphia (population 42,444), New York (33,131), and Baltimore (13,503).

13

Philadelphia, long dominated by Quakers and long having attracted and produced aristocratic community leaders of the first quality, was the wonder of America. Clean, orderly, and beautiful, blessed with theaters, learned societies, musical societies, and a college, it may have lacked the grandeur of ancient European cities, but it lacked their filth and poverty as well. European travelers no less than American were impressed that so new and primitive a country could have made such a city.

New York and Baltimore, by contrast, were more truly American: raw, crude, greedy, but also lean, hard, and self-confident. In a single generation New York had passed Boston and Charleston to become the number two American city, and Baltimore had mushroomed from a village with only a few hundred inhabitants. The leading men in both places were less staid than Philadelphians and less savory in their dealings with outsiders and possessed of extreme esprit de corps and local patriotism. This is not to suggest that, by standards that would later prevail, the two places were vulgarly democratic. Even there, in the negotiation of financial backing, gentle birth and proper connections still weighed heavier than mere talent or collateral; but ambitious and imaginative young men on the make, if they could show the prospect of semilegal or extralegal profit by trade in, say, the French or Spanish West Indies, could find opportunity and even sponsorship in New York and Baltimore, whereas in Philadelphia more conventional trade as well as established connections were the norm.

In the Georgian world that had flourished in colonial times, in the polite and orderly universe epitomized by Bach and Handel and the minuet, the way of the Philadelphians had prevailed. But that world had been sorely crippled by the American Revolution, and the French Revolution, just beginning, would deal it the death blow. In the new and less couth world that was aborning, the methods of New York and Baltimore would be the way to success. Moreover, Philadelphia had another handicap in the fierce intercity rivalry: back-country politicians in Pennsylvania worked against their metropolis when it appeared profitable and possible to do so. In 1785, for example, being temporarily in control of the state legislature, they had disregarded the interests of both state and nation and promoted their own interests by revoking the charter of the Bank of North America.

Finally, there was New England, whose complex economic system had evolved from adversity. For the most part, the area had no great agricultural staple. Farmers on the fertile flatlands immedi-

14

ately adjacent to the Connecticut River could, it is true, grow both tobacco and wheat, but those lands had long since been appropriated by a prosperous few. Farmers nearly everywhere in the region owned stands of timber, but except near the coast these were of little value to them, for lumber was too bulky to be transported economically to market. Instead, they burned the wood in the fields, processed it into potash and pearlash, and sold it as a cash crop in that form.

Such methods used up great quantities of land. A few decades earlier, when the land supply had still seemed limitless, proprietors of new towns had been able to make out reasonably well by burning off some of their acreage and selling much of the rest to new settlers, but by 1776 new land was all but gone in the southern two-thirds of New England. Because of an abnormally high birth rate and an abnormally low death rate—the more lethal germs of the times being unable to prosper in New England's wintry climes—the population grew rapidly, and the pressure of people on space grew proportionately.

Ever ingenious, patient beyond normal human tolerance by virtue of necessity and their rigid Calvinism, the Yankees had devised one means and another of coping with their adversity. In Connecticut, farmers had begun by mid century to raise workhorses for export to the West Indies, and that industry—sending more than eight thousand horses a year southward by the 1780s—kept many a barren farm alive. But the same industry prevented the development of a freighting business, or "carrying trade" as it was then called; for wooden holds that transported live horses were never again suitable for other cargoes. In Rhode Island, where almost every farm was within smell of the sea, farmers pooled their resources and outfitted trading sloops, to parlay their meager crops by bargaining their wares in ports of the American continent and the West Indies. The more lucky and more daring of them tried their hands at every form of trade, including slaving, and had no hesitation about using bogus papers, supplied by officials of the state government, to enable them to cheat outsiders.

But the broader and generally more efficient economic system of New England worked on other bases. Effectively mobilized, the area produced two commodities that had a large and profitable market: fish and lumber. The fish were caught off the Grand Banks by men who had long since forsaken the land for the sea; the lumber was cut in New Hampshire and Maine (then a province of Massachusetts) by men who perhaps preferred to be farmers, but were enticed into the industry by the prospect of cash wages. Fish and lumber were sold in the West Indies, to merchants who serviced the masters of sugar plantations, in return for raw sugar or molasses and cash. Sugar and molasses were made into rum, which was sold to fishermen and lumbermen, who consumed rum in abundance.

That left only the trade between Europe and New England, which in colonial times had been worked out successfully despite a huge imbalance in favor of Europe. Farmers had sold their potash and pearlash and lumber, and occasional foodstuffs, to retail or outport merchants. In exchange, outport merchants had supplied farmers with imported European goods, mainly from England, which they acquired through an aristocratic "class" of international importing merchants based in Boston and Newport. The outport merchants conducted the West Indies trade, from which they made profits large enough to overcome the deficit in trade with Europe—and thereby to balance the whole system.

When the Revolution came, most of the established international merchants in Boston and Newport became Loyalists. The outport merchants, joined by a number of former artisans and seamen who grew suddenly rich in privateering, moved up to take their place as the international mercantile "establishment" of New England. But in the process the commercial structure and patterns of the area were thoroughly disrupted, and what was worse, the usurpers of commercial leadership did not know how to perform their new roles.

When the independence of the United States was recognized in 1783, the new-rich merchants of New England, in their greed and ignorance, placed huge orders in London and naively expected to grow richer by supplying a long-pent-up demand. They failed to take into account several things: that New York City had been occupied by the British throughout the war and had supplied the surrounding countryside with European goods, that Philadelphia and Baltimore had regularly managed to smuggle in goods, that Virginia and Maryland planters would negotiate private arrangements with British houses, and so on. Accordingly, the newly dominant merchants of Boston and Providence (which supplanted Newport during the Revolution) were stuck with large quantities of imported goods that they could not sell. Moreover, even their traditional trade patterns were now more or less closed to them by postwar restrictions on commerce with Britain and the West Indies.

And there was one more element in the equation. By the end of the war, Congress and the state governments had taken on immense public debts, and a large portion of the "public securities" representing these debts had come to be concentrated in New England. Already by 1785 various Yankees had begun to notice the concentration, and soon they responded. Rhode Islanders moved to repudiate their debts through an issue of paper money. Massachusetts went the other way: Governor James Bowdoin introduced, and the state legislature passed, measures to collect taxes with which to pay the public debts. The merchants of Massachusetts, having acquired sizable amounts of the securities, cheered—but not for long. The public, under the nominal leadership of a former captain of the Continental Army named Daniel Shays, resisted; and the rebellion that bore Shays's name was one of the vital stimulants in bringing about the new United States Constitution.

The debts themselves remained largely unpaid, and not only in New England, as one of the most pressing and burdensome problems facing the new national government. No one could say how much they amounted to; educated guesses ranged from $60 million to $80 million, depending on how much "scaling down" one thought should be done to reflect wartime inflation. Congressional accounts were still being audited, and state debts had been handled in a wide variety of ways. Some states had virtually repudiated their obligations; others had striven valiantly but vainly to pay them off. A few had managed to service their own debts with some success and even to assume responsibility for the national bonds held by their citizens.

Only one thing about the public debts seemed certain—that there could be no easy solution to the problems they posed. Not to pay them was unthinkable, for the commercial dislocations that would result from such a policy would cause irreparable damage to the nation's economy; and besides, the larger holders of government bonds constituted a powerful and energetic lobby. On the other hand, to attempt to pay off the debts within a reasonably short time would require a tax burden so large as to paralyze all trade, as the experience of several states had so recently shown. For example, to pay all public debts, national and state, by the twenty-fifth anniversary of independence would require annual taxes almost equal to half the exports from the United States.

Even if these complex political and economic ingredients should be stirred skillfully and in the national interest, there was no guarantee that the new system would work, for it was by no means certain that the Americans were governable as one people. The Americans were in fact not one people but many, comprising cultures as numerous and variant as the British had a few centuries earlier.

A long succession of Europeans traveled to the United States after independence, and many of them wrote books trying to define the American character; but none could quite cope with its plurality.[3] A case in point, and one of the better early efforts, was the work of the Frenchman J. Hector St. John Crèvecoeur, who published his *Letters from an American Farmer* seven years before Washington took the oath of office as president. Crèvecoeur cited several attributes that he thought distinguished the Americans from their European forebears: they treasured their freedom, had no great extremes of rich and poor, had no distinctions between people based on hereditary status or religion, and depended upon their own unrestrained industry, especially in working the soil, as their means of livelihood. The country was spacious and bountiful, invariably working a regeneration on the immigrants from a variety of European nations who migrated to the "great American asylum" for the middling and the poor.

Crèvecoeur did not get far into his description, however, before he found it necessary to make exceptions. The New Englanders, he noted, were unlike other Americans: they were "unmixed descendants of Englishmen," careful and methodical in settling their territory, especially decent in manners, devoted to education, and more industrious than most of their countrymen. To account for the other differences between Americans, Crèvecoeur divided them into three broad groups—those who lived near the sea, those in the middle settlements, and those on the wild frontier. The maritime Americans he saw as bold, boisterous, enterprising, gregarious, and restless. The middle inhabitants, "by far the most numerous," were "wise and pure," but also litigious, proud, politically active, materialistic, selfish, devoted to comfortable living, and tolerant to the point of indifference in matters of religion. The frontiersmen would in time become like the middle inhabitants, but as long as they lived in the "great woods," they were uncouth, drunken, lazy, brutal, wasteful,

---

[3] The following analysis closely follows, and in some instances quotes or paraphrases, the analyses in Forrest McDonald, Leslie E. Decker, and Thomas P. Govan, *The Last Best Hope: A History of the United States*, 2 vols. (Reading, Mass.: Addison-Wesley, 1972), 1:229–230, and Forrest McDonald, *E Pluribus Unum: The Formation of the American Republic, 1776–1792* (Boston: Houghton Mifflin, 1965), pp. 64–68, 106–107. All three analyses are based upon the author's researches in primary sources.

contentious, and lawless, "no better than carnivorous animals of a superior rank."

This system of classification had some merit in regard to the inhabitants of the Middle States, but even there it was inadequate, for they were the least homogeneous of all Americans. In New York, a powerful Indian confederation still dominated the interior, confining whites to the Hudson River Valley, to Manhattan, Long Island, and Staten Island, and to frontier settlements westward along the Mohawk and northward to Lake Champlain. Among the white inhabitants, only about two-fifths were English, nearly half of whom were invaders from New England who occupied much of Long Island and Staten Island and whose fellow Yankees had spilled over into northern New Jersey. Of the remaining New Yorkers, nearly a fifth apiece were Dutch, Scotch or Scotch-Irish, and black, and most of the rest were Germans, French, Scandinavians, and Sephardic Jews. In Pennsylvania, where the eastern third and a narrow strip of the interior from Harrisburg to Pittsburgh were settled, and in well-settled Delaware and New Jersey, about a third of the people were English, another third were German, a fifth were Scotch or Scotch-Irish, and most of the remainder were Dutch, Irish, Welsh, Scandinavian, French, or black. In New York the Anglican Church was tax-supported and established by law; but adherents of Congregationalism, Presbyterianism, and various Dutch Reformed sects were considerably more numerous than members of the official church and were exempted from taxes for its support. In New Jersey these several sects were present along with a goodly number of Quakers. In Pennsylvania, Quakers, long dominant in public and private affairs, had been displaced as leaders during the Revolution by the more numerous Presbyterians and by a variety of Dutch Calvinists and German Lutherans.

New England and the South were something else again. As to New England, Crèvecoeur was on sound ground as far as he went, but he underrated the most important elements of all, the religious and the natural. The Anglo-Americans in New England had originally set out to fashion themselves in the image of God, as they conceived of God, but their image of God had been shaped over the course of a century and a half by the tangible evidence of Him in Nature. As it happened, Nature had been parsimonious in New England, and thus the evidence told the Yankees that God was cold, stingy, uncompromising, and especially given to putting people on trial. The New Englanders impressed outsiders as being much the same way.

19

So the Yankees wore a stereotype: they were puritanical, brittle, stern; they were greedy, stingy, shrewd; they were vulgar, mean, democratic. They had no comprehension of generosity, elegance, or taste; they drove sharp bargains, were too busy, talked too fast and through their noses, and built fences of stone, as if man's days on earth were not numbered.

This general outside view of New Englanders was not entirely accurate, though in fact the Yankees tended to live up to their reputation when they dealt with outsiders. The general outside impression of southerners and the South, on the other hand, was entirely inaccurate—though southerners, too, tried to live up to their image, whether in dealing with outsiders or with one another. Even in those early days of the Republic the white south was a mixture of pretense, illusion, and ideal: of generous and gregarious Cavalier gentry, of great slave-owning planters, and of republican aristocrats who stood above the crass pursuit of wealth. At best, the first two pretensions accurately described no more than a tenth of the white adult males in the South, and the third suited almost none, though the pretense itself was widespread and common. What was equally important, the South was even more diverse, from state to state, than were the other parts of the Union. On one extreme was the raw frontier state of Georgia, containing (in roughly equal portions, not counting the slaves) rice-plantation aristocrats like those of South Carolina, Yankee immigrants, and Scotch-Irish back-country men; but the overall quality of life in the state was very close to the barbarism that Crèvecoeur attributed to all frontier communities. On the other extreme was South Carolina, where the low-country planters were as decadently civilized as the nobility of ancient Egypt and where the up country was filled with rude, hard-drinking, politically disruptive Scotch-Irish cattle drovers. Virginia was still dominated by pseudo-Cavaliers and cultured republican aristocrats whose disdain for the commercial life was exceeded in intensity only by the avidity with which they pursued wealth; but in the piedmont's Southside, in the Blue Ridge foothills, in the Valley, and in the trans-Alleghany region the dominant element was the Scotch-Irish. As to Maryland and North Carolina, it is not a great exaggeration to assert that the one was a veritable Virginia infused with a conspiratorial style, in the manner of Restoration England, and that the other was a veritable Virginia watered down by a bumpkin's style, in the manner of the back country throughout America.

Finally, Americans were pluralistic in two other ways. One of these derived from their multiple forms of social stratification. Each local community—the town in New England, the manor in New York, the plantation and the county or parish elsewhere—had its own hierarchy, which sometimes did and sometimes did not correspond to the gradations of power and status in the state as a whole. For most ranks of the social ladder, one's wealth, occupation, and ethnic stock were the regular determinants, but the most important determinant was an irregular one, that of sponsors and family connections.

An equally vital dimension was the division of Americans along lines that would soon come to be called Hamiltonian and Jeffersonian, though they were well established when both those Founding Fathers were children. This was a division between town dwellers and country dwellers, between merchants and farmers, between international and outport merchants, between planters who were entirely dependent on commerce and those whose plantation units were largely self-sufficient as well as commercial. Most importantly, this was a difference in attitudes, between those who accepted the expansive and corrupt commercialism that had grown up in eighteenth-century Britain and those who rejected it and embraced the antimoney prejudices (though not the politics) of the British Tory Viscount Bolingbroke. This line of division cut across all others and defies precise definition by places and groups, but one set of generalizations that is at least loosely true can be made. The states that had matured as colonies in the seventeenth century—New England and the tobacco country—generally shared the Bolingbroke position, though Boston, Newport, Providence, and some of Maryland leaned in the opposite direction and though the two areas were otherwise poles apart, one having inherited the "Roundhead" or Puritan Commonwealth tradition and mythology of the seventeenth century, the other the "Cavalier" or royalist tradition and myths. On the opposite hand, colonies that had taken form in the eighteenth century—the Middle Colonies and the lower South—generally shared the values ushered in by England's financial revolution and the freewheeling commercialism that followed it.

Viewed up close, then, the Americans were an extremely diverse, not especially attractive, and possibly ungovernable people. It was only when they were viewed in broad range, *on the average,* and in comparison with the world's other peoples, that their virtues and their promise to mankind became evident. If there was any genuine likelihood of the improvement of the lot of the common man; if, as Americans believed, civilization was retarded rather than preserved by artificial and inherited barriers between men; and if the Americans could succeed in their effort to live together as one nation, despite the diversity of its parts; then Washington was right, and the United States truly was the hope of the future.

2

★★★★★

ESTABLISHING A GOVERNMENT
1789

The new government got off to a slow and erratic start, one suitably gauche for a band of yokels who had arrogantly declared themselves able to get along without the guidance of kings, nobles, or bishops. On March 4, 1789, the day appointed for the meeting of the First Congress, only a quarter of the members showed up. A week passed, and the Senate was still four members short of a constitutional quorum (half the membership), and the House of Representatives was twelve short of a quorum. Another week passed, and another, and another, until, at last, the House obtained a bare quorum by April 1, the Senate on April 6.

Then there was the matter of the presidency. Presidential electors had been chosen the previous fall, had met in the several states as the Constitution required, had cast their unanimous ballot for George Washington, and had made John Adams vice-president by giving him the second most votes. Everyone knew before the balloting began that Washington would be president, and the newspapers announced the results early in 1789. Any other man than Washington would have been in the temporary capital, New York, in time for the opening of Congress. But the Father of His Country was ever concerned with propriety, and since he would not be officially elected until a joint session of Congress tallied the votes of the electors, he stayed at home in Mount Vernon. When Congress obtained a quorum, counted the votes, and notified him accordingly, he still tarried, lest unseemly haste suggest that he was improperly eager for the office. He took a leisurely trip northward, incidentally wallowing in the popular adulation shown him in every hamlet along the way, and finally arrived in New York in time to be inaugurated on April 30.

Compelling practical considerations dictated more promptness from all quarters. Anti-Federalists had by no means given up in their efforts to defeat the Constitution, and every delay worked in their favor. More tangibly, there was the matter of revenues for the new government. Everyone knew that the old Congress of the Confederation was bankrupt, and everyone knew that the financial health of the new system would depend upon the funds derived from import duties. Everyone also knew that Americans normally did most of their importing in the spring and that part of the duties were paid when goods arrived from abroad, the remainder six months later. Thus if the new Congress failed to enact a schedule of tariffs before the spring importing season of 1789 was over, it could count on no appreciable revenues for twelve to eighteen months. In fine, unless someone acted quickly, the babe Constitution could die stillborn.

In these circumstances only one man appeared with the energy and awareness that the occasion demanded. Washington himself could not take the lead, for he had but a limited understanding of what was happening; and besides, he knew, if only instinctively, that he could contribute best by serving as a symbol. Nor could John Adams, he who had been so bold in seizing the initiative on the eve of independence, repeat his earlier performance; this pompous man was as devoid of understanding of present circumstances as he was lacking in followers. The Senate over which Adams presided, regarded by many as potentially the fount of enlightened leadership that the nation needed, quickly proved to be as inept as the vice-president. Most members of the House were scarcely better.

Fortunately for the infant States, James Madison was on hand, and Madison both understood and knew how to translate understanding into action. He had been instrumental in having the Constitutional Convention of 1787 called, had been instrumental in the work of that convention, and had been instrumental in bringing about the ratification of the Constitution. After 1789 he would lose control over, and sometimes lose contact with, the tide of events; but in 1789 he was the man of the hour.

24

Acceptance of the presidency was one of the most painful decisions of Washington's life. For years his abiding, overriding concern, amounting almost to an obsession, had been his reputation—or, as he put it, his desire for the "approval of his fellow-citizens" and for a favorable judgment from "posterity." Liberty and republicanism mattered to him, to be sure, but less for their own sake than because of their connection with his reputation: if they did not survive, neither would his reputation as the First Character of the Age, the Father of His Country. He had hoped that problems of government would solve themselves, for he had had little experience in dealing with them and had even less talent; but things had not worked out that way, and the call had come. He could not afford to refuse, and he could not afford to fail; for if he should fail now, his entire life's work would retroactively have been a failure.

Thus, despite his preferences and protestations, there had never been any likelihood that he would spurn the office. He was indispensable, and he knew it. As a man idolized by the people—almost all the people, whatever their station in life—he could make it possible for them to indulge their habitual adulation of a monarch without reneging on their commitment to republicanism. As a symbol of the Union, he could stimulate, at least for a time, the emotional attachment to the Nation that normally requires centuries in the building. As a man with a thoroughly justified reputation for integrity, dignity, candor, and republican virtue, he could inspire the trust that was crucial to the radical experiment in federal government. He could do these things, and no other man could. The circumstance stretches the imagination—possibly it was unprecedented in history, and it would certainly never recur in the history of the American presidency—but the fact is that Washington was the only man who measured up to the job.

Yet Washington was mean as well as grand, and it was the pettiness that showed most during his first few months in office. No sooner had he taken the oath of office than he found himself in a dilemma or, perhaps more appropriately, a tizzy. His large rented house in New York was overrun with visitors, a few there on serious business, most total strangers come to solicit jobs with the new government or simply to gawk at the Great Man. All acted as if they had every right to be there. Between invasions he found it impossible, from breakfast to bedtime, to be "relieved from the ceremony of one visit before I had to attend to another." He inquired as to the practice of his partial predecessors, the presidents of the old Confederation Congress, and learned that they had been "considered

25

in no better light than as a maître d'hôtel . . . for their table was considered as a public one." Thoroughly peeved, Washington published an advertisement in the newspapers, announcing that he would thenceforth receive "visits of compliment" only between two and three on Tuesday and Friday afternoons, would return no visits, and would accept no invitations.

The more austere republicans howled that the president was thereby proposing to shut himself off from the public "like an eastern Lama," forgetting that he was merely an official chosen by the people. Almost desperately, Washington now sent inquiries to several people—Madison, Adams, Alexander Hamilton, John Jay—asking advice on rules of behavior that would strike a balance between "too free an intercourse and too much familiarity" (which would reduce the responsibility of the office) and "an ostentatious show" of monarchical aloofness (which would be improper in a republic). It was a matter of the gravest moment, Washington said, for precedents set now would affect the course of government for many years to come.

Rules were worked out. Dinners were to be held every Thursday at four, the guests being only government officials and their families, invited in an orderly system of rotation to avoid charges of favoritism. As to the general public, Washington established two occasions a week for greeting them: a "levee" for men only on Tuesdays from three to four, and tea parties for men and women, held on Friday evenings. Anyone respectably dressed could attend either public function without invitation or prior notice, but at least the traffic was reduced. Habitually, Washington found the levees insufferable, for people came, saluted him, and otherwise ignored him while freeloading on the refreshments he provided. The tea parties, presided over by his wife Martha after she arrived at the end of May, were much more to his liking, for he loved to circulate among and charm the ladies. (Charming the ladies was not difficult for him. Abigail Adams, wife of the vice-president and a veteran of receptions at the Court of St. James, fully expected to dislike the president, but was almost moon-struck upon meeting him. He moved, she gushed, "with a grace, dignity, and ease that leaves Royal George far behind him.")

The program of entertainment was not unrelated to another delicate matter considered in the first few months. Washington magnanimously—or so it seemed—offered to serve without salary, asking Congress only to pay his expenses. Remembering that he had fared rather handsomely under such an arrangement during the Revolutionary War, the General was almost insistent, but Congress instead voted him a $25,000 salary and no expense account. Washington's concern is understandable when it is realized that his liquor bill alone ran to almost $2,000 in 1789.

Two other aspects of the presidency during the early months proved even more vexing. The first was that at first there was precious little for the president to do except entertain. Until the Congress should take some action, there were no national laws to enforce, no officers to appoint, not even any criminals to pardon. The one area in which the Constitution empowered the executive to act without legislation was the conduct of foreign relations, and even there the extent of his discretionary authority was not clear, for his powers were hampered by the requirement that they be exercised with the "advice and consent" of the Senate. Therein lay a second vexing aspect of the office. Washington was an experienced and skillful administrator, but he could function only with an expert corps of advisers—from whom opinions could be solicited and to whom authority could be delegated, but who had to be devoted to and obey the commands of the leader. The Constitution provided for no such body of advisers, and many persons, including Washington's neighbor and old friend George Mason, had opposed it at least partly for that reason. Instead, the document (which Washington interpreted literally, almost as if it were a manual of instructions) authorized the president to require "the Opinion, in writing," of department heads, whenever Congress got around to establishing the departments; otherwise, there was officially nothing but the advice and consent of the Senate.

For a time Washington made do with administrative relics of the defunct Confederation: John Jay, superintendent of foreign affairs, and his one-man diplomatic corps, Minister to France Thomas Jefferson; and Superintendent of War Henry Knox, who oversaw Indian affairs with the assistance of an authorized army of 840 men, of whom no more than two-thirds were actually in service and almost all were in arrears of pay. Through Jay and Knox, meetings were arranged between the president and foreign envoys already on the premises; and negotiations with various Indian tribes, already underway, proceeded for a time. Then it became necessary to issue further instructions in regard to the Indian negotiations, and a minor constitutional impasse ensued.

The president and the secretary of war conferred and decided that they were constitutionally bound to seek the advice and consent of the Senate. One Saturday morning, just as the Senate was beginning its deliberations, Washington and Knox sauntered in, told

27

the doorkeeper to announce their presence, and informed the senators that they were there seeking advice and consent. Knox handed a paper to Washington, who handed it to Adams, who read it just as several carriages were rolling by. Some could make out the word "Indians," but few heard anything else. When the reading was finished, Washington said something about seven points in regard to which advice and consent was requested, but outside noises again prevented anyone from hearing. An embarrassed silence followed. Senator Robert Morris of Pennsylvania, erstwhile Financier of the Revolution and one of the few intimates of the president, deferentially asked that everything be read again. Everything was read again, whereupon Vice-President Adams put the question: "Do you advise and consent?" on each of Washington's seven proposals, one by one. On point after point the senators, conceiving of themselves as a deliberative body, were disposed to debate and ended up postponing the question. Washington, accustomed to dealing with advisers as subordinates, grew visibly irritated, his face flaming red as his hair. Finally he rose and declared that "this defeats every purpose of my coming here," and general embarrassment pervaded the room. He gradually cooled down, and so did the senators; but after another confrontation the following Monday, it was mutually if tacitly agreed that advice, like consent, should come after and not before the president acted.

Trivial as the circumstances of that decision were, the decision itself was of considerable importance. For one thing, it ruled out the possibility that the presidency might evolve into something resembling the prime-ministership in Great Britain. For another, it set a pattern in the conduct of foreign relations. Thenceforth, Washington initiated foreign policy on his own, seeking no counsel from the Senate at all. Furthermore, ever after, only "weak" presidents, those who entrusted foreign affairs to the secretary of state, worked through the Senate as a matter of course; every "strong" president, like Washington, had as little to do with the Senate as possible.

For all its fumbling, the executive branch had a saving grace that the Senate lacked. Washington and his minions escaped laughability for much the same reason that Napoleon and his marshals later did: people who defeat the best armies of Europe are somehow not very funny. The upper house of the new government, lacking any such basis for pretensions, was a pretty sorry spectacle.

The comedy started almost with the first rap of John Adams's gavel. Unlike those who followed him in the office, Adams participated in as well as presided over the doings of the Senate. From the outset, he was disposed to interrupt the debates with pedantic little lectures or even speeches, alternately attempting to impress the senators with his learning and with his experience, both of which were in fact vast. Most of the senators, in their turn, seemed scarcely able to speak without citing a dozen ancient authorities, so as to display their erudition and prove the timeless rectitude of their views. It was as if a dialogue—or debate—were being held between Polonious and a Greek Chorus.

The comedy began in earnest when a hassle developed over the proper way to address the president. Adams, once a radical republican, had acquired a taste for pomp and ceremony during his many years as a minister in the courts of Europe, and he ardently desired that regal "dignity and splendor" be made a part of the American system. Characteristically, he rationalized the matter. Society, he maintained, was held together by customs, prejudices, and superstitions—a reasonable enough assumption, but from it he concluded that only an elaborate system of titles would instill in the people the awe and veneration that would give permanency to the government. A large number of the senators, conceiving of themselves as a virtual American House of Lords, agreed with the vice-president and proposed, for openers, a series of exalted titles for the president. After lengthy discussion "his elective majesty," "his excellency," and others were rejected in favor of "His Highness the President of the United States and Protector of the Rights of the Same." Only three senators opposed such nonsense, and two of them, curiously, were among the nation's richest men: Charles Carroll of Maryland and Ralph Izard of South Carolina, who owned thousands of acres of rich plantation lands and more than a thousand slaves between them. The third was William Maclay, a militant republican and back-country Scotch-Irishman from Pennsylvania.

The House of Representatives refused to concur in the Senate's resolution respecting a presidential title, and the Senate peevishly wrangled about whether to compromise on this grave matter. At one point Richard Henry Lee of Virginia, who strongly supported Adams, stood up and read off "the titles of all the princes and potentates of the earth," to show that the term "highness" was in almost universal use. At another point Adams interrupted the debate by declaring that the president could communicate to the Senate in three ways—in person, through a "minister of state," or through a personal aide. As everyone looked blank, wondering what this had to do with anything, Adams solemnly declared that "it may become a great constitutional question." The subject of titles, which had consumed almost all the Senate's time since April 23, was finally closed on May 14 with a general Senate endorsement of the principle of a title for the president.

The comic climax came four days later. Habitually and in keeping with British practice, colonial and state legislatures had, upon being convened, heard a speech by the executive and subsequently responded by calling on him and presenting an answering address of their own. The Senate called upon the president for that purpose on May 18. Adams, followed by the eighteen senators, filed into the president's levee room, where Washington stood with two aides. "His Rotundity," as Izard dubbed the fat vice-president, was trembling so badly that he was able to read only by placing the senatorial address in his hat and holding on to the hat with both hands. That made for some difficulty in turning the pages, but Adams finally managed to get through.

Washington had prepared a brief reply, which he now removed from his coat pocket, only to create a minor dilemma. He had the paper in his right hand and his hat in his left, and no hand left over to remove his spectacles from his vest pocket. After some Chaplinesque shifting of objects he got his hat under his left arm and the paper in his left hand, somehow extracted the glasses from their case and got them on his nose, but was left with the case occupying the right hand. He overcame this "small distress" by placing the case on the chimney piece. Then, "having adjusted his spectacles, which was not very easy, considering the engagements of his hands, he read the reply with tolerable exactness and without much emotion." The president then invited everyone to sit, but Adams, perhaps because he found it difficult to sit gracefully while wearing his sword, declined, and the Senate bowed and left.

Beneath all this nonsensical ostentation and formality, however, lay some deadly serious jockeying for power, collective and individual. On one level, the Senate was looking out for its interests as a body. The exaggerated deference toward the president was designed, at least in part, to ensure that if court politics developed, the senators would have first rank as courtiers. The exaggerated insistence on formality, on the other hand, was part of a design by the senators to protect their prerogatives against executive encroachment. Their jealously in this regard was revealed in June, when a move was made to require the president to have senatorial approval in removing as well as appointing executive officers. The senators were borne down on that occasion by doubts among their own members and by overpowering constitutional arguments emanating from the House of Representatives, led by James Madison; but the very effort was symptomatic of a trait that would endure.

On another level, the frippery in the Senate was the surface manifestation of a struggle for power inside the body. In broad terms, senators from Virginia and New England were seeking to re-establish the alliance that had triumphed in the old Congress and brought independence in 1776, and those from the Middle States and the lower South were groping toward reestablishing their own coalition, which had prevailed in 1774–1775. On this more personal level, Richard Henry Lee, mistakenly figuring that Adams controlled the New England senators, kowtowed to Adams to aggrandize his own influence. The New Englanders, overestimating Adams's influence with the president and misreading the doings of Lee and his southern supporters, sought to strengthen their own hands by backing Adams and Lee on matters that they regarded as trivial. And so on.

The proceedings of the Senate (unlike those of the House) were closed to the public, but had there been any careful and seasoned Senate-watchers, the man they would have watched was Senator Oliver Ellsworth of Connecticut. His fellow senators, in fact, began to watch him more and more as the summer progressed. And well they might, for he was a shrewder political operator than all the others combined. Moreover, Ellsworth had some grand schemes afoot, and when he executed them—so skillfully that his colleagues never knew quite how it happened—the Senate could claim a large share of the credit for the achievements of 1789.

James Madison, however, was the person most nearly in command of national affairs. Madison was and is perhaps the most difficult of all the Founding Fathers to understand. His contemporaries were almost unanimous in regarding him as remarkably learned, candid, open, and of a sweet and amiable disposition. On all counts but the first they were entirely mistaken: he was, in actuality, so carefully contrived and controlled that in comparison to him Hamilton, Jefferson, and even Burr were open books. Possibly the key to his character is that he was either an epileptic or a victim of epileptiform hysteria and that he devoutly guarded the secret of his infirmity, lest he be regarded (in keeping with the superstitious science of his time) as being insane. Almost certainly he had not yet worked out what various psychiatrists and historians have described

31

as the "identity crisis"—that is, making one's peace with one's own finiteness.

In keeping with the psyche that in many cases stems from such internal stresses, Madison had fervently embraced a cause, that of enlarging national power as a means of creating a balanced system of government; and in keeping with the dictates of a finely honed mind and a highly developed skill in manipulating other men, he had been engaged for some time and with considerable success in support of his cause. Without him, Virginia might never have ratified the Constitution; and without Virginia the Union was entirely unworkable. Patrick Henry prevented Madison's election to the Senate and gerrymandered his representative district to make it unlikely that he could win a seat in the House; but Madison conducted a veritable door-to-door campaign and won a seat in the House anyway. Now, almost awesomely versed in the immediate problems facing the new government, he was better prepared than anyone to take the lead in making it workable.

One large problem quickly proved itself to be temporarily insoluble, and Madison shrewdly preceived that it should therefore be treated as a means by which other problems might be solved. This was the question of the location of the permanent capital of the United States. Every town of any pretensions to consequence between New Haven and Norfolk vied for the honor and the expected wealth that would arise from the choice. More importantly, every politician of consequence sought to have the location fixed as close as possible to his own constituency, on the theory that proximity would influence attendance and therefore influence the locus of power. As a practical matter, the outside limits seemed to lie between New York City and Annapolis. As a practical matter also, James Madison doubtless foresaw that in the rivalry lay the ingredients of a deal, whenever there arose a controversy in which the stakes were large enough to justify some trading.

Meanwhile, there was another large problem, which was almost as thorny but had to be resolved quickly: the matter of a tariff law to raise revenue. Madison's thinking on the subject had been worked out in consultations with Washington but was much more sharply refined than was the president's. The two Virginians agreed that revenue measures should be so devised as to implement a second consideration of national policy—to discriminate somewhat against the nation's late enemy, Great Britain, and to give a favored position to its ally, France, and to those few European powers with which the United States had been able to negotiate commercial treaties.

32

Madison introduced a bill toward this end on April 8, the very first day on which the House settled down to serious legislative business. He proposed a schedule of specific duties (taxes of so much a gallon or pound) on imported rum, liquor, wine, molasses, sugar, tea, cocoa, and coffee, and duties ad valorem (taxes based on a fixed percentage of value) on all other imported commodities. He also proposed a graded system of tonnage duties—taxes on the carrying capacity of vessels—on ships and smaller cargo craft arriving from foreign ports. Vessels owned by Americans would pay the smallest duties, those owned by subjects of nations "in treaty" with the United States would pay somewhat more, and those of Great Britain and other "untreatied" powers, considerably more.

A conflict of interests immediately arose, to foreshadow every debate on every proposed tariff for more than a century. Thomas Fitzsimons of Pennsylvania suggested that the list of specific duties be expanded to "protect our infant industries," which is to say the handcrafted goods that were produced mainly in his state and surrounding states. Fitzsimons also had an ulterior motive, however, or at least so supposed William Maclay, his fellow Pennsylvanian in the Senate. Fitzsimons was an affluent importing merchant, and together with others of that description, including the erstwhile anti-Federalist Elbridge Gerry of Massachusetts, he apparently set out to delay the enactment of tariff legislation until the spring importing season was past. Meanwhile, merchants could raise their prices on the pretense that the duties were forthcoming, and thereby take in a million or two from their customers on their own account.

Besides such shenanigans, there were more substantial interests at stake, but few understood quite what their interests were. Madison's proposed discrimination was a bonanza to New England shippers, or so it seemed, at the expense of tobacco planters in Maryland, Virginia, and North Carolina. Because freight rates were such a large part of the cost of marketing American tobacco in Europe, southerners objected to discriminatory tonnage duties, on the theory that Europeans would thereby be taxed out of the trade and New Englanders, thus endowed with a virtual monopoly, could raise freight rates at will. In point of fact, precious few Yankees were in the freighting business, preferring instead to buy cargoes and sell them for their own accounts; and so their congressmen counted this proposal as no boon at all, even as the southerners wailed against it as an unfair advantage to New England. Simultaneously the New Englanders objected to Madison's proposed duties on molasses, as being destructive of their rum industry.

In this maze of interests, real and imagined, Madison and reason prevailed. Few were entirely satisfied with the measure as it finally passed both houses of Congress, which was to be the way of things with tariff legislation nearly ever after. The average duty was around 7 or 8 percent. The secondary considerations of policy that motivated Washington and Madison did not lead to law, for full discrimination against Britain was not carried, nor was the protective principle espoused by Fitzsimons. Moreover, the bill did not pass until the spring importing season was almost over. Even so, by midsummer the government had a regular and potentially large source of revenue, which meant that it might be able to survive. That, in itself, was a monumental fact, for the Confederation Congress and the British Empire itself had, within living memory, foundered on proposals to create just such a system of taxation.

As the tariff was being debated, Madison was already engaged on another front, that concerning a bill of rights to the Constitution. In 1787 the Constitutional Convention, with the wholehearted support of Madison, had rejected proposals for a bill of rights, on the logically impeccable ground that it made no sense to create a federal government by listing the powers it could exercise and then to cloud the issue by listing powers it could not exercise. But opponents of the Constitution had created a considerable stir by demanding a bill of rights and had used that commotion as an excuse for demanding the calling of a second constitutional convention, ostensibly to rectify the oversights of the first but actually to subvert the Constitution entirely.

Understanding the perils of what was involved, Madison announced on May 4 that three weeks hence he would propose certain amendments to the Constitution. The reaction was gradual and complex. Some of the staunchest Federalists in the House, including Roger Sherman of Connecticut and Fisher Ames of Massachusetts, adhered blindly to the original Federalist position and strongly denounced the very idea of a bill of rights. Anti-Federalists, the erstwhile champions of amendments, caught on one by one: Aedanus Burke and Thomas Sumter of South Carolina, Elbridge Gerry of Massachusetts, and James Jackson of Georgia, who less than a year earlier had tried to prevent the adoption of the Constitution on the pretended ground that it had no bill of rights, now joined the likes of Sherman and Ames to oppose the introduction of amendments.

But Madison understood that a bill of rights was not primarily a substantive issue, and fortunately for the Nation, a majority of his colleagues went along with him. He had meticulously studied the

34

proposals that had emanated from the various state ratifying conventions. Not counting North Carolina and Rhode Island, which so far had refused to ratify, formal requests for restrictive amendments had come in from five states, and informal requests had come from two others. Because he recognized that the motivation underlying the demand was more political than ideological, Madison disregarded the fact that only three of these states had bills of rights of their own. Instead, he gathered and organized the proposed amendments.

Eliminating duplicates, Madison found eighty proposals. From all nine states he catalogued requests for a prohibition against interference by Congress with the time and place of holding elections, for restrictions on the taxing power, and for a declaration that all powers not delegated to the general government should be reserved to the states. Seven states spoke for jury trials; six called for an increase in the number of members of Congress, protection of religious freedom, and a prohibition of standing armies in times of peace. Five wanted prohibitions against quartering troops and against unreasonable searches and seizures and demanded protection of the right of the states to control the militias, the right of the people to bear arms, and the rights of freedom of speech and of the press. Four states requested guarantees of due process of law, speedy and public trials, the rights of assembly and petition, limits on the power of the federal judiciary, and bans on monopolies, excessive bail, unconstitutional treaties, and the holding of appointive federal offices by members of Congress.

Madison dismissed the least popular and most impractical of these suggestions and reduced the remainder to nineteen substantive amendments. (He introduced one impractical proposal of his own: that the amendments be woven into the text of the Constitution, rather than tacked on at the end.) On June 8 the House resolved itself into a committee of the whole house to debate the proposals, and by August 24, after intermittent debates, it had approved the amendments. They differed little from Madison's original proposals, save for being consolidated into seventeen amendments and being so worded as to be added onto the end of the Constitution. As they emerged from the House, the amendments were designed to apply to state governments as well as to the national government. (Hence, for example, states as well as the national government would have been required to have trials by jury and prohibited from restricting freedom of speech.)

On September 2 the Senate took up the proposals. Right away,

35

that body removed the applicability of the bill of rights to the states (hence, for example, states remained free to tax all citizens for the support of established churches, as Connecticut did until 1818 and Massachusetts did until 1833). Otherwise, however, the Senate largely concurred, though it and a joint committee that met on September 25 further consolidated the amendments so that only twelve were left. The first two, concerning the number and salaries of congressmen, were never ratified; the other ten, known as the Bill of Rights, became part of the Constitution on December 15, 1791.

The next great legislative task—taken up after but completed before the drafting of the Bill of Rights—was also constitutional in nature, namely the creation of the executive departments. On May 19 Congressman Elias Boudinot of New Jersey opened the subject, but Madison soon took charge of the debate. It was readily agreed that three departments were necessary and that they should comprehend the same activities as the earlier administrative arms of the Confederation: Foreign Affairs, War, and Finance.

Only three serious issues arose during the debate. One surfaced when John Vining of Delaware proposed that a Home Department be created, to exercise general supervision over the records of the government, relations with the states, establishment of post roads, the census, western territories, patents, geographical surveys, and similar matters. Vining received little support and was barraged by some who argued that the functions should not be exercised and by others who held that they should be assigned to the three great departments. By and large, the latter group prevailed; not for many years would the various domestic departments begin to materialize.

A second and much more delicate matter concerned the Treasury Department. First a group of arch-republicans, led by Elbridge Gerry, expressed great concern at the enormous power that would be lodged in the department and proposed to render the power safe by vesting it in a three-man board (as the arrangement had been since 1784) rather than in a single secretary. Tempers flashed hot; it was really a renewal of an old controversy, that between those who had supported Robert Morris as superintendent of finance in 1781–1783 and those who had almost hysterically opposed Morris's administration. That controversy, in turn, had arisen from conflicts of personalities and interests as well as of principles and had pitted the Lee-Adams "junto" of Virginia and Massachusetts against Philadelphia and New York.

The advocates of a single secretary prevailed by a handful of votes, but the uneasiness aroused by the debate led to another decision that was of great consequence in both the short range and the long. Bit by bit, as the subject arose intermittently in the early summer, the House began to add restrictions on the powers of the secretary of the treasury—not to reduce his powers, but to tie them to the House instead of to the independent executive authority. The design was to curtail the executive and aggrandize the House. The effect, as things worked out, was to plunge the Treasury Department into the most important activities of Congress. Indeed, the way was unwittingly paved for a brilliant and energetic secretary of the treasury to become, for practical purposes, an American "prime minister," even as the chancellor of the exchequer served that function in Britain.

The third subject of dispute, the removal power of the president, has already been mentioned. Fear of executive power was widespread and strong. Repeatedly, the more cautious congressmen warned that some powers which might be safely entrusted to Washington were dangerous in principle, for Washington could not live forever, and that it was best to err now on the side of checking presidential authority by making it subject to senatorial approval. Madison and others in what might have been styled the "court party" argued persuasively that if the president could not remove appointees without the permission of the Senate, appointees would serve for "good behaviour" or even life, since the only other way of removing them was the cumbersome impeachment process. Doubtless a few congressmen supported Madison out of jealousy of the Senate's powers. In any event, the principle of unilateral executive removal of executive appointees passed the House by a margin of six or seven votes in each of the bills creating executive offices. When the Senate approved the House measures in July (apparently, more than once by a tie vote broken by the vice-president), the principle became a part of established constitutional custom. Along the way, it was also established that clerical and other "inferior" personnel could even be appointed without the Senate's approval, by the president or by the heads of departments.

The bills establishing the departments were enacted in the late summer. The Department of Foreign Affairs (redesignated the State Department on September 15) was created by law on July 27, the War Department on August 7, the Treasury Department on September 2. In addition, Congress also provided for two federal agencies that had less than departmental status. It established the office of attorney general, wherein a lawyer was to be placed on retainer to advise the president on matters of constitutionality and law, and the office of postmaster general, which was to oversee the execution of the Constitution's mandate that Congress establish post offices and post roads.

As the summer of 1789 progressed and as these various enactments became law, President Washington found himself with almost a thousand offices to fill. Several times that number of applicants for jobs besieged him, directly or through intermediaries, but Washington scrupulously declined to exploit the opportunity to develop a system of patronage. Only in one special sense were his appointments partisan: he appointed only persons "of known attachment to the Government we have chosen"—that is, he refused to appoint anyone who was a known enemy of the Constitution.

In screening applicants for the minor jobs, he generally followed one of three rules of thumb. The first was a reflection of the aristocratic life-style: if Washington did not know the candidate personally, he made inquiries until he found a trusted acquaintance who did; and no appointment was forthcoming unless someone Washington trusted attested to the applicant's good character. The second was that Washington allowed his upper-level appointees to choose their own immediate inferiors. The third rule was one imposed upon Washington against his will, the practice that came to be called "senatorial courtesy." The president nominated Benjamin Fishbourne to be naval officer of the port of Savannah, but when Georgia Senators James Gunn and William Few objected, the Senate, on the strength of their preferences alone, refused to confirm the appointment. Washington was miffed, but he withdrew the nomination, and subsequently it became regular practice to appoint no one to whom the appointee's senators personally objected.

In making the major appointments, Washington consulted with several intimates, notably Madison, and considered the matter carefully. For secretary of state, the position generally regarded as the most prestigious, he preferred John Jay; but Jay indicated that he wanted to be chief justice, and Washington granted his wish. Instead, to head the State Department, Washington chose Thomas Jefferson, who was on his way to Virginia on leave from his post as minister to France. Henry Knox was continued in the War Department, and at Madison's urging, Washington named his former aide-de-camp, Alexander Hamilton, to be secretary of the treasury. Rounding out the major appointments, Edmund Randolph of Virginia became attorney general, and Samuel Osgood of Massachusetts became postmaster general.

As to setting the executive departments into operation, three general philosophies of public administration—indeed three different philosophies regarding the proper nature of the presidency— were advanced. One was that held by a number of senators and others who believed the Senate should be the repository of power for a strong aristocracy, namely, that the Senate should serve as the president's executive council and, as had been the tradition with the upper houses of several colonial governments, exercise a full share of the executive authority. Washington was temperamentally opposed to such an arrangement, and any doubts he may have held were dispelled by the fiasco of seeking advise and consent from the Senate in person. Moreover, Madison's efforts in working out the laws establishing the departments were carefully designed to minimize the Senate's influence in the executive branch—in matters of administrative detail as well as such broader questions as the power of removal.

A second view, more subtle and more complex, is most closely identifiable with Alexander Hamilton. Hamilton preferred an executive branch modeled after that of Great Britain, where the ministers (including heads of departments), acting in the name of the Crown, in fact constituted "the Government." Such a ministry would not only implement policy, as defined by Congress, but would initiate policy as well, both by exercising an independent administrative power and by drafting legislation and guiding it through Congress. Hamilton's position ran counter to the ideas of both Washington and Madison, and decisions made before Hamilton took office prevented him from fully implementing his ideas. Nonetheless, the nature of Hamilton's responsibilities, carried out in the context of the administrative system that Washington chose to put into force, partially permitted Hamilton to have his way.

The view that prevailed was Washington's own, that executive authority was solely the president's, that the Senate had no share in it beyond that of approving or rejecting his appointments and treaties, and that department heads were responsible directly to him. Not even Hamilton settled any matter of consequence without consulting Washington and obtaining his approval, and all department heads submitted matters of both detail and administrative policy to him. In turn, Washington expected departmental subordinates to be responsible to their heads in just the way the heads were responsible to the president.

Administration was therefore highly personal, after the fashion of the pre-bureaucratic eighteenth-century world. That is to say, subordinate officials normally did not act in accordance with rules or objectively defined codes of procedure, but in accordance with the direct instructions of their immediate superiors. To be sure, it became necessary in carrying out many of the routine activities of the Treasury Department, such as the acceptance of merchants' bonds for the payment of customs duties, to work out strict and uniform procedures, and Hamilton labored effectively to systematize all such activities. But in general, administration was ad hoc and personal; and thus, for example, Congress normally voted money in lump appropriations to the several departments, leaving the administrators a wide latitude of discretion in the actual spending. Washington personally decided how much to pay American ministers abroad, and department heads and even their subordinates often spent money for one purpose when Congress clearly had intended that it be spent for another.

In day-to-day practice, Washington supervised the activities of his department heads closely. In keeping with the Constitution's stricture that the president could seek their opinions *in writing*, he kept them all busy penning reports on matters he had referred to their attention, opinions of proposed plans of action, judgments of the constitutionality of legislation, drafts of his public papers, and compendiums of information. Commonly, moreover, after an exchange of letters Washington would invite the subordinate to breakfast, where discussion would go on until the president was perfectly satisfied.

Jefferson's description of the way the system worked is an excellent one:

> Letters of business came addressed sometimes to the President, but most frequently to the heads of departments. If addressed to himself, he referred them to the proper department to be acted on; if to one of the secretaries, the letter, if it required no answer, was communicated to the President, simply for his information. If an answer was requisite, the secretary of the department communicated the letter & his proposed answer to the President. Generally they were simply sent back after perusal, which signified his approbation. Sometimes he returned them with an informal note, suggesting an alteration or a query. If a doubt of any importance arose, he reserved it for conference. By this means, he was always in accurate possession of all facts and proceedings in every part of the Union, and to whatsoever department they related; he formed a central

point for the different branches; preserved an unity of object and action among them; exercised that participation in the suggestion of affairs made incumbent on him; and met himself the due responsibility for whatever was done. . . . [Washington's system] gave, indeed, to the heads of departments the trouble of making up, once a day, a packet of all their communications for the perusal of the President; it commonly also retarded one day their despatches by mail. But in pressing cases, this injury was prevented by presenting that case singly for immediate attention; and it produced us in return the benefit of his sanction for every act we did.[1]

Some variations in the routine arose from differences in the talents and temperaments of the administrators. In affairs of the State Department, Washington believed himself an expert; and in the affairs of the War Department he unquestionably was an expert; and thus he was in practice his own foreign secretary and war secretary, Jefferson and Knox often being reduced virtually to clerical roles. Jefferson, who was not at all fond of clerical work, was not always as diligent an administrator as he might have been. Given a free hand on a subject that interested him, he worked promptly and thoroughly; but if he was given only a passive role or (as increasingly happened as time went by) Washington adopted policies that he disagreed with, Jefferson tended to obstruct things through studied lackadaisicalness. Knox was a diligent administrator who loved his work and loved his boss, never initiated or questioned anything, and executed orders with promptness and dispatch. Hamilton, on the other hand, was an expert on finance and commerce, matters clearly beyond Washington's ken and outside his area of interest. Necessarily, Hamilton had a freer rein than did his colleagues. But what was more, Hamilton was hyperenergetic, impatient, and a compulsive meddler; and he often took the liberty, when policies in the province of the War or State departments were of interest to him, of attempting to initiate policy by preparing unsolicited position papers for the president's attention and even by making private commitments that Washington was unaware of.

In regard to the Post Office Department, Congress kept the power of laying out post roads for itself, despite Federalist efforts to vest it in the president; and since Washington was not especially

---

[1] Jefferson to heads of departments, November 6, 1801, in Jefferson, *Works* (Federal edition), 9:310–312.

interested in the department anyway, its affairs drifted without presidential direction. Timothy Pickering, who succeeded Osgood as postmaster general, went so far in the discretionary exercise of authority as to drop the customary practice of advertising for bids for mail contractors, until Congress made the practice mandatory in 1792. Postmasters were appointed by the postmaster general, not the president, and were almost never removed from office.

The last grand constitutional task of the First Congress, that of creating the federal judiciary, was the only one carried out by the Senate. It was also the most complex, for it involved the settlement of knotty problems on three essentially unrelated levels: legal, ideological, and economic. In all three areas Senator Oliver Ellsworth took the lead and, with assistance from Senator William Paterson of New Jersey, was largely responsible for the outcome of the debate.

The legal problems were awesome. Anglo-Saxon jurisprudence, from which American law and legal procedures were derived, was itself a maze, involving as it did common law, equity, chancery, and statutory law as well as a myriad of both local and special variations. American law was Anglo-Saxon law compounded by a factor of thirteen. To cite but one relatively simple example, in regard to the manner of directing new trials when an appellate court found something wrong with the way a lower court had conducted a trial, New York, New Jersey, and Virginia followed the procedures of British common law; Massachusetts had long since worked out a different system and had recently confirmed that system by statute; Connecticut was in process of devising a new and especially fuzzy system.

Ellsworth, a man of limited formal training but great common sense and a most diligent and energetic student, had briefed himself as thoroughly on legal procedures as Madison had on bills of rights. He also drew from Paterson, tough minded and thoroughly trained, and Caleb Strong of Massachusetts, fairly short on intellect but long on training and experience. When their combined knowledge was not enough, Ellsworth simply incorporated Connecticut practice into the bill for the national judiciary or invented a commonsense procedure of his own. In the doing, he had the advantage of minimal political opposition to this aspect of the work. Senator Maclay and a few others grumbled, in accordance with an attitude that was widespread in New England and in the back country elsewhere, that the lawyers were making things unnecessarily complicated so as to preserve a secure and comfortable living for themselves; but such prejudice occasioned little opposition in Congress.

Ideological differences, on the other hand, were much less easily resolved. The basic issue in question was fairly simple: how far the power of federal courts should overshadow that of state courts. Extreme nationalists wanted to create a full network of federal courts, to endow them with as much power as the Constitution allowed, and to minimize the powers of the state courts. Extreme states' righters wanted to confine the Supreme Court to the narrow original jurisdiction prescribed by the Constitution, to vest it with as little appellate jurisdiction as possible, and to deposit most of the judicial power in the existing state courts.

Neither view was likely to prevail, but compromise would be difficult. Archfederalists feared state legislatures as the most dangerous enemies of union, but those who were trained in the law viewed the state courts with scarcely less anxiety. As for the anti-Federalists, the great republican orator Patrick Henry had predicted that the national government would swallow up the states and that the main agent of the devouring would be the federal judiciary; and his personal representatives in the Senate, Richard Henry Lee and William Grayson, echoed that sentiment.

Faced with such opposition, Ellsworth produced some creative innovations. He proposed that there be, in addition to a six-member Supreme Court, one district court for each state. The district courts would be federal, but the judges had to be residents of the state from which they were appointed. That insured the following of traditional local procedures except when different procedures were carefully specified by national law, and thus imposed little that was alien upon local lawyers. Moreover, Ellsworth and his associates proposed the creation of circuit courts, to consist of two traveling members of the Supreme Court and the district-court judge in the state in which trials were held, the main function of the district judge being to make sure that trials were conducted according to local rules. Finally, Ellsworth proposed to arrange jurisdictions so that in many cases state courts would have concurrent jurisdiction with federal courts, the sanctity of the Constitution being preserved by provision for direct appeal to the United States Supreme Court when the constitutionality of state law was in question. Such a mixture of jurisdictions confounded the enemy, and Ellsworth's court structure passed the Senate by a 14 to 6 vote and the House by 29 to 22.

The complexities underlying the judicial act in its third aspect, the conflict of economic-interest groups, were so tangled as to make the legal and ideological problems seem simple by comparison.

Those involving maritime law, admiralty courts, and similar commercial matters—which anyone learned in British law might have expected to occasion difficulties—were solved with surprisingly little friction. What was less simple was the matter of conflicting claims to land titles.

These conflicts were long in developing. Before the end of the seventeenth century, Americans had begun to realize that the great wealth to be reaped in their continent lay neither in farming for market nor in trade and shipping, but in acquiring large tracts of vacant land and selling it at a profit to newcomers from Europe. That land could be bought and sold like any other commodity was itself a departure from the European norm, and it was bound to have legal and political repercussions. By the 1730s political factions had begun to form in Massachusetts, Pennsylvania, Maryland, and Virginia, with rivalry over land grants and the means of paying for them as their base. By the 1750s and 1760s such rivalries were setting off conflicts that would (in conjunction with other forces) lead to revolution. During the Revolution and under the Confederation, conflicts over land claims were among the few genuinely vital determinants of political positions. In sum, for nearly a century the questions of "home rule, and who should rule at home," to employ Carl Becker's celebrated phrase, had had meaning largely in terms of the unspoken question, "Who shall have control over land grants?"

That was the larger background. The more immediate background had to do with the recent formation of large companies and groups of powerful individual speculators to obtain huge tracts of the public domain—lands acquired by the United States or by individual states as a result of the Revolution. In 1787 the Ohio Company (originally consisting of investors from Connecticut, Massachusetts, and Rhode Island, but ultimately consisting almost exclusively of Connecticutters) had arranged for the purchase from Congress of a million acres of land on the Ohio River at less than a dollar an acre and payable in public securities at their par value, though these bonds could be acquired from individual owners at less than twenty cents on the dollar. In 1788 a group of New Jersey investors, calling themselves the Miami Company, arranged a similar purchase. In 1789 the legislature of Georgia succumbed to large-scale bribery and made its first sales of "Yazoo Lands" (in what became Alabama and Mississippi) to outsiders for a nominal price. In the "western reserve" of Pennsylvania, claimed by Connecticut, dubious sales were also made. In the "triangle" of western New York, northwestern Pennsylvania, and the northeastern portion of the Ohio country, Oliver Phelps and Nathaniel Gorham purchased a huge tract, and it was rumored that every influential New England politician was in on the deal. New York and Pennsylvania speculator-politicians—including William Bingham, William Constable, Secretary of War Henry Knox, and Senator Robert Morris—negotiated and concluded a number of large-scale deals for acquisition of lands owned or claimed by individual states.

The Constitution potentially gave the federal courts jurisdiction over all the litigation that would arise from these various grants. Oliver Ellsworth and William Paterson, as investors in two of the companies that were sure to become involved in litigation, had an interest in seeing to it that jurisdiction was in fact lodged in the federal courts, for they, like other Connecticut and New Jersey investors, purchased directly from the federal government. After the Ohio Company and the Miami Company purchases, most speculators bought from state governments with rival claims and figured to fare better in the courts of the states from which they made their purchases. In short, it was as important to land buyers before 1789 that claims be adjudicated in federal courts as it was important to subsequent buyers that claims be decided in state courts. The judiciary act of 1789, as devised by Ellsworth and Paterson in the Senate and as defended by Roger Sherman of Connecticut in the House, loaded the deck in favor of federal adjudication.

Despite the narrow considerations upon which the judiciary bill turned, however, it was passed into law and became, for practical purposes, a part of the Constitution itself. As things worked out, the Supreme Court did not become especially important either during Washington's presidency or during that of his successor. Washington's appointments to the bench were distinguished enough: Jay as Chief Justice and, as associate justices, John Rutledge of South Carolina, James Iredell of North Carolina, John Blair of Virginia, James Wilson of Pennsylvania, and William Cushing of Massachusetts. But with few exceptions, the court was not called upon to adjudicate the pressing issues that faced the nation in the 1790s, and much of the time of the justices was taken up with the tedious, onerous, and largely fruitless business of "riding circuit." Moreover, when the court did begin to become important, it came under political attack, and demagogues ever after would exploit popular prejudice to attack the system on one pretense or another. And yet, despite revisions in 1801, 1802, and occasionally thereafter, the system created by Oliver Ellsworth and his associates and allies in 1789 would endure.

Congress adjourned on September 29, and then everyone—or almost everyone—took a breather. Congressmen went home to rest, congratulate themselves, tend to private business, and scheme for the second session, convening on January 4. Washington set off on a triumphal tour of the New England states.

The one man for whom there could be no rest was Hamilton. In keeping with Madison's plan to make the Treasury Department subordinate to the House of Representatives, the House instructed Hamilton to make a survey of the public debts and come up, by the time Congress reconvened, with a plan for servicing them.

The assignment was herculean, but Hamilton did it. In the doing, something quite unexpected took place: Madison's scheme backfired, for Hamilton himself emerged as the most powerful man in the government.

3

★★★★★

THE FINANCIAL DILEMMA

The House's orders to Hamilton specifically required him to find out how much the states' war debts were and how they were being serviced, ascertain how much of the certificates of continental debts were owned by state governments, and prepare a plan "for the support of the public Credit." Nobody had a comprehensive grasp of the first part of the assignment—that is, the information on which any reasonable plan for servicing the public debts must be based. Almost everybody had an answer to the second.

Hamilton's approach to the problem was radically different from everybody else's. Partly he saw things differently because he knew more than anyone else did: he studied his subject with a diligence that surpassed even that with which Madison had studied bills of rights and Ellsworth had studied the judiciary, and arrived at a greater mastery. Partly, too, he differed because he was disinterested: vast as was the wealth with which he dealt and great as was the opportunity for peculation, only the most hysterical of his enemies thought of accusing him of acting with a view toward personal gain or of favoring the interests of his state or section. But these were only incidental sources of his plan. The real roots lay deep in British history and even deeper in Alexander Hamilton's psyche.

For he schemed a scheme so grand and so audacious that almost no one, not even his staunchest supporters, understood it until it had been executed, and few understood it even then.

Some suspected. Thomas Jefferson, in a bitter and distorted

account of these years, written late in his life, came closer to the truth than he knew. He told of a discussion he had with Adams and Hamilton early in Washington's presidency, when the three were still on terms of cordiality and mutual respect. They were talking political philosophy, and Adams, or so Jefferson recalled with obvious distaste, opined that if the British system of constitutional monarchy could be purged of corruption, it would be the best system of government ever devised. Hamilton, to the utter horror of the arch-republican Jefferson, replied that the British system was the best possible form of government as it stood, for, purged of its corruption, it would not work.

That was the key: Hamilton set out to plant the British system in America, corruption and all, and to do so within the framework of the Constitution and American institutions.

Because the Revolutionary War had been financed on a hand-to-mouth basis, the tangle of obligations remaining at war's end was bewilderingly complex. Theoretically, war finance was to have been simple, the states being expected to supply the needed funds on an equitable basis and the Continental Congress being supposed to administer the disbursement. Things had not worked out that way. In addition to the prescribed method, Congress had raised many millions on its own account, and states had raised and spent many more millions directly, without working through Congress. Most such efforts facilitated the war effort, but they also added to the financial confusion when the war was over.

As matters stood when Hamilton inherited the problem, the public accounts fell into two broad categories. The first and by far the largest was not the "public debt," the sums owed by governments to citizens, but intergovernmental obligations and credits. The total amount that the state governments had spent during the war in the "common defense and general welfare" had been something over $100 million. Under the terms of the Articles of Confederation and various ordinances passed by Congress, evidences of such expenditures were to have been audited, a total arrived at, and shares of the costs apportioned among the states on the basis of the value of land within each. Those states which were found to have paid more than their share were to have been reimbursed from the general treasury; those that had paid less than their share were to have paid the deficit into the general treasury.

The sums at stake being so great, the procedure for settling the state accounts had occasioned as much acrimony as any other question that faced the Confederation Congress. Each state believed (or professed to believe) that it had spent more than its share, but each also feared that the accounting method adopted by Congress might not give it full credit. Southerners had been especially slipshod in recording expenditures for the war cause—or, as they phrased it, they had acted "in the true Spirit of a patriot . . . without taking any heed concerning the day of retribution." Accordingly, they insisted that a lax system of documentary proof of claims be followed, and even that sworn statements be acceptable in lieu of receipts. New England Yankees, by contrast, habitually got receipts in writing even in emergencies, and they feared that southern insistence upon lax accounting masked a design to justify fraudulent claims. And beyond regional distrust lay another source of contention, claims for military expenditures that had in fact been made in the interests of states, not the nation. Massachusetts and Virginia, in particular, insisted on charging to the Union the cost of such ventures—Massachusetts for an abortive raid that it had launched, without congressional authorization, upon Penobscot, Maine, in 1779; and Virginia for George Rogers Clark's foray into the Ohio country in 1778.

Congress began the process of auditing such accounts in 1782 but changed the rules almost seasonally until 1787. At that point a compromise, designed to expedite settlement, was agreed upon. Five regional commissioners were appointed, with instructions to accept all indisputable claims as rapidly as possible and to pass questionable claims on to the three-member General Board of the Treasury. Minor changes in procedure were subsequently adopted, but the crucial decision was that in 1789 the new Congress under the Constitution separated the whole matter of state accounts from the problem of public debts—that is, from the problem referred to Hamilton.

Public debts fell into three broad categories: foreign, national, and state. The United States had received from abroad $10 to $11 million in subsidies and loans during the war, mostly from France. This debt was politically neutral, since almost every American agreed that it should be paid as soon as possible, for reasons of both honor and expediency. To be sure, honor and expediency did not quite dictate identical policies. The debt to the government of France, something over $8 million, probably had first claim on America's honor; but the debt to private bankers in Holland, about $2 million, probably had priority as a matter of national expediency, since future loans were more likely to be forthcoming from Dutch bankers than from Louis XVI of France. For now, however, the distinction was too fine to worry about, for the entire foreign debt was well within the capacity of the newly reorganized American government to pay.

The second category of government obligations, namely the debts inherited from the old Congress by the new constitutional government, was for the most part likewise clean-cut. The old Congress had made direct expenditures in three main ways, not counting spending the proceeds of its foreign loans—by issuing unsecured paper money; by selling bonds called "loan office certificates" or issuing them directly for supplies; and by authorizing its officers and military commanders, in certain circumstances, to supply and pay the troops by signing promissory notes in the field. The paper money had depreciated almost to nothingness ("not worth a Continental") and had been officially devalued at a ratio of 40 to 1; and now the only question remaining was whether to disregard it entirely or redeem it at an extremely devalued rate. The loan office certificates, amounting to more than $11 million, and the field expenditures, nearly another $16 million, were generally regarded as ranking just below the French debt as a matter of national honor; indeed, it was these obligations that most Americans meant when they referred to the "public debt." But there was also the matter of accrued interest on these debts—virtually nothing in the way of interest except "indents," or promises of interest, had been paid since 1783—and this back interest was subject to some dispute. The dictates of national honor might be read either way, for it could be argued with equal plausibility that patriots should not profit from the weakness of government or that government should not exploit the patriotism of citizens. The dictates of expediency, on the other hand, were unequivocal, since no one would be disposed to lend money or services to the government in the future, if the government were unwilling to pay interest on what was loaned.

Finally, there were the debts of the states. The states had financed their wartime expenditures in much the same ways employed by the Congress, but they had one power that the Congress had not, namely the power to levy and collect taxes. Consequently, the states were slower to resort to large-scale deficit financing, and many might have emerged with little or no debt except for an emergency that had arisen in 1780. The Congress was bankrupt, having exhausted both money and credit, and until its affairs were reorganized by Superintendent of Finance Robert Morris in 1781, the states were called upon to pay and supply the army directly. They did so, and also compensated the soldiers for earlier pay in currency that had depreciated, and in the doing they took on debts about as large as those of Congress.

No one knew just how much the states owed at the end of the war, and the matter was even more muddled by 1789. Some states had, by then, almost wiped out their debts by levying heavy taxes payable in their depreciated securities; others had virtually crippled themselves by attempting to service their debts with hard money; still others had managed their finances so well that they were able to assume responsibility for the national debt owned by their citizens. The cardinal fact about the state debts, however, was not their amount but the reduced ability of states to service any debts, now that the Constitution had vested Congress with exclusive power over the most convenient and lucrative forms of taxation. For that reason, sentiment was widespread that the state obligations should be treated as properly being debts of the nation.

Ownership of the various forms of government debts was distributed unevenly, and the interests of public creditors were scarcely identical. At the time Hamilton was instructed to make his survey, holdings of state and national securities were still quite widely distributed, despite the natural tendency of securities to drift toward commercial centers. As recently as two years earlier, for example, nearly twelve thousand people in New York and Pennsylvania, or about one adult male in twelve, held Continental securities; and in Rhode Island about a sixth of the heads of families were creditors of the state. And despite intensified activity by speculators since 1787, between fifteen thousand and twenty thousand people owned certificates of the Continental debt in 1790, and possibly that many more were state creditors. Between 25 and 40 percent of the securities were still in the hands of the original holders—those who had served in the army or had supplied money, goods, or services in the war effort. All things considered, that was a surprisingly low turnover, representing alienation of original holdings at an annual rate of only about 6 percent.

It was not, however, the thousands of small and original holders who clouded the task of managing the public debt, it was the small concentrations of holders of huge amounts. The largest single concentration of Continental securities was in state treasuries, especially those of New York, Pennsylvania, and Maryland; all told, the states owned roughly $9 million in federal securities, not counting accrued interest, or about a third of the entire national debt. Next in size, perhaps, came the holdings of foreign investors, especially Dutch financiers, and their American agents. A Dutch syndicate headed by Peter Stadnitski, for example, began buying American securities in 1786 through a Massachusetts broker named Daniel Parker and had amassed $1.34 million before the Constitution was ratified in 1788. In 1789 Stadnitski, Nicholas Van Staphorst, and other Dutch investors added another $4 million to their holdings. By the time Hamilton took office they probably held nearly a fifth of the American national debt. Finally, there were large-scale American investors on their own account. In Massachusetts 107 individuals owned nearly $3 million of the federal debt between them by 1790, in Pennsylvania 78 individuals held more than $2 million, and so on. Eleven speculators, mainly from New York, acquired in 1789 more than $600,000 of the state debt of North Carolina.

The interests of the large holders were far from identical. Foreign investors in Continental securities were straightforwardly bullish, betting on the rise: they had bought at ten to fifty cents on the dollar and expected the new government to repay them at full par value. But many of them were strongly opposed to payment of state debts by the national government, on the theory that the additional burden would strain the national government's resources and jeopardize their investments. Many state creditors had opposed and continued to oppose a national system out of a similar fear.

More divisive were the conflicting interests of American speculators. In most parts of the United States a large portion, perhaps a majority, of the speculators on a grand scale were not "bulls" at all, but essentially short-sellers whose interest was in holding down rather than raising the market price of securities. That is to say, the bigger and bolder operators, following the American habit, had plunged deeply into land speculations, and they had done so in a way that would be most profitable if the prices of public securities remained low: they had contracted with Congress or state governments to buy vast tracts of vacant land, the purchase price being payable in several annual installments and in government securities *at their par value*. If securities could be bought on the open market at, say, 15 cents on the dollar, then a million acres of land at a dollar an acre could thereby be obtained for a cash outlay of $150,000. The prospects of profit from land speculation on that basis had been so high, and the prospects in securities so low, that most every man of means and a gambling instinct found investment in public lands irresistible. If, however, the market price of public securites should rise, their profit margin would decline; and a large rise would wipe them out.

Only two concentrated groups of American investors in public securities were bulls, betting their all on the hope that security prices would rise, far and fast. One was a group in New York, headed by William Duer and William Constable and working at least in part on the basis of inside information from the Treasury Department, who stayed out of large-scale land operations until the funding system proposed by Hamilton was in full operation. The other was the collection of new-rich merchants in Boston and Providence, perhaps 150 men in all, who had made extremely bad investments in imported British goods at the end of the war and had made what had long appeared to be equally bad investments in government securities. They were deeply indebted to British merchants for their imports, and the national and state governments were deeply indebted to them. If they could realize fully upon their second investments, they could recover handsomely from the first.

It is to be noted that the bullish speculators became aware of the nature of their interests before the land speculators did. The latter, and especially those in Philadelphia and New York, acted for a long time as if the supply of cheap public securities was unlimited. Thus Andrew Cragie, Robert Morris, and many another well-known speculator contracted to buy huge tracts of land on the terms just described, and simultaneously joined Duer and Constable in contracting with European investors to buy securities on the Europeans' account, apparently without realizing that in their second capacity they were to force security prices so high as to imperil their investments in land, or perhaps mistakenly thinking that they could play both ends against the middle.

Finally, there was the matter of conflicting state interests. At one extreme stood Massachusetts, Connecticut, and South Carolina: their public debts had been insupportably large even before the constitutional shift of the taxing power, and they obviously stood to gain if the national government assumed the obligations of the states. At the other stood Virginia, Maryland, North Carolina, and Georgia: they had retired the better part of their debts, expected to be owed much from the general treasury when the auditing of state accounts was complete, and were not anxious to be saddled with the burden of supporting the debts of states that had been less diligent than they in retiring their securities. In between were Pennsylvania, which owed little to its citizens and owned a sizable portion of the national debt, and New York, which had a large state debt but also owned a considerable amount of national securities.

In sum, the dictates of neither honesty nor policy were clear guides to determining who should be paid what, by whom, and when.

And there was still another dimension to the problem, the ideological or philosophical. Nonphilosophical as most Americans were, averse as they were to determining things on the basis of ideology, the long-range implications of the way the war debts were handled were too great to ignore. Accordingly, no small number of Americans, even some who had large financial interests at stake, rose above their personal concerns and advocated various policies on the basis of broad philosophical considerations.

Disinterested viewpoints, however, were neither less varied nor less vigorously defended just because they were disinterested. Indeed, guesses and fears and prejudices about the socio-political effects of servicing the public debts were so diverse and so intensely felt that any attempt to analyze them necessarily oversimplifies and underestimates the problem. Even so, some understanding can be had by observing the more frequently expressed of the extreme alternative positions.

The most radical position was that the debts should simply be repudiated. Not many people in public life, to be sure, openly espoused repudiation, but sentiment for repudiation of all but the foreign debt was actually common. Many persons in Congress advocated repudiation of accrued interest, and at least four members of the House of Representatives—Samuel Livermore of New Hampshire, Thomas Scott of Pennsylvania, Thomas Tucker of South Carolina, and James Jackson of Georgia—proposed that the principal of the debts be "scaled down" to their market value, which would have effectively repudiated three-fourths of their face value. Moreover, there was both precedent and justification for such a course. In 1780 Continental paper money had been reduced, by action of the old Congress, from a face value of $200 million to $5 million. Benjamin Franklin had defended the policy on the ground that the paper money had actually depreciated gradually before the official devaluation, costing but little to every person who accepted it and then used it to buy something, and thus that it had worked as an equitable form of taxation. John Adams had defended the official devaluation with the bald assertion that "the public has its rights as well as individuals."

Related to the advocacy of repudiation was the advocacy of discrimination between original and present holders of government paper. That is to say, many believed that original holders should be

54

compensated in full (with or without payment of accrued interest), but that persons who had acquired certificates second- and third-hand were considerably less deserving. Popular prejudice against speculators was widespread and intense, the term bloodsuckers being commonly used to describe them. But to discriminate would have been to set off nightmarishly complex problems. The old soldier who had sold his pay certificates to a speculator for ten cents on the dollar would be taken care of by discrimination, but what about the honest merchant who had accepted the soldier's certificate at or near face value in payment for goods; was he not entitled to something for his faith in the credit of the nation? Besides, as the opponents of discrimination argued, to refuse full payment to present holders would make all future government bonds nonnegotiable; in times of depressed credit in the future, the government creditor would find it utterly impossible to find anyone to buy his bonds, no matter how dire his needs.

And even among those who insisted on full compensation for all present holders of government paper, there was disagreement over whether state debts should be assumed by the national government. As indicated, many a pocketbook was involved in this matter, but feelings on the issue ran far deeper than that. Some viewed it simply: honor dictated that governments, like men, must pay their just debts; the state war debts were just, and that was that. Others feared the aggrandizement of national power implicit in assumption, and opposed it because it would in effect create a list of fifteen or twenty thousand pensioners of the national government. Ardent nationalists, on the other hand, advocated assumption for precisely that reason.

Finally, there was an emotionally laden issue that overlapped and often overrode all the others. In the simplest terms, this question turned on whether the debts should be repaid or merely "funded." Those who took the first position regarded a public debt as a public burden, necessitating a level of taxation that hampered economic development and also necessitating a government whose strength was inimical to personal freedom. The proper course to follow was therefore to retire the debt as quickly as possible—by levying taxes as high as they could be equitably imposed, pushing the sale of public lands for public securities, and keeping all government expenditures at a barebones minimum. The opposite point of view was to regard the public debt as a public blessing, as something which, if properly managed, could facilitate both growth and stability. To this way of thinking, provision should be made for making regular interest payments on the debt, but the principal should remain more or less permanent and should be managed through sophisticated fiscal techniques so as to serve as a basis for a uniform and elastic currency.

The roots of the second attitude, and the controversy surrounding it, went back to British experience early in the eighteenth century. During the wars that followed the Glorious Revolution in England (1689–1714), the English government had, in effect, invented the modern phenomenon of public debt by selling interest-bearing "annuities" to the public, principally London merchants. As an inducement to buyers, Parliament authorized a group of wealthy Londoners to create a corporation, the Bank of England, which as an institution rapidly became the largest single holder of government annuities. These devices worked handsomely to finance the war, but in a postwar speculative orgy the country perverted the mechanism and almost gambled itself into national bankruptcy. Then followed the long and astonishingly successful prime ministry of Sir Robert Walpole (1721–1742), during which the financial system was regularized—with significant consequences for the English-speaking world, and indeed the entire world.

Walpole set out to restore financial stability, and toward that end he created a "sinking fund," a treasury reserve built from the revenues of certain fixed taxes. The ostensible purpose of the sinking fund was to reduce and ultimately retire the public debt; the real purpose, it turned out, was not to pay the debt but to convince people that it would be paid. The very establishment of the fund restored faith in the government's credit, with the results that the market price of annuities rose and interest rates declined accordingly. To complement the illusion the Bank of England, in an effort to facilitate managing the wholesale marketing of government bonds at reduced interest rates, developed the practice of buying and selling annuities at retail on the London stock exchange. That kept the market high and steady, as anticipated, but had an unexpected effect as well. The general public became convinced that government bonds could always be converted into cash at or near their face value and began to accept ownership of them as a basis for granting private credit. The Bank of England thereby became able to issue notes, universally acceptable as money, against government bonds held in its vaults. In sum, the annuities supported the bank notes, and bank notes supported the annuities, and thus—without anyone entirely planning it—England's public debt became monetized. It was no longer either necessary or wise to reduce the public debt, for to do so would be to reduce the nation's money supply, shrink its credit reservoir, and jeopardize its prosperity and economic expansion.

But that was not all: this "Financial Revolution" had set off profound social and political changes as well. Traditionally, in England only landed estates were regarded as "real" property—all else, even gold and silver, being mere "personal" property—and power had flowed from ownership of the land. Now, in a single generation, personal property became both quantitatively and qualitatively more important. The traditional Tory squirearchy lost wealth and influence, or rather, retained them only to the extent that landholders participated in and profited from the newly monetized scheme of things. Power then tended to devolve upon a handful of great families, who through their liquid wealth controlled most of the seats in Parliament. Prime ministers could control Parliament only through open corruption: bribery, proffered in the form of money, place, or royal favor.

Both the monetization of English society and the corruption of English politics offended and outraged many in England as well as in America—even though the two instrumentalities were remarkably effective in bringing about freedom, prosperity, and peace. In Britain the ablest opposition spokesman was the Tory Henry St. John, Viscount Bolingbroke. This great reactionary theorist saw nothing but decay and evil in eighteenth-century English life, and saw money as the poisonous wellspring of it all. Earlier, he believed, when the gentry was supreme, relations were based upon ownership of land, honest labor in the soil, craftsmanship in the cities, and a system of deference wherein every man was secure in his place; honor, manly virtue, and public spirit governed people's conduct, and avarice and ambition were reckoned as the cardinal vices.

In America, the Walpolean system had met with greatest favor in the Middle Colonies, in the vicinities of New York and Philadelphia, and in the lower South, especially South Carolina. The "agrarianism" of Bolingbroke and his circle found adherents mainly in the tobacco-growing areas—Virginia, Maryland, and North Carolina—and in New England. By the time Alexander Hamilton became secretary of the treasury, these attitudes had become deeply rooted patterns of thought, with but two modifications. One was that many people in New England, and particularly in Massachusetts and Connecticut, had, in the 1780s, become disillusioned with the puritanized Bolingbrokism that had long prevailed in the area and were ready to have a go at the effeminate luxury and vice that would be theirs if Walpole's system were adapted to America's problems. The other was that since the orgy of denunciations of British corruption that had preceded the Declaration of Independence, few Americans were willing to come right out in public and admit that they advocated servicing the public debts in a way that would appeal to man's baser instincts.

Alexander Hamilton cast his lot unequivocally with Walpole. A great deal of ink has been spilled over the question of the origins of Hamilton's ideas on the subject. Certainly he was influenced by the earlier efforts and thoughts of Robert and Gouverneur Morris, and he solicited and clearly took into account suggestions from William Bingham, Stephen Higginson, James Madison, Samuel Osgood, Benjamin Walker, John Witherspoon, and Oliver Wolcott, Jr. In his reports on the public credit, he quoted or paraphrased Hume, Hobbes, Montesquieu, Necker, Montague, Vattel, and Blackstone. Perhaps, most of all, he was indebted to Malachy Postlethwayt's *Universal Dictionary*, which explained and defended Walpole's system and served as Hamilton's primer in all matters of economic theory and practice.

But the creative contribution was largely Hamilton's own, for he mastered the British system, thoroughly acquainted himself with the ingredients of the American problem, added his vast (and possibly almost instinctive) understanding of man and society, and emerged with a plan uniquely adapted to American needs. His plan was partly revealed—but only partly—in his "Report Relative to a Provision for the Support of Public Credit," presented to the House of Representatives on January 14, 1790. Two more reports, for "Further Provision" for the public credit, were presented to Congress eleven months later, and the three must be taken together to understand what Hamilton was about.

In the first report, Hamilton spelled out in detail his plans for funding the debts. In quick, decisive strokes he disposed of repudiation, either of principal or of accrued interest, and justified his position on grounds of both honor and policy. He likewise disposed of discrimination, drawing on Postlethwayt and others to demonstrate that no one would lend money to government "unless they could have the privilege of buying and selling their property in the public funds, when the occasion demanded," and also to demonstrate that to make public securities nonnegotiable would be to freeze an enormous amount of liquid wealth and thereby to paralyze the economy. Then, in a careful blending of logic with the available facts and figures, he estimated the debts: foreign, $11,710,000, including principal and arrears of interest; national, $27,383,000, plus $13,030,000 in accrued interest and an allowance of $2,000,000 for old accounts not yet liquidated; and state, for which Hamilton proposed to allow $25,000,000. All these debts, Hamilton said, should be funded, but he proposed some concessions to expediency: the interest rate should be reduced from the existing 6 percent to a little over 4 percent, and in certain ways the debts should be subjected to minor scaling down.

He called for a new loan to the United States government, the subscriptions being payable in old securities. Creditors could receive new securities on a variety of bases. They could choose to receive two-thirds of the value of their subscriptions in new government bonds (called "stock") that bore 6 percent interest and the remainder in western lands at twenty cents an acre. They could take the full value of their subscriptions in 4 percent "stock," and be compensated for the reduced interest by receiving seventy-nine acres of western lands for every hundred dollars subscribed. If the creditors were uninterested in western lands, they could take all their subscriptions in stock: "sixty-six dollars and two thirds of a dollar" of each hundred dollars of old securities subscribed would be exchangeable for new stock bearing 6 percent interest; the remaining $33.33 would entitle the holder to $26.88 in new stock bearing no interest for ten years and 6 percent thereafter. Any subscribers who agreed to pledge half in old securities and half in gold or silver would receive stock bearing 5 percent. Finally, any old creditors who refused all these options could keep their old securities and receive 4 percent on them, but their interest would be payable only if, in a given year, there was a treasury surplus after servicing the subscribed debt.

Two or three other features of the plan were of importance. State securities were to be subscribable to the new loan on the same terms as Continental securities, with two key stipulations: the states would be charged, in the final settlement of accounts, for all debts assumed, and no interest would be payable on new stock issued for state debts until January 1, 1792. Old Continental paper money would be acceptable at the rate at which it had last been devalued, namely 40 for 1. Most importantly, there was to be no maturity date for any of the new stock; it was to be redeemable only at the pleasure of the government. Redemption, moreover, was to be accomplished through a government commission "either by purchases of stock in the market, or by payments on account of the principal, as shall appear . . . most adviseable." Hamilton made it clear that the function of such operations would be what in a later day would be called "pegging the market"—that is, pushing the market value of stock "up to its true standard as fast as possible."

What he did not make clear, just yet, was a much more sophisticated plan he had in mind. He recognized that given the interest rates that prevailed in the world and given the questionable credit reputation of the United States, it would be difficult if not impossible to support the entire proposed new debt at par. He also recognized that it would be dangerous to do so; for speculators in western lands, having bargained to pay for their purchases in installments and in public securities at par, and expecting to acquire those securities at great discounts, would be wiped out if government stock should rise too high, too fast. One part of his plan to protect land speculators was implicit in the funding proposal itself: they could take up to a third of their subscriptions to the new loan in land at twenty cents an acre, rather than at the dollar per acre for which most of them had contracted to pay. But they would be additionally protected by his unspoken intention that the government's market-pegging operations should push prices up only gradually and to an average of only about three-fourths of par—around eighty-five cents on the dollar for 6 percent stock and between fifty and sixty cents on the dollar for deferred sixes. And there was another prospective advantage in maintaining prices high but below par and variable. The face value of the new domestic debt would be around $65 million; supported at 75 percent of par, that would make the nation's credit reservoir around $49 million. If the economy should become sluggish, another $1 million could be added to the reservoir simply by raising the pegged price of government securities a cent or two, and if it became overheated, it could be cooled by dropping the pegged price.

To make the system work, treasury agents (or, more properly, agents of the sinking-fund committee) would have to have hard money or an acceptable equivalent at all times—though not very much, for all that was necessary was to convince people that they could always sell their bonds at a good price in cash; if they were so convinced, most of them would not bother to do so. But the need for a continuous, if small, source of money posed a problem. The tariff already enacted by Congress would be supplemented by assorted other taxes proposed by Hamilton, but import duties would remain the principal source of government revenue. Because goods were imported mainly in the spring and merchants customarily paid half the duties when the goods arrived and half six months later, government revenues came in two floods, one in time to make interest payments in July and another in January, which is when Hamilton proposed to make the payments. But if the treasury was to peg the market in bonds, it would have to have access to money every day of the year.

The only possible way to get money on such a basis was to borrow it from a bank, and for that reason Hamilton saw no alternative but to emulate the British example all the way, to create a national bank and use the new government bonds as the basis for the nation's money supply. There were, to be sure, three private banks already in existence in America, and theoretically they might have performed the functions that Hamilton had in mind. But Hamilton had had experiences with the Bank of New York and Philadelphia's Bank of North America, experiences sufficient to convince him that bankers were not boundless sources of wisdom and virtue and, indeed, that it would be foolhardy to put the short-term credit of the government at their mercy.

Accordingly, in December of 1790 Hamilton proposed (as he hinted he would do in his January Report) that Congress charter a national bank, to be known as the Bank of the United States. It would be capitalized at $10 million, one-fifth of the stock to be subscribed in cash by the government. The bank would immediately lend the government's $2 million back to the government on a ten-year loan, to be paid in equal annual installments. All the remaining stock would be sold to private investors, three-fourths of their subscriptions being payable in the new 6 percent government bonds, the remainder in specie. The bank would be hedged in by restrictions designed to make it safe: its obligations (not counting deposits) could not exceed its capital; its charter would last twenty years and would be exclusive during that period; foreign stockholders would not be able to vote; and the secretary of the treasury could remove government deposits, inspect the books, and require periodic statements. The bank, once organized, would issue its notes in the form of commercial loans and short-term government loans; and these notes, along with those of the state-chartered banks, would be the nation's principal circulating medium, its paper money. To facilitate the circulation of the national bank's notes equally with gold and silver, the government would accept them at par for all taxes and other obligations. In addition, the bank would serve as the depository and fiscal agent of the government, making payments, transferring funds, and otherwise expediting government business.

There were two foundation stones remaining to be placed in the edifice Hamilton proposed to build, both involving taxation for purposes that transcended the mere raising of revenue. The first, which Hamilton recommended on advice from Madison, was an excise tax on the producers of "spiritous liquors." The excise would fall heaviest on big New England and New York rum distillers, and would in fact be a valuable source of revenue; but there was another consideration as well. About a third of the nation's liquor came from the whisky stills of small and medium-sized distillers in the West. Most whisky distillers were full-time operators who bought their grain from neighboring farmers, thus providing an important market for the farmers. Most people involved in the business were also Scotch-Irish frontiersmen who had a hearty lack of respect for the new national government, and Hamilton agreed with Madison that these westerners should be made to feel the lash, as well as the benefits, of government.

The other measure was more complex. Hamilton proposed to exempt land from federal taxation and to rely on import and excise taxes, but to do so in a way that would encourage national economic development: that is, he would make the tariffs discriminatory. On goods that could not be produced economically in the United States, he would impose tariffs for revenue. On manufactures that Americans could and should produce, he would impose tariffs high enough to give Americans a decided competitive advantage. The resulting loss of revenues would be made up by rapid economic growth—which, in turn, would be stimulated by the protective tariffs and also, in the more traditional lines of agriculture and commerce, by Hamilton's policy of not levying direct property taxes. That policy would indirectly subsidize the agricultural interests of the country, even as the state governments were to be directly subsidized.

The man who worked out this magnificently integrated system was the most brilliant bastard in American history. Hamilton had been born out of wedlock on the British West Indies island of Nevis, the son of an erratic Scottish planter and a French (and possibly Jewish) mother. His precocious intelligence as a teen-ager attracted attention in New York and won him a patron who sponsored his education at King's College (later Columbia). His native intelligence and burning ambition—both derived, no doubt, from the nature of his parentage—made him a flaming revolutionary, then aide-de-camp to General Washington. Subsequently he fell passionately in love with and wooed and wed Elizabeth Schuyler, a daughter of the leading member of New York's manor-lord aristocracy; and partly through that connection he became an eminently successful New

York lawyer. Until the day of his death, however, his ambition was never sated; and his compulsion to attain legitimacy through Fame, the secular variation of Christian immortality, could never have been sated.

But his abnormal drive was tempered, in the interests of the nation, by three great gifts that he brought with him to the office of secretary of the treasury. The first was a command of the intricacies of finance that surpassed even that of Robert Morris. The second was a capacity to recognize his mistakes and grow as a result of them. The third was a love of the United States as United States, free from the taint of provincialism, and a commitment to making it into a great nation.

Hamilton's views about how the United States could be made great have been as misunderstood as his views of man and society. He was and has been regarded as the patron saint in America of nationalism, capitalism, and conservatism. The first two descriptions, if properly defined, are reasonably accurate characterizations of what he was about, the third considerably less so. He has also been depicted as a monarchist, which he was, and as a believer in aristocracy, which he was up to a point. But his belief in monarchy, far from implying advocacy of authoritarianism, derived from the conviction that a limited monarchy was the surest guarantee of individual liberty; like most Britishers and many American Federalists, he was skeptical of the proposition that popular government was compatible with personal freedom. As to his belief in aristocracy, the matter has been distorted beyond recognition. He never said that government should be the province of the "rich and well-born"; that was John Adams's idea. He never talked of a "natural aristocracy" which should govern mankind; that was Thomas Jefferson. Nor, at the other extreme, did he share Thomas Paine's democratic view that if a government would "give the people the truth, and freedom to discuss it, all will go well." Indeed, Hamilton distrusted authority that was exclusively lodged anywhere in particular: "Give all power to the many," said he, and "they will oppress the few. Give all power to the few, they will oppress the many."

Therein lies the key to Hamilton's view of mankind and his vision for America. His notions about human behavior were remarkably similar to those of modern anthropologists, including the controversial Robert Ardrey. Hamilton understood a great deal about role-playing, rank, status, and cultural habit. He dismissed, almost with a wave of the hand, what Ardrey calls the "romantic fallacy": the notion that man is inherently "good," perfectable, or rational. "A

63

great source of error," Hamilton wrote, "is the judging of events by abstract calculations, which though geometrically true are false as they relate to the concerns of beings governed more by passion and prejudice than by an enlightened sense of their interests." Chief among the governing passions, he believed, were avarice and ambition—desire for property or "territory" and power or "status." Accordingly, "the safest reliance of every government" was not the goodness of the people, but "men's interests," thus defined.

The Constitution provided a theoretical framework whereby men could act in accordance with the dictates of their baser passions and yet have those actions neutralize one another in such a way that, *on the whole*, the public good would be served and personal liberty would be protected. Hamilton, however, had grave reservations about the efficacy of what he called "that frail fabric, the Constitution," for its viability rested on the willingness of people to adhere to its rules. He thought the balance of interests in the society would have been better preserved if provision had been made for something resembling a hereditary monarchy and a hereditary aristocracy; and he feared that the state governments, unless they were thoroughly checked, or even repressed, would undermine the nation in the same way that so many feudal barons could undermine a king.

His financial program was designed to overcome these "deficiencies" in the Constitution. The absence of a permanent system of status in America would be compensated for by the continuation of landed aristocracies and the creation of a financial aristocracy. The quasi-feudal power of the states would be reduced by making them virtual economic dependencies of the national government. Every important economic-interest group in the nation would stand to profit from his system, but every one would be required to bear a part of the burden as well. Most importantly, every person and every group in the highly pluralistic American society would have to deal directly or indirectly with the national government in order to conduct even the most ordinary of business transactions, for the money supply itself would be a creation of government. Of such stuff, Hamilton believed, a nation could be forged—one that would be prosperous and, despite itself, free.

President Washington's role in Hamilton's grand doings wants a little explanation. Washington had nothing whatever to do with the preparation of the great Reports: partly out of observation of the nicety that Hamilton was acting on instructions from Congress, partly because the whole subject was beyond him, the president volunteered neither questions nor suggestions. In administrative matters that were clearly executive—the short-range borrowing and disbursal of funds, for example, or the preparation of reports for executing an act regarding lighthouses—Hamilton continued to report directly as a subordinate and to act only upon orders from his superior. In the larger area of public finance, Washington left him alone except in one instance, when an issue of constitutionality rather than of policy arose.

But there was more to the matter than just that. Washington and Hamilton were both aware that the president's silence would be generally regarded as approval and that Washington's tacit sanction was necessary to the success of the system. As Hamilton later said, Washington was an indispensible *aegis*—shield—for his measures. The president's willingness to provide the aegis, in turn, arose from several springs, all more or less intuitive. Washington's life as a Virginia planter might have disposed him toward the anticommercial prejudices held by so many of his neighbors, but for his character and personal history. As to character, he abhorred slipshod or dishonorable conduct, and he operated his plantation on a businesslike basis; and thus the payment of just debts, public or private, was a crucial matter of honor with him. As to personal history, events in the recent past made it possible for Washington to equate opposition to Hamilton with opposition to himself. Toward the end of the war, many of his fellow Virginians had vehemently fought Robert Morris, then superintendent of finance, with the same kinds of arguments they would soon use against Hamilton. Morris's enemies had been much the same people as those who had conspired to deprive Washington of his command, and Morris, for his part, had come up with the money that had made the victory at Yorktown possible. Washington was accordingly as suspicious of Hamilton's critics as he had been of those of Morris. Finally, the nationalistic implications of Hamilton's program appealed to Washington far more than its anti-agrarian implications might have upset him.

And so Washington provided the shield for Hamilton, and knew—or at least sensed—what he was doing.

4

★★★★★

HAMILTONIANISM

To have devised the Hamiltonian system was a monumental achievement; to have brought it to life without stirring up great opposition, even with Washington's endorsement, would have been a miracle. It potentially flew in the face of the richest, most powerful, and most avaricious interest groups in the nation, despite Hamilton's subtle efforts to minimize conflicts; and its nationalistic implications alarmed state-oriented politicians from the moment his first report appeared.

For these reasons and because of his skepticism about man in general, Hamilton thought it would be foolhardy to entrust the fate of his program to the goodness and patriotism of the members of Congress. He did, for whatever it might count, marshal a brilliant exposition of the various parts of his plan, but he did so, one suspects, more as an intellectual tour de force than from an expectation that logical argument would prevail. Too many members of the Congress would not understand the intricacies of the system, and even more, perhaps most, would not appreciate the delicate inter-dependence of all its parts. They would, he believed, adopt the funding and assumption portion of the program only if enough of them thought they or their favorite constituents could profit from it. As for the rest of it, they could be induced to support this part for one reason and that for another. Given skillful enough management, they would end up adopting it all without fully understanding what they had done. Without such management they might destroy the system without understanding what they had done. So that is the way Hamilton chose to play it, and for most of the members of Congress his judgment was confirmed: a few understood and agreed, and most submitted to artful management.

But Hamilton made some grave miscalculations, the most important being that he failed to anticipate the opposition of his recent ally James Madison and then grossly underestimated Madison's skill as a politician. The miscalculations, operating in tandem with the dynamism of Hamilton's program itself, set in motion quite a train of unexpected events, and these, in turn, raised a number of problems that were not readily resolved. Adjustments in federal-state relations had to be made; the executive "cabinet" had to be transformed; a functioning system of loyal opposition had to be evolved; a major financial panic had to be dealt with. In the doing, patterns and habits would be established, and these, as long experience had shown, would not easily be broken.

Public finance was not a subject about which James Madison pretended to have any genuine expertise. Indeed, when Hamilton asked him, after Congress adjourned late in 1789, for advice in formulating his Report on the Public Credit, Madison replied that he had not "revolved" the matter enough in his mind even "to form any precise ideas." But he was an adroit manipulator of men and had ambitions as powerful as Hamilton's own; and for these reasons alone, conflict between the two men was inevitable as soon as Hamilton seized the initiative, thereby threatening Madison's position as the most influential man in Congress and as the president's most trusted adviser.

Conflict arose also from another source, from differences in political styles and political necessities. Hamilton, as an appointive official, found it both expedient and compatible with his temperament and talents to engage in "court" politics to bring his programs into existence. Madison, as an elective official, found it necessary to engage in popular politics as well as court politics. Powerful though Madison was in the House of Representatives, his footing in his Virginia constituency was still tenuous, and to save his political life he had been steadily moving away from the position that he and Hamilton had shared as coauthors of the Federalist Papers in 1788. To win and hold his congressional seat he had, among other things, to deemphasize his nationalism, orate in behalf of the rights of the states, champion a bill of rights, and vociferously oppose Great Britain and all things that smacked of British institutions. On all counts, such posturing placed Madison in direct opposition to Hamilton.

And Madison's constituents were in no mood to be easily placated. For one thing, the bottom had just fallen out of the tobacco market, not even partly to return for eight years, and thousands of Virginia planters were convinced that their misfortunes derived directly from the manipulations of financiers to the north. This conviction reinforced and was reinforced by the planters' republican variety of Bolingbrokism, the notion that all moneyed men—merchants, bankers, speculators—were leeches who lived by sucking the blood of honest farmers. That Hamilton's program exempted planters from taxes on their land and slaves, and that some people might regard living on the labor of slaves as rather different from honest toil, were not considered on the Virginia tobacco plantations. That the program would cost and restrict the actions of everybody, including the moneyed men, but promised prosperity to almost everyone, including the farmers, was invisible from that vantage point. From there, it seemed obvious that Hamilton was working for the exclusive gain of the bloodsuckers.

Moreover, tangible evidence abundantly supported what the planters knew by virtue of prejudice. New York and Philadelphia teemed with speculators, brazenly hovering around and even invading the very halls of Congress; and in January of 1790 several fast ships, laden with speculators and money, sailed from those two cities to southern states in the hope of buying state securities at depreciated prices before the locals heard of Hamilton's proposal to assume the state debts. There was, to be sure, an opposite side to all the frenzy. Virginians (along with North Carolinians) had written off a large portion of their state war debts in one way and another, thus demonstrating their belief that public obligations were less than sacrosanct. Moreover, many a back-country southerner was engaged in sharp practices, hoping to dump worthless paper on the northern city slickers and then keep it worthless by defeating any proposal to assume the state debts. But everything pointed in the same direction as far as the Virginians were concerned: they had little money for paying the taxes that Hamilton's program entailed, stood to gain little from the funding and assumption of the debts, and had a deep-seated prejudice against everything the program implied.

Madison therefore had no need for hesitation before taking his stand—except that the breadth and depth of Hamilton's proposals caught him flat-footed, without any plans for opposition. Accordingly, when the debate began in the House on January 28, 1790, he could at first only temporize, and in his initial effort he was thoroughly outflanked. After Congressmen James Jackson of Georgia and Samuel Livermore of New Hampshire took the lead, Madison attempted to rally the opponents of funding into an effective combination by advocating discrimination. Pay the foreign debt, said Madison, for that was dictated both by honor and by the hope for future loans. But as to the domestic national debt, discriminate between original holders and speculators, yet do so in a way that gave "justice" to both. Give the present holder a bond equal to the highest market price it had reached; give the original holder a bond equal to the difference between that and the original face value.

The maneuver was futile, for Hamilton had anticipated and refuted the argument in his report. As he had pointed out, to discriminate between holders would be to announce, at the inception of the new government, that the United States would not honor its pledges—for the old Congress had expressly pledged, in a circular letter dated April 26, 1783, and ironically authored by Madison himself, that it would honor its obligations without discrimination among holders. But again Hamilton took no chances with mere argument: in keeping with his preference for artful management over logic, he allowed his congressional supporters to circulate a lie that no one but he could really check, namely, that the condition of the records made it impossible to distinguish original from present holders.

When Madison's counterproposal came up for a vote on February 22, it was roundly defeated, thirty-six votes to thirteen. The roster of his supporters indicates the weakness of his efforts in the early stages: several were anti-Federalists who had opposed ratification of the Constitution, more than half were old republican ideologues, nine were Virginians, and eleven were from the South. Nor was this coalition any more effective in trying to undermine other parts of the funding program. True, it was partly as a result of their objections, but mainly because of modifications suggested by friends of Hamilton's system, that two minor departures were made from the original proposal. In regard to subscribers to the new loan who chose not to take any western lands, the House voted that old evidences of debt be redeemed at their full face value rather than at Hamilton's proposed figure of $93.54 on each $100. It also provided that overdue interest on Confederation debts should be exchanged for a third type of bond bearing 3 percent interest from the date of issue. The entire package of funded domestic debt, now consisting of "sixes, deferred sixes, and threes," was approved in the spring of 1790, along with provision for retirement of the foreign debt.

Debate on the remainder of the bill—the proposal to assume the state debts—was already well under way, and on that matter the opposition was more formidable. It was also more complex, arising from three general sources. The first was Madison and his immediate circle of followers, whom he had begun to call the "republican interest." Their rhetorical grounds were that assumption would saddle the young republic with an outrageous burden and that it would favor and perpetuate a national special-interest group. Doubtless some of them believed what they said; but most of them, like Madison, were also unreconciled to their defeat on the funding issue and perceived that to defeat assumption was to defeat the entire program. The second source of opposition derived from unabashed local interest, opposition that included the congressmen from New Hampshire, Pennsylvania, North Carolina, and Georgia, which states had either retired or successfully managed much of their debts. The third source was the special cases of two states, Virginia and Massachusetts, which threatened to block assumption unless they were expressly compensated, in the settlement of state accounts, for the private military ventures they had undertaken during the war. Massachusetts had an additional axe to grind, for it owed much more than anyone could reasonably expect to be assumed (as the law was finally passed, Massachusetts was left with almost $2 million not provided for).

There were, however, also those who supported assumption out of concern for the interests of their states or of themselves. New York, for example, had its own debts well under control, but stood to gain so much from Hamilton's program as to make state taxation unnecessary for a decade; South Carolina had a huge debt, which it had found difficult to manage; Connecticut's economy had been virtually unable to function for several years because of the burden of state debts there. As to individual congressmen, Nicholas Gilman of New Hampshire held over $1,000 in state securities, and other members of his family held far more; Theodorick Bland (the first Virginian to desert Madison's leadership) owned nearly $5,000 in state securities; William Smith, Aedanus Burke, and Thomas Sumter of South Carolina held nearly $20,000 in state debts between them; Abraham Baldwin of Georgia held $2,500, George Gale of Maryland $4,200, and Elbridge Gerry of Massachusetts $20,000. In addition, Michael Jenifer Stone of Maryland ($3,814), George Partridge ($2,195) and Theodore Sedgwick ($1,680) of Massachusetts, Hugh

71

Williamson of North Carolina ($2,600), and George Clymer ($12,584) and Thomas Fitzsimons ($8,314) of Pennsylvania had large holdings of various kinds of securities. Of the large holders of state securities, four—Bland, Gerry, Burke, and Sumter—had earlier been anti-Federalists, opposing ratification of the Constitution, but now followed their interests and supported assumption.

But the balance in Congress was close, the outcome turning on the positions taken by Virginia and Massachusetts. Partly because he had not anticipated Madison's opposition, Hamilton had ignored Virginia and concentrated his backstage efforts on Massachusetts, employing an artful combination of persuasion and bribery. He virtually seduced a former enemy, the old republican Stephen Higginson of Boston, by deferentially seeking his advice on financial and commercial matters; and Higginson, in turn, exerted his own great influence on the Massachusetts congressmen. The ablest of these was Fisher Ames, a brilliant young lawyer who became Hamilton's staunchest supporter in the House. More important, Hamilton quietly made a deal with the state: he would see to it that all of Massachusetts's debts would be absorbed by the national government, one way or another. If the amount to be assumed by law proved inadequate, there was another way—namely, whether the expenses of the Penobscot expedition were allowed or not, the auditors of the accounts of the states with the old Congress could see to it that the United States ended up owing Massachusetts most of the difference between the state's public debt and what was to be legally assumed.

For a time it appeared that the House, thus managed, would approve assumption almost as readily as it had approved funding the national debt—but then the Virginians came up with some ingenious maneuvers, designed to make enrichment of Virginia a condition of passage of the measure. First, Alexander White moved that assumption be restricted to the amounts which, after the final auditing of accounts, were found to be due from the old Congress to the state governments. Representatives from Massachusetts, Connecticut, and South Carolina, desperately hoping to relieve their states' burdens as quickly as possible, responded in alarm; for White's motion would have delayed assumption for perhaps two or three years. They were successful, and the motion was beaten, thirty-two votes to eighteen. But Madison followed with another stratagem. He proposed that assumption be tied to liquidation of state accounts and that in the auditing, the accounting procedures be lax enough that—he worded it more delicately—all of Virginia's claims for expenditures would be accepted, including those for the George Rogers Clark expedition. This proposal was carried, for it seemed to remove some of the objections to assumption.

Madison, however, had only begun in his efforts to either benefit Virginia or sandbag the whole program. Now he rose with an amendment aimed at securing his state's interests in the assumption itself, even if something went wrong in the final settlement of accounts: he moved that provision be made for the assumption of all state debts, including those that had been retired since the war. That would have increased the public debt enormously (contrary to one of the postures Madison had been taking) and would, by making the states themselves full pensioners of the national government, have increased national power even more so (contrary to another of his postures). Madison and his supporters, who included most of the southern congressmen except those from South Carolina, were making their position clear—that, despite their rantings, they had no real objection to wallowing at the public trough if they and their constituents got in on the wallowing.

This amendment was defeated, twenty-eight to twenty-two, but Madison was gaining ground through his tactics, for the support for assumption on Hamilton's terms was flaking away. Some congressmen who had large holdings of national debt and little or no state securities, notably Clymer and Fitzsimons of Pennsylvania, had previously supported assumption as part of the larger package; now they began to think of dropping assumption so as to save the funding portion of the bill. Some of the supporters of assumption, by way of compromise, offered to limit the amounts assumed to specific sums, less than the actual debts in each state; as a result the total was reduced from Hamilton's proposed $25 million to $19.3 million. What was more telling, the delay occasioned by the continued debate and the rash of amendments gave time for three recently elected congressmen from North Carolina to arrive, as Madison doubtless anticipated. By April 6, when the third North Carolinian showed up, Madison was able to muster twenty-seven votes against assumption on Hamilton's original plan, as opposed to twenty-nine favoring it. A week later, foes of assumption had a majority and were able to delete it from the main bill, thirty-one to twenty-nine. In that form the bill was passed and sent to the Senate.

In the Senate there was no James Madison in the opposition, Oliver Ellsworth and Robert Morris were present to lead the supporters of Hamilton's plan, and a large number of members had invested deeply in every manner of public securities. Consequently the Senate not only concurred in the passage of the funding portion of the bill but restored provision for assuming the state debts.

The Senate's action set the stage for a complex political deal. Pending also at the time was a bill for fixing the location of the permanent capital of the United States. Madison had long since perceived that the depth of feelings on this subject, arising from considerations of both power and wealth, made it a prospective issue over which bargains might be struck; and allies in Virginia wrote him to suggest, even as the Senate considered the funding-assumption bill, that he might be able to get the capital located on the Potomac in exchange for allowing assumption to pass. Various Pennsylvanians had a similar idea, thinking that some of the four representatives from Pennsylvania who had voted against assumption could be persuaded to change their votes, in exchange for which some New Englanders who favored assumption but also insisted on New York as the permanent capital would opt instead for Philadelphia. On learning of the Pennsylvanians' scheme, Madison was inspired to move quickly; but he lacked a pretense, consistent with his recent rhetoric and the polite conventions of the time, whereby he might approach Hamilton on the matter.

Hamilton himself unwittingly provided the occasion. Worried to a frenzy that his grand plan would be wrecked in the disagreement over Senate and House versions of the bill, he chanced upon his cabinet colleague Thomas Jefferson in the street in front of the president's house, and pleaded with Jefferson to try to persuade some Virginia congressmen to support assumption. Jefferson, only recently arrived in his post, maintained a cordial if formal relationship with Hamilton and professed (probably truthfully) to have neither much knowledge of nor interest in the subject of public finance. But Jefferson was also friendly with Madison—as intimately so as Madison's secret affliction would allow—and he countered Hamilton's plea with a suggestion that they meet the next day for dinner and discuss what might be arranged.

For word of this encounter and of the dinner meeting that followed, we have only Jefferson's recollections, penned nearly three decades later. Jefferson claimed then that Hamilton outwitted him and Madison, who also attended the dinner, by persuading them to induce two Virginia congressmen to support assumption, in exchange for northern votes in behalf of the Potomac as the permanent capital. All the available evidence, however, suggests that the persuading was the other way around. After the meeting, two Virginians in the House, Alexander White and Richard Bland Lee, did change their earlier positions and voted for assumption. But White had $1,619 in old Virginia securities, which he exchanged, under the act as finally passed, for new United States government bonds; and it is possible that Lee had made similar investments. As to the state of Virginia, it received an impressive set of advantages afterwards. For one thing, it got the permanent national capital, after an interim period in which the national seat was located in Philadelphia. For another, when the House agreed to restore assumption to the funding bill, Virginia's quota of the assumed debt was increased by $500,000 and North Carolina's by $800,000, and it was provided that if individual holders of state debts failed to subscribe the authorized amounts, the state governments themselves could pocket the difference, becoming creditors (or pensioners) of the national government. Finally, the rules of auditing state accounts with the old Congress were changed, in some mysterious ways. Population replaced land as the basis for reckoning the individual states' proportions of the common expenses, which made Virginia's share of the cost quite large; but a year's extension was granted on the presentation of claims, and during that time the Treasury Department stopped its practice of blocking tenuous and undocumented claims. The result was to swell Virginia's credits far beyond previous expectations. Thus, for example, in 1788 Virginia had dared ask only $500,000 as compensation for Clark's expedition to secure the Northwest Territory, but in the months following the Hamilton-Jefferson-Madison dinner that claim rose to $1.25 million and was allowed. All told, Virginia was allowed more than $19 million, which came within $100,000 of wiping out what it owed the nation; and even that amount was quietly dropped, along with $500,000 that North Carolina ended up owing. Finally, because the padded assumption allowance turned out to be excessive, the Commonwealth of Virginia emerged as a creditor of the nation in the amount of half a million dollars, rather than a debtor in the amount of several millions.

In any event, Hamilton's general program had carried, and on August 4, 1790, Washington signed it into law. A few more changes in his proposals were adopted at the last minute, but these did not significantly alter his larger plan. The assumed debts were placed on a slightly lower footing than Continental debts: subscribers of old state paper were to receive four-ninths of their subscriptions in 6 percents, two-ninths in deferred sixes, and three-ninths in 3 percent bonds; and no interest would be receivable on the sixes and threes until April 1792.

Four months after the funding-assumption bill became law, Hamilton followed through with his proposal for a national bank. His lengthy report on the subject was dated December 13, 1790, and shortly thereafter a bill to incorporate the bank on the terms he proposed was introduced in the Senate. After a month of secret debates the bill passed the Senate on January 20. On February 1 the House took up the Senate bill.

It is probable that Madison and his friends were again caught flat-footed by the sweep of Hamilton's proposals, despite his indication in his first report that he would later propose a bank. After all, in spite of the rhetoric and teeth-gnashing, the funding-assumption act had, at worst, only been a bit of large-scale boondoggling, and they had arranged to get more than their share. The bank, however, was something else again: once the report on it appeared, the magnitude of Hamilton's plan to transform America along Walpolean lines began to emerge. This issue, unlike the first, was therefore a matter of principle rather than interest.[1]

The Madison republicans were genuinely alarmed, but there was not much they could do. There was no contesting the fact that the bank could be of great utility to the government, and in regard to it there was no tangle of interests that could be manipulated, as there had been with assumption. Jackson of Georgia, Michael Jenifer Stone of Maryland, and a few others denounced the proposal on grounds of "class" interest, protesting that it would benefit merchants and do nothing for farmers. Madison took a different tack, employing a rather shakily constructed argument that the bill was unconstitutional. To no avail: after only a week of debate, the House passed the bill by a large majority, thirty-nine to twenty.

President Washington, however, was disturbed by the constitutional questions Madison raised, even though, in general, he agreed with Hamilton that a bank was desirable. To resolve his doubts, he asked Attorney General Edmund Randolph and Secretary of State Jefferson for written opinions on the constitutionality of the legislation. Both wrote opinions arguing that the bill was unconstitutional;

---

[1] In all likelihood, however, there was a more mundane dimension to the Virginians' opposition to the bank. According to Fisher Ames, they feared that if the bank operated in Philadelphia for ten years, the permanent national capital would never be removed from Philadelphia to the Potomac, despite the compromise legislation of 1790. Winfred E. A. Bernhard, *Fisher Ames, Federalist and Statesman, 1758–1808* (Chapel Hill, N.C.: University of North Carolina Press, 1965), 172–173. In my opinion, Ames's observation rings true, for it is complementary to the "gut" and philosophical reactions.

their grounds were similar, but Jefferson employed far more artful sophistry. The main ground of each was that the Tenth Amendment, then in process of ratification, prohibited the national government from exercising any power not expressly delegated to it, all such power being reserved to the states or to the people. (Actually no such word as "expressly" or "specifically" was in the amendment; Madison, in drafting the Bill of Rights in 1789, had opposed such a narrow restriction of national power.) But Jefferson went beyond this statement of the doctrine of "strict construction" and filled his opinion with a great deal of impressive legal obfuscation: he declared that, among other things, the bill violated the traditional laws of mortmain, alienage, descents, forfeiture and escheat, distribution, and monopoly.

To Washington, who was quite unlearned in the law and hypersensitive regarding questions of constitutionality, all this legal jargon was a bit bewildering. But he took seriously his oath to defend the Constitution, believing that the veto power was designed solely for that purpose, and to defy the constitutional opinion of three trusted fellow Virginians was more than he was willing to risk. Accordingly, he bluntly told Hamilton that he would not sign the bill unless the secretary of the treasury produced a written opinion that outweighed the arguments of the Virginians. Dumbfounded, then angered, Hamilton took up his pen, but he had to hurry, for the constitutional period of ten days for executive approval of congressional bills was fast running out. Meanwhile James Madison took up his pen, too, but in a triumphant spirit, for Washington asked him to draft a veto message.

Hamilton made his deadline with forty-eight hours to spare, delivering his celebrated "Defense of the Constitutionality of the Bank" to Washington on February 23. The well-known part of the defense spelled out the "loose constructionist" doctrine of the Constitution. The Constitution, said Hamilton, defined only in general terms the broad purposes for which the federal government was created, for it was not feasible to specify powers in minute detail. If Congress determined to achieve an end authorized by the Constitution, it was empowered by the final clause in Article I, Section 8 ("Congress shall have power . . . to make all laws which shall be necessary and proper for carrying into execution the foregoing powers"), to use any means that were not prohibited by the Constitution. That argument registered with Washington, but possibly of equal importance was Hamilton's devastating critique of Jefferson's finer points of legal disputation; to employ words that Henry

77

Adams used in another connection, Hamilton was almost "shouting with a schoolboy's fun at the idea of . . . teaching the Virginia democrats some law." The defense convinced Washington, and on February 25 he signed the bank bill into law.

In view of the wily machinations so far described, of the un-bridled greed and ambitions that were at work, and of the bitter and vituperative politics that were soon to come, it is well to pause and recall that the late eighteenth century was still a time when gentlemen behaved themselves as gentlemen, when all persons knew their place and comported themselves with the deference and decorum that befitted their stations, when even the crassest activities were conducted with careful attention to polite social convention, and when political and public affairs turned more upon personal considerations than upon any other pivots.

Many examples are to be seen in Washington's own conduct. He not only refused to exercise the veto power to express differences with Congress over policy, but also refused to propose legislation or interfere with its enactment. Given his great prestige, he could, had he so chosen, have influenced the make-up of Congress by endorsing or opposing candidates, but he was ever alert to prevent even the impression that he approved or disapproved a candidate. In 1792, for instance, Congressman John Francis Mercer of Maryland, an erstwhile delegate to the Constitutional Convention, claimed in his campaign for reelection that the president had told his nephew Bushrod Washington that Mercer was the best representative that "ever did go" to Congress from Maryland. Washington immediately denied the assertion publicly and huffily wrote Mercer that he had never expressed any "sentiment respecting the fitness, or unfitness of any Candidate for representation . . . conceiving that the exercise of an influence (if I really possessed any) however remote, would be highly improper."

Another example is afforded by a letter that Richard Henry Lee wrote in 1792 to Thomas Willing, who had become the first presi-dent of the Bank of the United States. Lee was an ally of Patrick Henry's and an old anti-Federalist, though one who (like Henry) would switch his allegiance to Federalism when Madison and Jeffer-son completed their switch the other way around. Lee was seeking a job as cashier of the Richmond branch of the bank for a man named Robert Pollard; stripped of pretensions, the letter was merely an effort by Lee to "lean on" Willing and get a friend of a friend in on the federal spoils. Yet the language Lee used was the epitome of eighteenth-century graciousness. "If gentlemen of great honor and judgment have not misinformed me," Lee wrote, implying far more than he said, "Mr. Pollard is a person who in every respect deserves the countenance and protection of worthy men. I think," he added, "that you will confer a favor on a grateful man, by obliging Mr. Pollard; and you will be thanked by one who has the honor to subscribe himself, Sir, your friend and most obedient servant Richard Henry Lee."

Still another example is observable in the relations between Willing and his business partner Robert Morris. Morris was the Financier of the Revolution, the agrarians' symbol of all evil, America's supermerchant and superspeculator. He was also involved, so deeply that it would ultimately ruin him, in ventures that he lacked the wherewithal to finance. Yet for nearly two years he refused to approach his partner Willing, in Willing's capacity as president of the bank, for a loan that might have made his affairs much easier to manage. Late in 1793, when in desperation Morris did broach the subject of a loan from the bank, Willing refused on grounds of propriety and forthwith dissolved his connection with the partnership.

Another and more subtle aspect of the same code of behavior is discernible in the correspondence between Hamilton and Jefferson. For several months after the dinner meeting that settled the controversy over assumption, relations between the two men remained quite cordial. They exchanged a number of letters, mainly over a proposal to establish a national mint, and such phrases as "with affection and esteem" were invariably incorporated into their complimentary closings. Then came the break over the bank; thereafter, the closings of the letters never again included the word "affection," though they still read "your most respectful and obedient servant." The minor shift in phraseology spoke volumes, expressing an unbridgeable gulf, and both men knew it.

The outcome of the disagreement over the bank was, in fact, a deeply traumatic experience for both Jefferson and Madison. To understand how it affected them, one must move beyond mere convention and ideology and plunge into the labyrinthine psyches of the two men.

At the age of forty-eight Thomas Jefferson had achieved nearly all a man could hope for, save the most important—measuring up to his image of manhood. His attainments as an intellectual, as a statesman, and as a humanitarian were almost awesome; but he was not, in his own terms, half the man his father had been. In those terms, to have written the Declaration of Independence was not nearly so important as it might have been to have fought Indians, subdued a tract of wilderness, or otherwise proved one's self to be a man among men, to be virtuous in the classical sense that virtue meant manliness. Indeed, on the one occasion of his public life when such manliness was called for, the British invasion of Virginia when Jefferson was governor in 1781, he had proved to be something scarcely distinguishable from a coward. In due course, as president, he would accomplish everything he thought a man should accomplish. In the meantime, suffering, he accommodated living with himself in two ways, not counting his considerable successes in the old Congress and as minister of the Congress in Paris. One was that he took in his care a wide variety of cripples, weaklings, misfits, and unfortunates and was a loving father to them all: people had only to show weakness and they had Jefferson's gentle paternal care forever. The other was that he looked for a superman father himself, to replace the natural father who had deserted him by dying when the son was a boy of fourteen.

In Washington, Jefferson thought he had found such a man, and his love for Washington was nothing less than adulation. But then, in the winter of 1790–1791, Washington betrayed him, as Jefferson saw it, succumbing to the wiles of the corrupt, effeminate, despicable Hamilton. That was simply too much for Jefferson to bear.

Madison was quite another case. As an epileptic, or victim of epileptiform hysteria, in an age in which such seizures were regarded as certain signs of insanity, Madison became the most guarded of men. Never to reveal one's malady, that was the inviolable rule; and that compulsion, together with a great, shrewd, canny intelligence, propelled him far in public life. Ever wary of the subtlest changes in his own psychic and physiological state—for, by being alert, he could anticipate and within limits even prevent the seizures—he learned to be similarly aware of the subtlest nuances in the behavior of others. Such awareness is the stuff of which master politicians are made. And fear of being found out, Madison's inner force, was far more potent than the relatively uncomplicated ambition and avarice that Hamilton believed to motivate men.

In the spring of 1791, shortly after Washington signed the bank bill, the psyches of Jefferson and Madison came together. Smarting from their recent defeat, they took a "botanical" trip to the north, hoping along the way to induce Aaron Burr and Governor George Clinton of New York to join them in forming a coalition of supporters of republican-minded candidates for the presidential election of 1792. Washington proposed to retire after one term (indeed, he asked Madison to prepare a draft of a farewell address), so such "campaigning" seemed entirely reasonable.

In a moment, more will be said about Clinton's own activities at that juncture. For now, a more mundane episode is what was important. After sailing to Albany and accomplishing their political missions, Jefferson and Madison sailed up Lake Champlain, and in stormy weather Madison became violently seasick. So far the record: now conjecture. When one is seasick, self-control becomes impossible even in the most iron-disciplined of humans. Confined in his cabin, Madison would have had one of his epileptiform seizures, and Jefferson would have witnessed it. *Mirabile dictu*: instead of feeling contempt upon seeing Madison's weakness, Jefferson was able to love him precisely because of it. Until that time Jefferson was a Madisonian; thereafter, Madison was a Jeffersonian.

Whatever the mechanism—and this conjecture could be entirely unfounded—the transition did take place in the spring of 1791. Jefferson did become the leader, and Madison the follower, whereas before it had been the other way around. And both, for all their continued protestations of loyalty, were thenceforth committed to the destruction of the Washington administration; for the administration, in their minds, had become the ministry of Alexander Hamilton.

Jefferson and Madison needed quite some time to work out, ideologically, the problems of being loyal in opposition, and neither Washington nor Hamilton would ever become reconciled to the idea that opposition could be loyal at all. Meanwhile, the Hamiltonian system would be shaken to the core by the doings of men who were devoid of concern for any ideological questions.

George Clinton was in his fifth three-year term as governor of New York. Like his archrival Hamilton, Clinton was driven by lust for fame, not money, and he had worked out a Clintonian system that was every bit as sophisticated in using men's ambitions and avarice to win loyalty to his state as Hamilton's system was in winning adherents to the nation. In the 1780s Clinton had made thousands of voters pensioners of the state, had enriched no small number of influential men and party adherents, and had satisfied the vanity of others, mainly through careful management and manipulation of public debts and confiscated Loyalist property. In 1790 the fruits of those activities grew far more bountiful, for Hamilton's funding and assumption scheme filled the state treasury to the point of overflowing. Forthwith, the governor and his cohorts set out to use these newly gained resources in an energetic program designed both to win more loyalties and to develop and aggrandize the state; for though the Clintonian's rhetoric was often strikingly like that of the Bolingbroke republicans in Virginia, they in fact operated an activist state government which vigorously supported capital ventures. Thus between 1790 and 1792 the State of New York invested in the stock of both the Bank of New York and the Bank of the United States, became a banker itself by lending $554,600 to its citizens against land as security, proposed a road system to open its interior, ordered the survey for what ultimately became the Erie Canal, and authorized a variety of related promotional enterprises.

As a part of these activities, the Clintonians determined early in 1791 to dispose of most of the vacant lands in the interior of the state, and in March the legislature enacted the necessary authorization. To be sure, New York did not own all its interior, for title to roughly the western third belonged to Massachusetts. That state, in turn, had alienated three million acres through the Phelps-Gorham purchase, by the terms of which a syndicate agreed to pay several annual installments in public securities. Because of the rapid rise in security prices in 1789–1790, however, the syndicate proved unable to make its payments; and though some of the land was hastily sold to other speculators, most reverted to Massachusetts. Massachusetts promptly resold the land to Robert Morris, who kept a large tract and sold the rest in separate transactions to one group of speculators in London and another in Holland. All that land lay idle in the hands of what Clinton denounced as land "jobbers," people who held it solely for the purpose of waiting for the rise in value that would ultimately and automatically accrue. But close to six million acres did belong to the State of New York, and the Clintonians were determined that it should be sold, under the 1791 law, to "promoters," men who could bring about a "speedy settlement" of the land by retailing it to yeoman farmers.

In accordance with that determination, the state land commissioners, with Governor Clinton presiding, considered applications for purchase of the lands in the summer of 1791. Before summer's end, the commission approved thirty-five "grants," comprising 5,542,170 acres, for a total sale price of $1,030,433, mainly payable in installments. Nine-tenths of the purchases were of extremely large tracts.

At that point the careful plans of both George Clinton and Alexander Hamilton began to go awry. Among the boldest, greediest, and least scrupulous speculators in the nation was a syndicate, or informal partnership, of four New Yorkers: William Duer, Alexander Macomb, Daniel McCormick, and William Constable. Duer, an intimate of Hamilton's, had served as assistant secretary of the treasury until he resigned (under a cloud) in April 1790; and though Hamilton himself was careful to avoid revealing plans that could be improperly exploited for private gain, Duer wantonly betrayed his trust, he and his associates making enormous profits by speculating in securities on the basis of "inside" information.[2] Macomb, the second member of the quartet, was a merchant prince and an erstwhile Federalist but also an old friend of Governor Clinton's who began drifting toward Clinton's party late in 1790. McCormick, a former Tory, was a Clintonian and a cohort of the governor's. Constable, a Federalist and sometime adviser to Hamilton, was the agent of the group in London.

This feculent foursome, cashing in their winnings late in 1790, looked about for new ways to pyramid their wealth and thought they saw another sure thing in land speculation—now that the market in securities had apparently peaked. Duer teamed up with various Philadelphians and acquired from Massachusetts two million acres in Maine; the others turned to New York. Inviting several loyal Clintonians in as minor participants, they acquired almost two-thirds of the entire amount of land disposed of by the state in 1791: a tract of 3,635,200 acres, comprising nearly all the land between the Adirondacks and Lake Ontario and from the Mohawk to the Canadian border. They also received the most favorable of terms, for the price was to be eight pence an acre, a total of about $300,000,[3] in money or public securities, with no down payment and

[2] Duer, the son of a British West Indies nabob, was a friend and neighbor of Philip Schuyler's and a man whose lavish displays of wealth dazzled one and all, Hamilton included. Hamilton was particularly vulnerable to the seductiveness of such "great men," and he hung on to the friendship long after good judgment should have convinced him that Duer was a thoroughgoing scoundrel.

[3] New York, like the other states, still reckoned money in pounds, shillings, and pence as well as in dollars. The rates of exchange varied considerably: In New York and North Carolina 8s. equaled one Spanish-milled dollar, a pound being $2.50; in Pennsylvania, New Jersey, Delaware, and Maryland 7s. 6d. made a dollar, the pound being $2.67; in New England and Virginia 6s. made a dollar, the pound being $3.33; in South Carolina and Georgia 4s. 8d. made a dollar, the pound being $4.28. In sterling money, 4s. 6d. made a dollar, and a pound was worth $4.44. In New York the shilling (12 pence) was worth 12½ cents, one pence being thus 1.041 cents. The total consideration for Macomb's purchase was therefore $302,739.46.

Hamilton, Jefferson, and Gouverneur Morris were primarily responsible for the decision to keep the accounts of the United States in dollars. One of the

with one-sixth payable in a year and the remainder in five equal annual installments. As a result of these purchases the Duer-Macomb-McCormick-Constable group reversed their earlier speculative positions; heretofore they had been bulls or "longs," betting that security prices would rise, and now they were bears or "shorts," betting that prices would hold steady or drop. Thereby they joined company with Robert Morris, William Bingham, and other Philadelphians and no small number of speculators in Maryland, New Jersey, and elsewhere.

They guessed wrong, for the market in public securities was about to take a spectacular rise. One element in the new rise was that throughout 1790 and 1791 certain important American speculators remained unreservedly bullish: the Boston merchant-speculators headed by William Philips, Nathaniel Prime, Samuel Breck, David Sears, and Jonathan Mason, and their counterpart group in Providence headed by John and Nicholas Brown, Philip and Zachariah Allen, John I. Clark, Joseph Nightingale, and Welcome Arnold. These men needed as large an appreciation of security prices as possible to enable them to pay for more than a million dollars in British goods imported in 1784 and still mostly unsold. British creditors were hounding them and threatening to haul them into the new federal courts, and forced payment would mean bankruptcy for most of them. Only if public securities rose considerably above the levels they had reached in 1790 would they be saved; if prices went to par or higher, these men would make a killing. Given their limited resources, these New England bulls could not, even with liberal loans from the Bank of Massachusetts, manipulate the bond market. But they perceived the crucial interdependence of parts of the Hamiltonian system. Since subscriptions to stock in the Bank of the United States were payable one-fourth in cash and three-fourths in 6 percent government bonds at par, the price of bank stock would dictate the price of government bonds. The trick then was to make bank stock go up; and because of the stock's relative scarcity, that would be easy enough, even if fake transactions had to be resorted to.

The bank stock was offered on July 4, 1791, and the rush for it proved so great that all the Yankees had to do was help nature take its course. Hamilton had originally proposed that subscriptions be

most effective collaborations between Hamilton and Jefferson, in fact, concerned the establishment of the gold and silver contents of the dollar, and the resulting relative values of state currencies.

taken in Philadelphia in April, that payments for the $400-par-value stock be made in four equal biennial installments, and that the first $100 payment be due at the time of making the subscriptions. As a result of various pressures, however, the date was set up to July; a number of shares were made available in Boston, New York, Baltimore, and Charleston; and the initial payment was reduced to $25 —for which the subscribers received certificates, or "scrip," entitling them to buy the stock subsequently at par. When the books were opened under these revised conditions, most of the $8 million in stock available to the public was subscribed in less than an hour. Moreover, active speculation in scrip began immediately, and prices soared. On August 10 scrip reached $325; the 6 percents, previously selling at 75 to 80 cents on the dollar, reached 130, and even 3 percents and deferred sixes, previously going around 40 cents, rose nearly to par. Talk of a new South Sea Bubble reached and alarmed the secretary of the treasury, but there was not much he could do.

Then the bubble burst. Prices plummeted, bank scrip falling to $160 and, in some panic selling, to $100 and even as low as $50. This was something Hamilton was prepared to cope with, and he did: operating through the Bank of New York and the Bank of North America and with authorization from the sinking-fund committee to spend $300,000 to $400,000 for the purpose, he poured money into open-market purchases. Six percents were supported at par, deferred sixes and threes at 60 cents. Prices sagged a little below those levels, but within a week the panic was over.

The real speculative boom, however, was only beginning. The wily Duer, inaccurately accused along with Constable of being behind the July bubble,[4] protested his innocence to Hamilton—and, in so doing, wormed out of the secretary just the information he

[4] Historians have generally credited the accusation; see, for example, John C. Miller, *Alexander Hamilton: Portrait in Paradox* (New York: Harper & Brothers, 1959), pp. 270–271. But Miller overlooks the activities of the New England operators—which the author has pieced together from Boston and Providence newspapers and manuscripts in the Massachusetts Historical Society, the Massachusetts Archives, and the John Carter Brown Library—and also the fact that Duer was "short" or "bearish" at this point because of his land speculations. Moreover, Rufus King, an astute observer and, as a director of the Bank of New York, a person in a position to know, told Hamilton that Duer had been engaged only in ordinary and "correct" transactions. King to Hamilton, Aug. 15, 1791, in Harold C. Syrett and Jacob E. Cooke, eds., *The Papers of Alexander Hamilton*, 9:61 (New York and London: Columbia University Press, 1965). King's letter also gives useful information on the panic, as does much of Hamilton's correspondence at that time.

needed to begin a new bubble of his own. Hamilton confided in Duer that $190 was about the right price for bank scrip, and the price he would seek to maintain; a little simple arithmetic, and Duer knew the price at which Hamilton would peg government bonds in the future. Knowing that, Duer and his associates soon reversed their positions again and set out to buy all the bonds they could lay their hands on.

The course they took was determined, in part, by the course taken in the organization of the Bank of the United States. Stockholders and directors of the existing state banks (those in Boston, New York, and Philadelphia and a new one in Baltimore) had feared the establishment of branches of the national bank in their cities, and Hamilton himself opposed branches, lest local and intercity jealousies undermine his whole system. In July and August the banks of Massachusetts and New York sought to protect themselves by attempting to become "partners" with the national bank—the one by seeking to buy 250 shares of the national bank's stock, the other by offering 300 shares of its own stock to the Bank of the United States—and Hamilton strongly favored such arrangements. But then, in October, the directors were elected—five from New England, six from New York, ten from Philadelphia, one each from Maryland, Virginia, North Carolina, and South Carolina; and though all were staunch Hamiltonian Federalists and conservative businessmen, they proved no more controllable than were the speculator Federalists. The board promptly, after choosing Thomas Willing as president, voted to establish branches in Boston, New York, Baltimore, and Charleston. At Hamilton's urging, each of the branches was allowed to have its own board of directors, but that was the only concession he got.

In these doings Duer saw opportunity to pull off the greatest of all his speculations. Throughout the fall, while quietly buying both United States bank stock and government bonds, Duer and Macomb took advantage of the uncertain future of the Bank of New York to begin buying that bank's stock as well. In December they drafted an agreement "for speculations in the debt of the United States and Bank of New York." Then they gathered an assortment of New Yorkers who were "disappointed in the direction of the existing banks," and they stirred up a movement to charter a new state bank. In early January 1792 "a bancomania" took form in three separate projects to create new banks: the "Million Bank," to be capitalized at $1 million but immediately oversubscribed by $10 million; the

"Merchants Bank," also to be capitalized at $1 million; and the "Tammany Bank," to be capitalized at $2 million. After a few days of frenzied promotion the projects were combined and a united petition was submitted to the legislature for a charter of a bank, first known as the Million Bank and later as the State Bank, which was to be capitalized at $1.8 million.

The purposes of this promotion, from the point of view of the Duer group, were threefold. The first was to depress the price of stock in the Bank of New York, making acquisition of it easier; soon, they had four hundred of the bank's seven hundred shares, and so frenzied did their buying become that it was said that at one time they had committed themselves to buy more shares than there were in existence. Their second objective was implicit in the first: to control the Bank of New York and thereby to obtain a source of financing their larger speculations. The third was more devious: to force a coalition of the United States Bank and the Bank of New York, which (after the proposed Million Bank had quietly been dropped) would send stocks of both skyward. With the rise in national bank stock, of course, 6 percent government bonds would rise as well, and the members of the "Six Per Cent Club" would profit handsomely. And it all seemed reasonably safe, for Duer knew the levels at which Hamilton proposed to use government funds to put a floor under the market.

But there was another group of speculators at work, and they proved Duer's undoing. Chancellor Robert R. Livingston and his numerous and aristocratic clan ardently supported the proposed new state bank. They did so partly because they wanted a bank to finance their own speculations and partly because they saw what Duer and his friends were about; and they set out to profit by betting the other way. That is, seeing that Duer and associates were buying wildly, they went "short," selling at high prices (for future delivery) securities they did not own. Keeping the Million Bank proposal alive was one way to depress the market, and the Livingstons made a portentous political commitment toward that end: they threw their weight behind George Clinton in his campaign for reelection in the spring. More directly, they "cornered all the gold and silver in New York; then, drawing the specie from the banks, they forced down the price of securities, prevented the banks from discounting and obliged them to call in their loans. Duer and his associates, having gone heavily in debt to the banks, were caught in the middle of a ruinous credit squeeze."

Duer and Macomb soon were done, and in the wake of their

collapse a large portion of the American economy collapsed as well. The Treasury Department entered the market again, but this time to little avail. Duer went bankrupt and was jailed, and Macomb soon followed. The banks and many private creditors, weakened by the inability of Duer and Macomb and their allies to pay, moved to protect themselves by calling in other outstanding loans, with the result that merchants had to liquidate their stocks of goods at panic prices and were unable to pay for spring imports that were arriving.

Elsewhere, scores of land speculators had been wiped out by the spectacular rise in security prices that preceded Duer's failure, and in other parts of the nation panic had already set in. By the fall of 1792 both financial and commercial affairs were settling down, but the whole episode was a crushing blow to the proud Hamilton. Not the least of his humiliations was that financial distress in New York was alleviated by the doings of George Clinton: the Clinton-dominated legislature revived its "paper money" act of 1786 and made credit available on mortgage loans. Moreover, the Clintonians, strengthened by the addition of the Livingstons to their ranks, were about to give Hamilton a measure of political comeuppance as well.

And not the least of the implications of the financial panic was that Washington found himself unable, in the circumstances, to fulfill his hope of retiring after one term in office. Things were simply too unsettled; and so, with great reluctance, he put away the farewell address that Madison had written for him.

5

★★★★★

A FEDERAL SYSTEM OF POLITICS
1791–1792

National politics in the eighteenth century was a game of intrigue and counter-intrigue that was, for the most part, played in a vacuum: the courts of the Hanoverians in England, of the Bourbons in France, of Frederick the Great in Prussia carried on their business without much regard for what happened or what was desired in the provinces. Similarly, the "court politicians" of George Washington's administration—from Adams and Lee to Maclay in the Senate, from Hamilton and Knox to Jefferson in the Cabinet, from Ames and Fitzsimons to Madison in the House—acted out their parts with little or no relevance to the real and felt needs and aspirations of people in the several states of the Union.

What Jefferson and Madison set out, ever so tentatively, to do in their "botanical expedition" of 1791 was to find counterparts or kindred souls in state politics, reach an understanding with them, and thus bring matters of national concern into some measure of synchronization with matters of local concern. The old alliance of anti-Federalists was not suitable for that end: in light of the spirit of nationalism that now pervaded the land, it was no longer acceptable to defend one's beliefs in terms of localism, in terms of the needs of Virginia, Ulster County, or the Town of Fitchburg. Some higher cause, something conceptually as grand as the Constitution itself, was necessary as a rallying point of opposition to the administration.

The cause with which anti-administration politicians chose to identify themselves was one that almost every American believed in, namely, republicanism. The technique was not a new one. In 1787, advocates of the Constitution had seized the initiative and had perverted the language to their advantage by grabbing the term "Federalists" for themselves and thus derogating their opponents to the unappealingly negative position of anti-Federalists. The label Federalists was, in 1787–1788, a misnomer; and so, now, in 1791–1792, was the label Republicans. Almost all Americans (as Jefferson was to observe in his presidential address in 1801) were both federalists and republicans. What counted was the evocative emotional content of labels. And therein lay the origin of the first American party system.

In Washington's court, as in the courts of Europe, a variety of small cliques came and went, but by 1792 these had hardened into two more or less cohesive factions. Each vied with the other for the favor of the president, and each conspired to make its leader the president's successor. The president, for his part—unlike most of the crowned heads of Europe—refused to participate in intrigue himself, remaining majestically and impartially above it all.

At the head of one faction was the secretary of the treasury. Circulating around him, in orbits of their own, were three sets of satellites—in the administration, in the House, and in the Senate. In the administration, the most important men were Secretary of War Henry Knox, whose attitude toward Hamilton was almost as subservient as his attitude toward Washington was; Hamilton's able young assistant secretary, Oliver Wolcott of Connecticut; and a large number of lesser officials, including what seemed to anti-Hamiltonians to be a small standing army of tax collectors.

In Congress Hamilton could count on regular (and almost unquestioning) support from about a third of the members in each house and consistent (though sometimes questioning) support from a clear majority. Subordinate leadership was most important in the House, both because of its larger and more diverse membership and because Madison was there. Heading the Hamiltonian opposition to Madison was Fisher Ames of Massachusetts, who was quite Madison's equal as a theoretician and orator and not far from his equal as a political manipulator. Ames's most able cohorts were William Loughton Smith of South Carolina and Theodore Sedgwick of Massachusetts. In the Senate, pomp and pretension disposed many members toward Hamilton's "high-toned" (the phrase is his) form of Federalism, and Ellsworth and Robert Morris, along with Rufus King of New York, provided Hamiltonian leadership.

Beyond these sources of support, Hamilton could count on three others that he manipulated or tried to manipulate directly. The first, moneyed groups that Hamilton influenced by the prospect of profits, had clearly got out of hand in 1791 and 1792, if indeed they had ever been under control. But his programs benefited them and they knew it; and few of them, whether conservatives or speculators, were likely to oppose Hamilton on any major matter. The second of the secretary's important groups of backers were the Treasury Department officials, especially customs officers, who were posted in the principal towns in every state and kept Hamilton informed about political activity as well as official business in all corners of the nation. The third was the propaganda arm: various printers, including Benjamin Edes of the *Massachusetts Centinel*, John Carter of the *Providence Gazette*, Samuel Loudon of the *New York Packet*, John Dunlap and David Claypoole of the *Pennsylvania Packet*, and J. V. Burd of the *Charleston Evening Gazette*, all of whom supported Hamiltonian policies out of nationalistic convictions, concern for the sensibilities and prejudices of their major clients, and an eye for profitable government printing contracts.

As his primary means of guiding the opinions of the more influential members of "the public," however, Hamilton relied chiefly on the printer John Fenno. Fenno had established his daily newspaper, the *Gazette of the United States*, some months before Hamilton took office, and dedicated it to the function of endearing "the GENERAL GOVERNMENT to the PEOPLE." He praised all administration measures from the outset and grew positively lyrical over Hamilton's various doings. Understandably, Hamilton soon saw to it that Fenno received the lion's share of the government printing. Equally understandably, whenever Fenno found himself in financial difficulties—despite the government printing and the fact that his was the nearest thing to a nationally circulating newspaper in the United States—Hamilton or his friends supplied him with loans on generous terms.

At the head of the other faction, by 1792, was Secretary of State Jefferson. Like Hamilton, Jefferson had satellites in three parts of government. Among high administration officials, Jefferson could count on Attorney General Edmund Randolph as strongly as Hamilton could count on Henry Knox (Postmaster General Samuel Osgood had also leaned toward the Republicans, but he resigned in 1791 and was replaced by the arch-Hamiltonian Timothy Pickering).

91

Republicans were strongest, of course, in the House, where Madison continued to exert a powerful and sometimes dominant influence and where Clerk of the House John Beckley served as a more or less full-time secretary and general factotum for the faction. In the Senate they had gained enormously since 1789. The senators from Virginia and from the recently admitted states of Rhode Island and Vermont were anti-administration in their views, and what was more ominous for the Hamilton faction, Hamilton's erstwhile law partner, the plausible superschemer Aaron Burr, had managed through artful manipulation to succeed Hamilton's father-in-law, Philip Schuyler, as a senator from New York. Despite his abilities and his almost irresistible charm—or perhaps because of them—Burr sometimes made Jefferson uneasy, for he was clearly his own man; but he offered his services as a subordinate member of Jefferson's faction, and there was no way the offer could be refused.

On other levels, the Jeffersonians were far weaker. For one thing, they had no organized body of interest groups to support them. In various portions of the back country, especially in Pennsylvania, whisky distillers and farmers who sold grain to the distillers objected to the excise tax levied by Congress in March of 1791, but they scarcely constituted a major interest group. Most other groups except tobacco planters appreciated the advantages of the Hamiltonian system, even if they had to help pay for it. For another thing, Jefferson's staff of administrative assistants, concentrated in the capital at Philadelphia, was miniscule compared to the administrative corps under Hamilton's control. A third and even more telling weakness was the virtual absence of a propaganda arm. Edward Powars's *American Herald* (Boston), Thomas Greenleaf's *New York Journal,* and Francis Bailey's *Freeman's Journal* (Philadelphia), almost alone among major newspapers, had opposed ratification of the Constitution and had survived to be highly critical of Washington's administration, and none of these could reasonably be called Jeffersonian. Powars's paper folded late in 1789, and the other two supported local political groups who, in state affairs, happened to oppose men who, in national affairs, supported Hamilton —George Clinton and his allies in New York and the erstwhile Constitutionalist party in Pennsylvania.

In 1791, to overcome this deficiency, Jefferson and Madison established a subsidized anti-administration (or, more properly at first, anti-Hamilton) newspaper. For the purpose they sought out Philip Freneau, who had been a close friend of Madison's at the College of New Jersey (Princeton) twenty-five years earlier, had turned his literary gifts to the cause of independence as the "Poet of the Revolution," and had in recent years worked as a journalist and a poet, neither with much success. Madison appealed to Freneau's unreserved hatred for Britain and for monarchists, who, Madison assured him, were taking over the federal government; Jefferson arranged Freneau a job as a translator in the State Department, a post that would support him but require virtually none of his time; and the two Virginians arranged financial backing from the New York printer Francis Childs. Thus induced, Freneau established the *National Gazette* in October 1791. From its very first issue, the *National Gazette* excoriated Hamilton as dishonest, corrupt, and the veritable head of a monarchist conspiracy and hailed Jefferson as an "illustrious Patriot" and "Colossus of Liberty" who stood almost alone in defending the nation against Hamilton's cabal.

The launching of Freneau's newspaper dramatically illustrated the change that came about when Jefferson emerged as the leader of the "republican interest," replacing Madison. With Madison in charge, the faction had been a disciplined and controlled instrument for seeking the legislative enactment of its principles and interests; his role had not been to stir up mischief, but to perform the more constructive work of organizing and rendering effective a group of otherwise impotent dissidents. He was therefore able both to retain favor with Washington and to cooperate with Hamilton whenever it suited his purposes to do so. Jefferson played an entirely different game. As John C. Miller has put it, quite in addition to conflicts of ideology and personality, "the two secretaries were engaged in a struggle for power; and the question who would be the heir apparent of President Washington was never far removed from the forefront of their consciousness." Believing that his rival must be destroyed, Jefferson convinced himself of Hamilton's total wickedness, then set out to convince Washington and the world. Thus, whereas Madison's opposition leadership had been compatible with the continued success of Washington's administration, Jefferson's was less responsible, more reckless, and far more dangerous.

The destructiveness inherent in Jefferson's personal attack on Hamilton, through Freneau, was made worse by certain flaws in Hamilton's character. Out of his deep-seated insecurity deriving from his illegitimacy, Hamilton had developed an exaggerated concern for his reputation as a man of honor and integrity, especially among those he regarded as persons of eminence. Moreover, he identified himself with Washington, with the administration, and with the nation; and like the president, he was quite unable to imagine that opposition could be loyal opposition. Thus when Freneau's shrill attacks began to come, they struck hypersensitive nerves, and Hamilton's reaction was very nearly hysterical. In vain, John Jay counseled him to ignore the barbs and defend himself only if and when, on retirement, he sat down to write his memoirs. That was easy enough for Jay to advise, for Jay was secure (if self-righteous and pretentious) about his birth and his aristocratic station; and besides, it was not he who was under fire. For Hamilton, to remain aloof was impossible. He responded with attacks in kind, and what was worse, he stooped to defend himself in every miniscule particular.

In the summer of 1792 the rivalry reached its nadir, both men descending to pettiness, to backbiting, to whining, and to what in some circles is called bitchiness. In one respect Jefferson retained a bit more of his dignity: he persuaded Freneau, Randolph, and others to do most of his writing for him, whereas Hamilton wrote lengthy newspaper diatribes in his own behalf under a half-dozen different noms de plume ("Caesar," "Catullus," "Scourge"), devoting so much time to the doing, indeed, that he was scarcely able to tend to the routine affairs of the Treasury Department. Jefferson worked more directly: in a series of interviews he told the president that Hamilton had encouraged the growth of corruption and a speculative spirit that were poisoning the government, that he was conspiring to make the Treasury Department so powerful as to swallow up the executive branch as soon as Washington retired, that he had denounced the Constitution itself as "a shilly shally thing of mere milk & water" which was useful only "as a step to something better," meaning a monarchy. After all that, and after the incessant attacks on Hamilton through Freneau, Jefferson had the nerve to complain to Washington in September that Hamilton was villifying him in the newspapers.

The rivalry between Washington's two most important department heads was rooted deep in their two psyches, but there were more conscious, more rational, more philosophical roots of division as well. The latter group of differences is epitomized by the differences between the conceptions of the presidency harbored by Hamilton and his followers and by Jefferson and his. In Federalist essay number 70, Hamilton had said that "energy in the Executive is a leading ingredient in the definition of good government," and he specified the elements that constituted executive "energy": unity, duration, an adequate provision for its support, and competent powers. To make the executive safe "in the republican sense," he added, the only requirements were "a due dependence on the people [and] a due responsibility." In essays 71 and 73 he made his position clearer: "It is one thing," he said, for the executive "to be subordinate to the laws, and another to be dependent on the legislative body." In other words, the executive authority must operate independently and with a wide range of discretion in its field, the Constitution and laws providing only broad guidelines and rules.

In Jefferson's view, and in that of most Republicans, such discretionary authority was inherently dangerous and smacked of monarchy. The more extreme Republicans preferred to check executive power by making the executive departments nearly independent of the president and by having committees rather than individuals in charge of the departments; committees were admittedly less efficient than individuals, but for that very reason they were safer. Neither Jefferson nor Madison went that far, but both preferred that the balance of discretionary power be vested in the legislature, particularly in the popularly elected branch of the legislature, and that within practical limits the president and his appointees be confined to carrying into execution the laws enacted by Congress. Or so, anyway, did they profess to believe until after 1800, when control of the executive branch came to be lodged in their own hands.

Beneath these antithetical conceptions of the presidency lay equally antithetical notions about the nature of man and society. There was a difference in preferences, for the commercial, urban style of life ("The busy haunts of men, not the remote wilderness," said Hamilton's friend Gouverneur Morris, "are the proper school for statesmen") or for the more relaxed rural style ("Those who labor in the earth," Jefferson said, "are God's chosen people"); but even these differences ran far deeper. Hamilton and his followers believed that men were inherently evil, governed by greed and lust and love of power and a host of even less endearing passions. In a society in which roles were fixed by law and custom, these passions were suppressed; but in a free society, they believed, the community could best protect itself and promote the happiness of its members by recognizing and accepting man's baseness, rather than by denying or attempting to reform human nature. Indeed, private wickedness could be harnessed to the public good: if individuals found it in their own pecuniary interest to act in accordance with the public interest, they would do so.

The Jeffersonians believed that man was inherently neither good nor evil, but a tabula rasa, a blank slate, destined to become whatever the accidents of birth and environment made of him. It followed that some men were wise and good, others stupid or evil. A society would grow better, not by so arranging its institutions that the wicked could thrive, but by stripping social and governmental institutions to the bare minimum so that the natural aristocracy might rise to the top. The natural aristocracy would in turn improve every man's conditions of birth and environment, and thus mankind would move ever upwards toward infinite perfectability.

(It does not mitigate the vitality of either set of beliefs to point out that each set of adherents confirmed Hamilton's skepticism by embracing the philosophy most compatible with its personal interests. Speculators, merchants, and opportunists, both political and economic, found Hamilton's view entirely palatable, for it encouraged them to do what they would have done anyway. Virginia planters found Jefferson's opposition to powerful external institutions similarly palatable, for they could readily conceive of themselves as "natural aristocrats," ruling as they did the scores of thousands of slaves on their plantations and resenting as they did any efforts by outsiders to interfere with that arbitrary rule.)

Washington, for his part, was a marvelous combination of sophistication and naiveté, and thus it was just as well that he chose to stand above the partisanship of his subordinates. On the one hand, he handled the affairs of administration with a skill born of long experience as a military man and as master of a vast plantation, and he so managed his rival subordinates as to keep them functioning despite their hostilities. On the other hand, he understood little and thought even less about the fine points of speculative disputation from which Hamiltonians and Jeffersonians derived justification for their conduct. Moreover, he was a man of unimpeachable honor and integrity who could continue to believe that most other men were, too, because he surrounded himself only with people who could comport themselves in accordance with his own unfeigned standards of honorable conduct. Even when Jefferson whined and accused and Hamilton delivered subtle knives into his adversary's back, both behaved, whenever Washington was present or looking, with the most careful attention to decorum. Such a gap between self and reality is inherent in the presidency. Thus Washington could continue to see things through honor-colored glasses until, two years later, the rantings of a partisan press brought into question both his personal integrity and the integrity of the presidential office.

Meanwhile, around the nation, politicians were vying for power in state governments. As would become the norm in America, these local rivalries originated in matters of local concern, but as would also become normal, they were influenced by and exerted an influence upon national affairs.

Almost from the outset of the new federal government the states found it necessary to rearrange their internal affairs, and some of these adjustments entailed significant shifts in local power structures. Most such shifts were in a conservative direction, undoing some of the radicalism of the Revolution. In Pennsylvania, for example, Philadelphia-based conservatives and nationalists, having suffered long under the radically democratic state constitution of 1776, were able in 1790 to bring about the adoption of a new constitution, modeled after the federal charter, that greatly weakened their back-country opponents. Georgia had performed a quite similar constitutional shift in 1789; like Pennsylvania, Georgia abandoned its earlier experiment with what was essentially an all-powerful unicameral legislature and moved toward a system based upon separation of powers and upon checks and balances. South Carolina also adopted a new constitution in 1790; that state preserved the extremely conservative distribution of power that had prevailed in colonial times and under the constitution of 1778, making concessions to back-country "democrats" only by reducing somewhat the high property qualifications for voters and officials and by providing a dual system of local administration, one for the low country and one for the middle and up country. In all three states, moreover, the reins of conservative control were tightened even more than they appeared to be, for in each the continuing influx of Scotch-Irish immigrants was rapidly tipping the balance of population in favor of the frontiersmen, but the new constitutions prevented numbers from being translated into political power.

Changes in administrative procedures and practices were likewise necessitated by the increase in national authority, and these, too, were generally in the direction of Hamiltonian "conservatism." The most striking change was in the nature of taxation. The Constitution vested the national government exclusively with the most desirable—which is to say the most painlessly collected—source of revenues, namely, import duties, and left the states with the most onerous, namely, direct property taxes; but the Hamiltonian system all but abolished the need for state taxes. Before the Constitution was adopted, Massachusetts was levying a million dollars a year in direct property taxes, New Jersey well over $100,000, Connecticut more than $200,000, almost totally for servicing public debts—the "civil lists," or regular expenditures, in each state being but a few thousand dollars. So heavy had the tax burdens been, indeed, that public creditors in Connecticut had faced the anomalous prospect of having their real property sold for nonpayment of taxes that had been levied to pay them as public creditors; Massachusetts farmers had taken up arms to prevent the collection of taxes; and most states had considered and some had adopted plans to issue unsecured paper money as a means of retiring public debts. Upon the funding of the national debts and the assumption of state debts in 1790, these tax burdens disappeared or became only nominal. Three states found it unnecessary to levy any direct taxes at all during the 1790s, and in almost every state the ordinary landowner became as free from taxation, except for immediate local needs, as he had been in the halcyon days before 1763.

These fiscal relocations, of course, also relocated influence, in accordance with the political maxim "Wherefore lies the money in government also lies the power." The larger area of profit, for most politicians in America, continued to be in the disposition of the public domain of unoccupied lands; but there, too, a shift toward the federal government was taking place. To be sure, western lands south of the Ohio River remained property of the states, but north of the river they belonged to the nation; and everywhere the clearing of titles and efforts to make the land habitable depended upon actions of the national government. The Washington administration (working more commonly through Secretary of War Knox than through Secretary of State Jefferson, for Washington considered Indian relations as primarily a military rather than as a diplomatic problem) sought vigorously to clear the land for white American speculators or settlers. Its efforts were scarcely an overwhelming success, for Indian wars were the norm on both the northern and southern frontiers throughout Washington's first administration, but the administration's policy was teaching every interested party to look to the nation, rather than to the states, for protection.

Then there was the matter of the apportionment of congressional districts, which signaled a problem of federal-state political relations for the future. In eighteenth-century Britain and British-America, plural officeholding was common and so were "rotten boroughs," minor jurisdictions with minimal populations which were entitled, by one accident of history or another, to legislative representation despite the lack of otherwise adequate population. Republican principles of political theory held that representation should be proportionate to the voting population, that officials should be confined to a single office, and that the electorate (however defined) should have the right to instruct its representatives. The Constitution, with its temporary, arbitrary apportionment of representation in the House and with its provision for reapportionment based upon a decennial census (the first being taken in 1790, effective for the 1792 elections), accorded with republican theory. It also, however, made republicanism equivalent to nationalism, in a subtle sort of way. The more republican-oriented states happened to gain a seat or two apiece in Congress by virtue of the census reapportionment, which directed their attention toward more, rather than less, active participation in the affairs of the nation. Moreover, the enactment, in accordance with republican principles, of "exclusion bills"—acts like the one Maryland passed in 1791, preventing the holding of seats in Congress simultaneously with seats in the Maryland House of Delegates—strengthened Federalist representation in Congress while weakening Federalist power in state governments.

In some states, on the other hand, local politicians turned local prejudice to advantage and minimized the shifts of power inherent in the adoption of the Constitution and the enactment of the Hamiltonian system. Rhode Island, the thirteenth member of the Union, managed to have its creditors benefit doubly from Hamilton's measures, but preserved its otherwise-minded reputation by electing anti-Federalist congressmen and by continuing to use state officials to help traders avoid customs regulations, even though these were now regulations of the United States. North Carolina, the twelfth state, flatly refused to amend its constitution despite glaring incompatibilities with the federal Constitution, refused to remit duties it was collecting on imports from other states, and openly challenged the authority of the federal judiciary as established by Ellsworth's act of 1789. In New York, as has been observed, the Clinton administration partially frustrated Hamilton's efforts to bind private interests to the nation, profiting as well as turning the loyalties of pensioners and speculators toward the state; and in Massachusetts the Hancock administration likewise accepted Hamilton's largesse but turned it at least partially to the political advantage of the governor and his supporters.

Of greater portent in the short run—and, curiously, in the long run as well—were local struggles for power. In several states, to be sure, there were no contests of moment. Bickering in Connecticut, New Jersey, and Delaware was considerable, but no amount of local quibbling could abate the nationalism of the voters, and so those states remained solidly Federal throughout Washington's first administration. Contrariwise, in the newly admitted frontier states of Vermont and Kentucky factionalism existed, but none of the factions was especially enamored of the national government or the Hamiltonian system. In Rhode Island, rivalry between national- and state-oriented factions was intense, but anti-Federalists were clearly dominant; in South Carolina a pattern of political division along sectional lines was more or less regular, but the low-country aristocrats were totally dominant and staunch in their Federalism; in New Hampshire, local rivals supported Federalism despite the localism of most voters. The partisan and factional alignments in the remaining eight states, however, were of some consequence to the nation.

State politics in Pennsylvania, geographically the center of national politics, had recently undergone as many convolutions as had the politics of the nation. The old Constitutionalist and Anticonstitutionalist parties of the Revolutionary and Confederation periods had broken down, and so had their successors the Federalist and anti-Federalist "parties" of 1787–1788. Personal friendships and habits of alliance had not changed appreciably, however, and they formed the basis of a new party system that emerged in 1790 and 1791. A clique of Philadelphia merchants and lawyers, headed by Robert Morris, Thomas Fitzsimons, James Wilson, and George Clymer—all of whom were Hamiltonian in national politics—sought to have General Arthur St. Clair elected as the first governor under the new state constitution. A rival clique of Philadelphians, led by Charles Biddle and likewise Hamiltonian, backed General Thomas Mifflin; whereupon many of the old Constitutionalist-anti-Federalist leaders began campaigning for Mifflin, if for no other reason than their habit of opposing any man or measure supported by Robert Morris. When Mifflin was elected (for the first of three three-year terms), something resembling a permanent "party" began to crystallize around him. And though Mifflin himself was rather conservative, most of his leading supporters—the likes of William Findley, John Smiley, Albert Gallatin, Alexander James Dallas, Blair McClenachan, and Jonathan D. Sergeant—were far more democratically inclined.

In New York the party alignments of the 1780s continued into the nineties, but with an aberration. The Clinton organization remained powerful; indeed, despite the momentum the Federalists had gained through ratification of the Constitution, the party of Hamilton, Schuyler, and Jay was unable in 1789 to defeat Governor Clinton's bid for a fifth consecutive three-year term. In 1792, however, the Federalists were determined to go all out to unseat Clinton, and their prospects brightened when Jay himself agreed to be the candidate, even though he refused on grounds of propriety "to make any effort to obtain suffrages." Then, in 1792, two new elements entered the equation: there emerged a powerful Republican faction, based in the city and headed by Senator Aaron Burr, and an equally powerful faction that Robert R. Livingston led out of the Federalist ranks. As a result, there were three "parties" in opposition to the Federalists instead of one, and each was headed by a wily and ambitious leader. If they worked together, they could thoroughly dominate the state, despite Hamilton's influence among merchants in the city and Schuyler's control of much of the tenant vote on the Hudson River manors. In the more likely event that the Republicans behaved suspiciously and treacherously toward one another, the state would belong to the Federalists.

Affairs in Massachusetts were more muddled. Governor John Hancock, still petulant about the choice of John Adams instead of himself as vice-president and no more interested in actually exercising power than he had ever been—the governorship was mainly a matter of vanity with him—nonetheless held together a potent political organization whose orientation was toward the state rather than the nation. Several factions opposed him. One consisted of enemies whose political position derived from national concerns: arch-Federalists Fisher Ames, George Cabot, Stephen Higginson, and others who would later be known as the Essex Junto. Popular support for this group was strong in all the eastern part of the state except Boston, Plymouth, and Cape Cod, and in the extreme west from the Connecticut River Valley to the Berkshire Hills. A second faction consisted of dissident "Old Republicans" (the likes of Samuel Adams, James Warren, and Elbridge Gerry), who regarded Hancock as a fraud and a traitor to the cause of republicanism. Support for this group came mainly from those parts of the east where the Federalists were weakest. Still another faction, potent only among the artisans and mechanics of Boston, was headed by Benjamin Austin; it stood, in the ideological spectrum, about midway between Hancock and the Old Republicans, though its stance was governed largely by concern for the interests of its working-class members and by the political ambitions of its leader. Finally, there were the truculent, conservative farmers of Worcester County in the heart of the state, who tended to vote alike but lacked leadership and rejected association with the other factions.

In four southern states—Georgia, North Carolina, Virginia, and

Maryland—the emerging internal political arrangements were even less systematic than those in Massachusetts. The central fact in Georgia life was that the state owned title to some 35 million acres of land in what would ultimately become Alabama and Mississippi —a virgin wilderness, entirely unoccupied except for a few hundred Spaniards and a few score thousand Cherokee, Creek, Choctaw, and Chickasaw Indians. Of what ended up being Georgia, only the northeastern third was settled; of that portion, the seacoast below Savannah and the lands adjacent to the Savannah River were mainly taken up with extremely prosperous, slave-manned rice plantations, and the rest was occupied by small and moderate-sized farms and tobacco plantations. In the rice country the white population was aristocratic, English (except for a few Germans and Scots), and mainly Anglican; elsewhere it was Yankee-Congregationalist and Scotch-Irish–Presbyterian or Baptist. Most political leaders came from the first group. What they did in public office was grow wealthier, and incidentally antagonize the frontiersmen, by granting vast tracts of the state's unoccupied lands to outsiders.

These doings came to have a relationship to national affairs. In 1789 Governor George Walton was signing land warrants granting as much as 50,000 acres to individual speculators; five years later Governor George Mathews was signing away 1.5 million acres to a single person. Meanwhile, the legislature was selling the same land: all told, lands in twenty-four counties, amounting to 8.7 million acres, were so frequently granted that patents for them totaled 29 million acres by 1796. In 1789 three "Yazoo Land Companies," named for the Yazoo River, were organized—one each for South Carolina, Tennessee, and Virginia—and the Georgia legislature sold them 16 million acres for a payment to the state of $200,000 and undesignated payments to the legislators. Then in 1790 President Washington, who took seriously his custody over Indian relations, warned Georgia and the speculators alike that Indian treaty rights would be respected. The next year he concluded a treaty confirming the Indians in title to most of the granted lands. The speculators went broke or dumped their dubious holdings on other outsiders. Northeast Georgians divided into two political camps, one supporting and one opposing the Washington administration, and planned new and more grandiose land grants for the morrow. Frontiersmen almost uniformly cheered the Washington administration, partly for its stand against the speculators, partly for moving to confine the Indians to specified territorities by treaty, and partly for moving to enforce the treaties with troops of the infant United States Army.

In North Carolina a similar situation prevailed. Tidewater planters, having embraced the Revolution in the 1770s in no small measure because absentee English landowners had engrossed much of the interior of the state, had in the 1780s appropriated most of that land (which included what became Tennessee) for themselves. Settlers in the interior had opposed the easterners so vehemently in the seventies as to become Loyalists, and in the eighties so vehemently as to become secessionists; and their enmity continued into the nineties. At issue in the rivalry was the ownership of land. The source, however, lay much deeper, in xenophobia, in hostility toward the stranger or the outsider: the interior uplands were populated by Scotch-Irishmen, Scots, and Germans, the lowlands largely by Englishmen. Most of the lowlanders, except for a commercially oriented group around Edenton, opposed the Hamiltonian system and the very idea of national power, even as they had opposed British power earlier, and thus became "Republicans." Their back-country opponents, true to habit, leaned toward "Federalism."

Virginia followed perhaps the most peculiar course of all. As Madison and Jefferson moved toward the states' rights position, they usurped the ground once dominated by the anti-Federalists Patrick Henry, Richard Henry Lee, and George Mason. By 1792 Lee and Mason were dead, and Henry had more or less retired from politics, seeking to provide for his old age through legal and speculative activity (including a plunge into Yazoo lands). That left the president virtually alone among eminent Virginians in the ranks of ardent nationalists, except for an assortment of relatively minor characters like Henry ("Light-Horse Harry") Lee and John Marshall. "Jeffersonians," as they could be properly called in Virginia, were dominant in all the piedmont plateau but the Southside (the Scotch-Irish Baptist portion of the lower piedmont) and in portions of the tidewater country as well. Federalists were predominant in and around Norfolk, in the Northern Neck, in portions of the Shenandoah Valley, and in Trans-Alleghany (what became West Virginia). The Federalist Henry Lee became governor, but that was essentially an honorary office; and Republicans could normally count upwards of 60 percent of the state's voters as being their own.

In Maryland, as in Pennsylvania, the factional system of the eighties had broken down, and there was virtually no continuity into the nineties of the alignments over the Constitution. A new polarization, geographical in nature, took place in 1790 in the dispute over the location of the permanent national capital: a Chesapeake faction emerged, comprising Anne Arundel (Annapolis),

Baltimore, and Harford counties on the western shore and all the eastern shore except the southernmost two counties; its opposite was the "Patowmack" faction, comprising the rest of the state. The former was loosely identifiable as anti-Federalist or anti-administration, the latter as Federalist or pro-administration. By 1792 the Potomac-Federalists had developed sufficient regular electoral machinery to qualify as something resembling a party, but there was no symmetry in the system; for the Chesapeake faction, though opposing the Potomac locally, was by no means its opposite nationally. Lines were still fluid, and the development of a regular two-party system awaited other issues, other stimuli.

These were the ingredients that the "national" politicians Hamilton and Jefferson had to work with in the elections of 1792. The combination of circumstances operative in that year's elections would never, or almost never, be duplicated. With a few exceptions, local and state elections were essentially unconnected with national elections; nationally prominent figures vied for office up and down the federal ladder; and most importantly of all, the presidency was uncontested. Washington had hoped and expected to be able to retire after one term; but the financial panic of 1792, the open break between Hamilton and Jefferson, and the storm clouds that were developing over Europe all conspired to make him change his mind. Moreover, almost every major leader of almost every major faction in American politics urged him to serve again. He bowed to pressure, and nobody dared challenge him for the office, and that was that. Quite early on, Jefferson and Madison decided to support Washington and to concentrate their efforts on unseating Vice-President Adams and attempting to elect Republican-oriented congressmen.

Pivotal to any strategy they might devise was the course of events in New York, where the state elections were held at the end of April. In those elections, a scandal erupted. After a spirited contest, Clintonians won an eight-vote majority in the Assembly, but the governor drew several hundred votes fewer than Jay, out of about sixteen thousand votes cast. Jay was not, however, elected: Clintonians, in control of the state's electoral machinery, threw out the votes of three frontier counties on the technical ground that the wrong persons had delivered the ballots to the secretary of state for counting; and that gave Clinton a plurality of 108 votes. Federalists howled, held popular meetings, circulated petitions, erected liberty poles, and even talked of a Lockean reversion to original principles and of an armed uprising to prevent Clinton's reinauguration. Their efforts were in vain, but the episode embarrassed the Jeffersonians. They needed a northern candidate in their move for the vice-presidency—Clinton himself had seemed ideal—and they coveted New York's twelve electoral votes (to be chosen by the state legislature), but their political posture was as champions of the people against aristocrats and corrupt schemers.

For a time there was talk of making Burr, rather than Clinton, the Republicans' vice-presidential candidate. Indeed, some efforts (none by Burr himself) were made to persuade Jefferson, Madison, and their ally, the erstwhile Virginia anti-Federalist Senator James Monroe, to take that step. The matter was laid to rest, however, at a caucus held in Philadelphia on October 16 and attended by Melancton Smith, representing the Clintonians, by John Beckley, representing the Virginians, by Mifflinites from Pennsylvania, and by Senator Pierce Butler of South Carolina. It was decided that Republicans everywhere would support Washington for president and Clinton for vice-president.

Already, Republicans had formulated and announced their party "platform." Madison had done so through Freneau's *National Gazette,* and Thomas Greenleaf's Clintonian *New York Journal* had echoed Madison's sentiments. "There are," the prospective voters were told, "two parties at present in the United States." Distinctions between Federalists and anti-Federalists were declared to be no more, since everyone now supported the Constitution, though it was hinted that the former anti-Federalists supported it more diligently and correctly than Federalists. Rather, one party was the Aristocrats, "endeavoring to lay the foundations of monarchical government" in America; the other was the Republicans, "the real supporters of independence, friends to equal rights and warm advocates of a free elective government."

If the rhetoric smacks of hypocrisy, it is only because the Republicans understood, far better than the Federalists did, the necessary techniques of popular politics. Nor did the hypocrisy end there. The overwhelming majority of the more ardent and active Republican "anti-aristocrats" were owners of large numbers of slaves and vast holdings of land, and they treated nonslaveholding farmers with a contempt and arrogance that one would never suspect from the way they glorified the "honest yeomanry" in their political tracts. Moreover, in New York the active supporters of the abolition of slavery were Federalists like Jay and Hamilton, whereas Clinton gave lip service to the cause but actually obstructed emancipation; and in Pennsylvania the Quakers, most of them staunch Federalists, were also staunch abolitionists. As to advocacy of the "rights of suffrage" and the principle of majority rule, Republicans were by no means democratic. In Pennsylvania, for example, the old Constitutionalists had deprived urban workers of the right to vote in 1786; and in 1792 their successors the Mifflinites attempted, vainly, to have congressional seats apportioned by gerrymandered districts because they knew they would lose in any contest of the state's voters at large. Proto-Republicans in Maryland and North Carolina followed similar courses. In Virginia and South Carolina, Republicans blocked all attempts to reapportion representation in such a way as to reflect the distribution of the free population.

Hamiltonian Federalists had not learned in 1792—in fact, they never entirely learned—how to play the popular political game. They viewed seduction of the voters as dangerous demagoguery, inevitably leading to tyranny, and had no stomach for it. It was true, as their enemies charged, that Hamilton and many of his followers believed in government by corruption, in the manner of Walpole; but such a belief was not only ill suited to, but actually quite naive in the sophisticated context of, the public politics that emerged in the United States in the 1790s. In their hearts, for all their philosophical distrust of "the people," the Hamiltonians believed that it was enough to govern well, and they trusted that the voters would recognize their services and respond accordingly. And thus, far from being the hard-boiled realists they fancied themselves as being, the Hamiltonians did not even understand the first maxim of popular politics: that the object of the game is to win.

The Republicans failed in their more obvious objective for 1792, that of defeating Adams for the vice-presidency. The choice was, in fact, not a matter of popular politics, for in nine of the fifteen states all the electors were chosen by the state legislatures, and in Massachusetts eleven of sixteen electors were so chosen. Washington received 132 votes out of a possible 136, and was thus reelected; Adams got 77, Clinton 50, Jefferson 4, and Burr 1.

In the matter of congressional elections the outcome was more complex and more interesting. Some historians and historical agencies, having a confidence in their surmises of what was then going on that the participants themselves lacked, have asserted that Democratic-Republicans won 57 seats in the House as against 48 Federalists, and that Federalists retained a 17 to 13 majority in the Senate.[1] Certainly, enemies of the administration and of Hamiltonian policies gained in the elections; and if due allowance is made for representatives tending toward an anti-administration position, as such a position had so far been defined, the Federalists clearly lost control of the House.

Things were not, however, so simple as all that. Participants in national politics were dealing in one set of terms, and participants in local politics were, with few exceptions, dealing in quite another. In Maryland, for example, there was no way that voters could express their approval of "aristocrats" or "democrats," the terms by which national (or court) Republicans defined the positions in the election, nor could they even vote a generally nationalist or generally states' rights ticket. Three candidates for congressional seats in Maryland ran as anti-Federalists, and two were elected, though that label had long since been consigned to the scrap heap of terms of opprobrium. Of the many candidates who ran as Federalists there, six were elected, but one was soon calling himself a Republican, and most of the Federalist party organizers in Baltimore were soon to desert the party they had organized.

For the most part, voters in every state expressed their attitudes about local concerns, even in their choices of national candidates, as they would continue to do for two hundred years. Counting up the national returns therefore became, as it would be a century and more later, a matter of counting up the aggregate of local sympathies. As indicated, Maryland went Federalist, though having little of the two-party national system in its bounds. All the other southern states, save South Carolina alone, went Republican. Delaware and New Jersey were overwhelmingly Federal, but the two big Middle States, New York and Pennsylvania, were split. New York elected its congressmen by districts, and so was divided; Pennsylvania chose its congressmen at large, and so was predominately Federal. New England went Federal overwhelmingly: in Rhode Island the advantages of the Hamiltonian system at last became so clear and the organization of the Providencers so strong that Federalism finally triumphed; and in the other Yankee states, voters had

---

[1] Bureau of the Census, *Historical Statistics of the United States, Colonial Times to 1957* (Washington, 1960), p. 692. Charles A. Beard, J. D. S. Bassett, Joseph Charles, and Orin G. Libby, among others, also thought they could assign more or less precise party affiliations to the congressmen elected in 1792; see their works, cited in the Note on the Sources and the Historiographical and Bibliographical Note.

virtually come to rank Hamilton with Calvin, and thus the Federalist candidates prevailed despite local habits of disputation.

Even as the elections were being held, Hamilton's most ardent enemies were attempting to destroy him in the rarified atmosphere of court politics. Convinced as they were that he misused public funds in his private interest as well as to corrupt government, they were nonetheless wary of bringing any formal charges against him; for an earlier such effort, brought rashly and without evidence, had enhanced rather than ruined Hamilton's reputation.[2] Late in 1792, however, a pair of developments seemed to expose him to successful attack, and the Republicans, smelling blood, swooped in for the kill.

The first development came in November, when Hamilton recommended to Congress that the government borrow $2 million from Dutch bankers at 5 percent interest and that it use the proceeds to pay in full its debt to the Bank of the United States, on which it paid 6 percent—thus saving $20,000 a year in interest payments. Republicans, suspecting a sinister scheme to provide the bank with more money for corrupt purposes, pushed through the House a demand for an explanation of the handling of earlier foreign loans; and there they found Hamilton somewhat vulnerable. Contrary to the intentions of Congress, he had intermixed funds from two separate loans, authorized in 1790 and totaling $14 million, and had used some of the funds for unauthorized (albeit legitimate and necessary) purposes, including his open-market bond operations during the panics of 1791 and 1792. Moreover, the reply he submitted on January 4, 1793, offered no explanations: it consisted merely of a number of tables and a brief, formal covering letter.

With Representative William B. Giles of Virginia leading the attack, but with Jefferson directing every move from backstage, the Republicans pushed through Congress five resolutions demanding a detailed accounting of the handling of all foreign loans, of all transactions between the government and the Bank of the United States since its inception, of all operations of the sinking fund, and of the current state of government monies. The Senate adopted a similar set of resolutions. The Republicans' expectations was that Hamilton

---

[2] In 1791 General Arthur St. Clair had suffered a disastrous defeat by Indians in the Ohio country, and Republicans charged that corruption in supplying the troops by treasury agents was the reason. Upon formal investigation by a House committee, it turned out that there had been no misconduct and, in fact, that Hamilton had offered advice which, if it had been followed, would probably have resulted in a victory by St. Clair.

could not possibly submit the reports before the Second Congress finally adjourned on March 3, and thus that the charges Giles made in introducing his resolutions—charges that Hamilton had concealed shortages in the accounts, had unlawfully favored the Bank of the United States, and had drawn money from Europe to America for the benefit of speculators—would be generally believed and be regarded as proven fact by the time the Third Congress convened in December. In the meantime Giles, at the head of a Committee of Fifteen, conducted his own investigation of the Treasury Department, of treasury officials, and even of Hamilton's private business, confident that endless dirt would be dug up in the doing.

The Republicans miscalculated on both counts. By dint of herculean labors Hamilton finished the last of the required reports by February 20; and the congressional committee unearthed no evidence that Hamilton's private finances had been in any way improper, none that relations between the government and the bank were improper, none that European money had been used by government to aid private speculators, and none, indeed, that Hamilton had ever acted without Washington's approval. All that remained were the technical charge about intermixing the proceeds of the 1790 foreign loans and the well-grounded fact that Hamilton had been high-handed and far from full or punctual in keeping Congress informed about treasury affairs.

Already, however, and overconfidently, Jefferson had drafted, for Giles to introduce, a series of resolutions condemning Hamilton for much the same things that the *National Gazette* had charged him with and demanding his removal from office. In the face of Hamilton's reports and the disappointing inquisition, Giles had no choice but to drop the more extreme of Jefferson's resolutions. Moreover, when nine diluted anti-Hamilton resolutions were offered, the Republicans were defeated on every count. Partly because a censure of Hamilton implied a censure of Washington, even Virginians deserted the Republican ranks: only five members of the House, including James Madison, voted for all nine resolutions.

In regard to the other development that took place at the same time, Hamilton was far more vulnerable, but in a different kind of way. In 1791 Hamilton had fallen prey to the feminine wiles of Maria Reynolds and her confidence-man–husband, James Reynolds. Hamilton and Maria had a bizarre and apparently passionate sexual relationship for more than a year with the full knowledge of her husband, whose feigned outrage was assuaged by regular blackmail payments. Then, in December of 1792, Reynolds and his partner

Jacob Clingman were arrested and imprisoned for defrauding veterans in a complex swindle. At first Reynolds was confident that Hamilton would intervene in his behalf rather than have the scandal disclosed; when Hamilton refused to do so, he began to rant that he had information that would "hang the Secretary of the Treasury." Word reached Republican Congressman Frederick Muhlenburg of Pennsylvania, who had once been Clingman's employer; and since rumors had been abroad for some time that Hamilton was involved in shady dealings with Reynolds, Muhlenburg hastened to the prison to interview the felons. Encouraged by the interview but possessing nothing tangible, Muhlenburg confided in his friends and Republican colleagues James Monroe and Abraham Venable of Virginia. The threesome then interviewed both Reynolds and his wife, heard grave charges against Hamilton (but not a word of what the actual relationship had been), and received letters written by Hamilton which seemed to prove that he had been speculating in government securities through Reynolds and others as intermediaries.

On the morning of December 15, 1792, the three congressmen called upon Hamilton in his office with their accusation. The secretary promised them evidence that would prove beyond doubt that his relationship with Reynolds in no way compromised the integrity of his official conduct, and he invited them to his home that evening to examine it. They accepted, and that night—with Assistant Secretary of the Treasury Oliver Wolcott present as a witness—Hamilton laid bare the whole sordid story, complete with letters of documentation that he had been prudent enough to save. The three Republicans accepted the explanation, agreed that no facts had been presented to compromise confidence in Hamilton's official integrity, and—as eighteenth-century gentlemen—pledged themselves to eternal silence about the affair.

But Monroe was not a gentleman, and he wasted no time before passing the secret along to Jefferson and John Beckley. Figuring that the scheme to discredit Hamilton through Giles's maneuvers was sure to succeed, the Virginians temporarily held back the information, perhaps planning to use it as the *coup de grâce* later in the year. Whatever their motivation, however, they let the opportunity slip through their fingers early in 1793, for the time abruptly ceased to be ripe. Five weeks after Congress adjourned, Citizen Edmond Charles Genet landed in Charleston as minister from revolutionary France, and almost immediately the country was racked with division over the wars that had begun in Europe. Republicans could always use the Hamilton-Reynolds scandal in the future, and in time they did; but in 1793 the scandal and even the Hamiltonian financial system itself ceased to be newsworthy.

For the survival of the nation, or of republican government, or of both was suddenly at stake.

6

★★★★★

FOREIGN ENTANGLEMENTS: 1793

The blessing of international peace vanished during Washington's fourth year in office. For the remainder of his presidency—indeed, for most of the time under his three successors—Europe was at war, and the United States was an unwilling pawn in the struggle.

Events in Europe were exceedingly complex, and those in the United States, reflecting what happened in Europe as well as expressing internal forces, were almost equally so. France erupted in a revolution that quickly turned into a movement to republicanize the world; the crowned heads of Europe trembled, then snarled, then joined in a coalition to destroy the revolutionaries. The Americans, sentimentally bound to the revolutionaries, were legally bound also; for the treaty of 1778, whereby France assisted the United States in its fight for independence, was a treaty of "perpetual friendship and alliance." But they were bound to Britain, too, by ties of heritage and commerce; and when Britain joined the coalition against France, American feelings became as intense as they were divided. Moreover, interests entered the equation as well, interests so vast as to dwarf those involved in the Hamiltonian financial system. The key to these was western land, and the key to the land was, besides the behavior of France and England, the activities of Spain and the interior Indians.

Neither as a matter of sentiment nor as a matter of interest was it easy for Americans to be consistent in their positions, because none of the other players stood still in this grand and deadly game.

113

France went through a half-dozen forms of government in as many years, and its ideological stance changed even more kaleidoscopically. Britain formally joined the coalition against France but in reality opted to sit out the war for a considerable period, determining instead to plunder what was left of the French empire in America. In a span of three years Spain was a neutral, an anti-French belligerent, a neutral again, and then an ally of France's. The Indians were forced to shift positions almost continuously.

In these circumstances President Washington was torn. He might have assumed genuine leadership of the American people, for it is in the conduct of international relations that the executive power is constitutionally least fettered, whereas in regard to domestic concerns, which dominated Washington's first term, presidential power is formally quite limited. On the other hand, it quickly became clear to him that to hold to a firm position was by definition to become entangled in the personal and partisan rivalry that had separated his department heads, the Congress, and, in considerable measure, the nation. Moreover, his sentiments were with France, at least at first; but his judgment told him that the best interests of the United States lay in neutrality, which in the context of events meant rejecting the French alliance in favor of peace with Britain.

To some extent Washington sought to deal with his responsibility by avoiding it, by opting to continue to "preside" rather than to lead or to direct. This meant that the rival factions of court politicians—the Hamiltonians and the Jeffersonians—could continue their contention for favor and power. Soon, however, the president had to take a stand, and the stand he took made Jefferson's position in the cabinet untenable. It also added a new dimension to the presidency: henceforth the president was not only chief executive and chief administrator, but head, at least in a titular and symbolic sense, of his party as well. Washington despised and resisted and renounced the role, but he could not avoid it.

The proximate cause of the French Revolution was the American Revolution. For all the decadence, corruption, and inefficiency of the Old Regime, the beginning of the end for the Bourbon king Louis XVI came with his virtual bankruptcy as a result of the war against Britain and for American independence. Late in the 1780s, even as the Americans were writing and ratifying their Constitution, Louis reached the end of both his wits and his treasury; and thinking to extract additional revenues from his subjects, he resurrected an ancient institution known as the Estates General. The Estates General consisted of representatives from each of the great classes in France—the clergy, the nobility, and the people. Leaders of each "estate" welcomed the call (the Estates General had not met for nearly two centuries), each in the expectation that it could improve its own position by gaining concessions from the absolute monarch, and could prevent the others from doing so.

The Estates General met in May 1789. Controversy arose immediately over the method of voting. The first two estates (having three hundred representatives each) expected to vote by orders—one vote for the clergy, one for the nobility, and one for the commoners. The third estate (represented by six hundred delegates) insisted that the three estates be combined for voting purposes and that each delegate have one vote. When they did not get their way, they effectively seceded and, in the celebrated Tennis Court Oath of June 20, vowed not to adjourn until a limited constitutional monarchy had been agreed upon. Louis, desperate, accepted their demands and persuaded most representatives of the first and second estates to rejoin the third on a one delegate–one vote basis. Actually that seemed safe enough, for the third estate was dominated by the bourgeoisie—merchants and financiers who lived in the cities—and their influence was not expected to be especially radical.

But the summer produced foretokens of things to come. On July 14 mobs in Paris, hungry because of crop failures the fall before, got out of hand and attacked and "liberated" the old prison and symbol of tyranny, the Bastille. Shortly afterward a "Great Fear" swept the countryside, and peasants went berserk in an orgy of jacqueries, looting and burning the manor houses of the nobility throughout the kingdom. In response, on August 4 the Constituent Assembly, as the Estates General had now become, abolished feudalism and a host of aristocratic privileges. A National Guard was established under the command of the Marquis de Lafayette, late of American Revolutionary glory, and it temporarily restored order in Paris. The Constituent Assembly settled down to its constitutional task, its most notable product being the celebrated Declaration of the Rights of Man and the Citizen (August 27, 1789), an amalgam of the real or supposed rights of Englishmen and Americans with a few abstract rights thrown in for good measure. In October the Paris mobs marched out to the palace at Versailles and terrified the royal family, but Lafayette and his National Guard brought things under control—or seemed to. Lafayette became the hero of the hour and the most important influence upon the king—or seemed to.

Up to this point most Americans applauded what they knew of

what was going on in France and avidly sought to learn all they could. They bought, for example, an enormous number of copies of Thomas Paine's *The Rights of Man*, written from France in response to Edmund Burke's hostile *Reflections on the French Revolution*, and Paine's work was serialized in many newspapers. Lafayette sent Washington the key to the Bastille as a symbol of Franco-American friendship and of solidarity in the love of liberty, and Washington happily accepted the gift in that spirit. Even Hamilton, at first, said the news from France filled him with the passions he had felt in 1775. His ardor soon cooled, for he foresaw that a demand for absolute liberty would lead to absolute tyranny; but most Americans continued to cheer the Revolution throughout 1790 and until the middle of 1791.

In July of 1790 the king (who Americans had managed to convince themselves was a great friend of human liberty) approved a constitution that limited his own power and provided for a measure of representative government. A few danger signs appeared—clubs of Jacobins and Cordeliers (republicans if not indeed democrats or something even more radical) teemed in Paris and cropped up in other cities—but the Feuillants (moderate monarchists led by Lafayette and the Comte de Mirabeau) seemed to have the situation well in hand. In America various clubs, supporters of the revolution in France and of increased democratization at home, began to appear; and on patriotic occasions Americans lavishly and interchangeably drank toasts to Louis XVI, Washington, liberty, and the "late revolution in France." Many in England, Scotland, and Ireland responded in a similar fashion.

The illusion was shattered in June of 1791 when the king, in disguise, was arrested in a wild attempt to flee the country. Henceforth, Louis was a prisoner in his own kingdom, and the whole world knew it. Americans became sharply divided in their attitudes toward France, the more conservative of them expecting and fearing that increasingly radical turns were in the offing and the more radical devoutly hoping so. European kings were disturbed, not because of sympathy for Louis (indeed more than one smelled an opportunity to take for themselves various parts of France), but because the French were setting an example that their own subjects might aspire to follow. King Frederick William of Prussia and Emperor Leopold of Austria met in Pillnitz in August to consider invading France, but neither was willing at the moment to trust the other, since they were at that moment on different sides in the perpetually changing game of international intrigue designed to devour one's neighbor. Thus, instead of invading, they issued a declaration that when and if a coalition of all major European powers were formed, they would take action to restore Louis to his throne and to absolutism. Their hope was that a threat of force would curb the radicalism in France.

Instead, France moved both leftward and toward war. The king was restored to the throne in September, when he took an oath to support a revised constitution. The Constituent Assembly dissolved, and a Legislative Assembly, elected under the new constitution, convened in October. A new party, made up of dedicated republicans called Girondists, was the most vigorous group in the Legislative Assembly, and they saw war as a sure means of deposing Louis forever. Lafayette and the Fueillants, desperately trying to hold power and preserve the constitutional monarchy and believing that war would solidify royal authority, worked covertly with the Girondists toward that end. Then on February 7, 1792, war drew imminent, for Prussia and Austria overcame their differences and signed an alliance against France. Ten weeks later, on April 20, France declared war on Austria. The War of the First Coalition had opened for a five-year run.

For the next five months France was a veritable disaster area. Its armies met repeated defeats in the field, many officers joining other nobles in leaving the country, the soldiers deserting in droves. Inflation and disorder racked the countryside. On August 10 occurred what the historian Georges Lefebvre has called the Second French Revolution: a well-planned insurrection, which was directed by Jacobins and employed recruits from all over the country, resulted in the seizure of the royal palace in Paris (the Tuileries), the "suspension" of Louis as king, and the virtual abdication of the Legislative Assembly. A new National Convention, to be elected by universal manhood suffrage, was called for late September. Meanwhile, Lafayette's troops deserted, he was captured by the Austrians in the Ardennes, northeast of Paris, and the Prussians took Verdun, 150 miles east of Paris. Austrians and Prussians moved inexorably toward the capital; order was retained there and fragmented French armies were kept in the field only by resorting to what Lefebvre has called the First Terror—the execution of well over a thousand political and criminal prisoners and the imprisonment of many more suspected enemies of the Revolution. Still the Prussians and Austrians advanced. It appeared uncertain who would get to Paris first, the members of the new National Convention, scheduled to meet on September 21, or the foreign invaders.

Then on September 20, 1792, at the village of Valmy, a miracle

117

happened. A ragged army of eighteen thousand Frenchmen under General François Kellermann, ill-equipped and armed mainly with enthusiasm, took a stand against the mighty, machinelike Prussians, whom all Europe thought invincible; and the French held. The Prussians, stupefied, retreated; they did not know they had witnessed the birth of the modern popular army, but they knew they had seen something awesome. The poet Goethe, who watched the battle, recorded that it would have infinite repercussions; and it did. The very next day the National Convention proclaimed France a republic. In the weeks to follow, Valmy was repeated again and again, and France's inspired citizen armies took the offensive, sweeping over the Austrian Netherlands. On November 19 the National Convention, drunk with freedom and power, issued a manifesto urging all the world's peoples to cast off their rulers and declaring that any who thus embraced the cause of liberty would be supported by France's conspiratorial skill and armed might. Almost as an anticlimax, on January 21, 1793, Louis XVI was beheaded. Ten days later France declared war against Great Britain, Holland, and Spain.

But this was not a mere fit of enthusiasm; the Jacobins, now in charge, were coldly calculating and deadly earnest. To conduct the war of world "liberation," the French resorted to *levées en masse*, a nationwide recruitment and conscription system that soon made it possible to put a million men in the field. The discipline of the regulars was skillfully blended with the ardor of the conscripts and volunteers; and under the brilliant direction of the military engineer Lazare Carnot, the troops were well equipped and well supplied. To restore discipline at home, the Jacobins resorted to totalitarian rule and the Reign of Terror—whereby twenty thousand traitors, aristocrats, and alleged enemies of the Revolution were beheaded. The Church had long since been stripped of wealth and power, and now even the Christian calendar was abandoned, and the worship of Reason was encouraged. Reason really meant the state and the Revolution: government became totally centralized and all-powerful, and both liberty and law disappeared.

In the months immediately following Valmy the French unquestionably assumed that the Americans would join them in their holy mission of world revolution. The United States, after all, had become the first revolutionary republic with France's aid, and the French image of America was that of Revolution fulfilled: a land where all the oppressive institutions of the Old World were nonexistent, where man had returned to an ancient state of innocence. Besides, there was the matter of the treaty of 1778. It was for the purpose of cementing that alliance that Citizen Genet was sent as a special emissary. Ironically, but typically for the turbulent times, Genet was almost obsolete by the time he arrived in Charleston on April 8, 1793. He was a Girondist, and the Girondists had already fallen to the Jacobins, who would soon be rounding Girondists up and herding them to the guillotine.

In America the reaction to Valmy and its aftermath was far more complex than the French had expected it to be. New Englanders, long accustomed to despising and fearing France when it was a Papist monarchy, despised and feared it all the more as an atheistic revolutionary republic. Elsewhere conservatives, including Hamilton and his followers, saw the Revolution as a peril to law and liberty everywhere, believing that the revolutionary manifesto was a thin disguise for a design of conquest and that the United States was a prime and vulnerable target of French conspiracy and arms. Most other Americans, including Jefferson and his followers, had regarded the formation of the coalition as the first step in a plan to destroy republicanism everywhere and to dismember the United States, even as Poland had just been dismembered. Accordingly, their reaction to the events between September 20 and January 21 was one of relief and a joy that bordered on delirium. The more extreme Jeffersonians were convinced that the Hamiltonians were domestic agents of an international monarchist conspiracy; the more extreme Hamiltonians were convinced that the Jeffersonians were domestic agents of an international Jacobin conspiracy.

Reinforcing these "gut" emotional reactions lay conflicts of economic interests, tangible and vast, and conflicts between the ways of life that those interests represented. One relatively uncomplicated tangle of interests was involved with the Hamiltonian system. Most federal revenues came from import duties, and by far the majority of American imports came from Great Britain and its possessions. Since 1783 efforts had been made both in France and in the United States to substitute Franco-American trade for the traditional pattern of Anglo-American trade, and in February of 1793 France went so far as to put American goods and ships on the same legal footing as those of French citizens. All such efforts were vain: Americans simply preferred British goods, and France could neither produce economically the things that Americans were accustomed to buying nor absorb what Americans had to sell. Most important of all, British merchants could and habitually did extend long-term credit to Americans, thereby financing American business with British capital, and French merchants were unable and unwilling to deal on those terms. For all these reasons, the entire Hamiltonian system—which, in the eyes of Hamiltonians, anyway, held the nation together—depended entirely upon the continuation of commercial relations with Great Britain. Since France and Britain were now at war, to support France would be to go to war with Britain and thus, ipso facto, to undermine the American government.

But the Hamiltonian system of "paper-jobbing," however much it did for the nation, remained alien to most Americans; as has been indicated, they devoutly embraced schemes of getting rich quick, but most preferred to do their gambling in the more manly business, as they saw it, of land-jobbing. Nor was land speculation a game confined to the rich or to such gigantic operators as Morris, Macomb, and Duer; it was played on all levels of the society and by adherents of every political faith. Even Alexander Hamilton, who scrupulously avoided private investment in the bonds and stocks he managed as a public trust, had plunged into investments in land speculations in upstate New York and the Ohio country. For the most part, speculators tended to invest in vacant lands near home, partly because they could exert more political influence with the granting governments there. In gross terms, New Englanders invested mainly in lands in Maine and Ohio, New Yorkers invested on the Canadian border, Pennsylvanians in western New York and Pennsylvania, Virginians in Kentucky, North Carolinians in Tennessee, and South Carolinians (along with many from Virginia and North Carolina) in the Yazoo lands of Georgia. That pattern of speculation formed a matrix that conditioned the attitudes of Americans toward Revolutionary France.

For there were two political arenas that vitally affected the profits or losses of land speculators. One was that of the granting or selling agency, namely, the state or federal governments. The other was international: title to interior lands was worthless unless it could be cleared of Indians, and clearing it of Indians depended, in large measure, upon the policies and activities of Spain and England. Prior to the outbreak of war in February of 1793, American relations with Spain and England were on one footing. After that time they were on quite another.

Strategic considerations in the interior are best understood from the perspective of the Indians. The Indians had recognized, when the United States won its independence, that the land-hungry Americans could not be kept east of the Appalachians, but they believed and hoped that American settlers could be confined to the valleys of the Cumberland, the Tennessee, and the upper Ohio. All that was necessary to bring that about, in fact, was for the British—with whom the Indians had fought as faithful allies for nearly ten years and with whom they had been peacefully allied for ten years before that—to retain the area north of the Ohio and continue to maintain their military posts there and in the Great Lakes country. But in the peace negotiations in 1782 the Shelburne ministry myopically overlooked the Indians and thereby doubly betrayed them: by the treaty of 1783 the lands between the Ohio and the Great Lakes were ceded to the United States, and Britain agreed to evacuate its forts "with all convenient speed." In vain did the British attempt to explain to the Indians the legal nicety that the treaty did not give the Indians' lands to the Americans, but merely conferred upon them the exclusive right to negotiate for title to the lands. On their own initiative, chiefs of the various tribes, led mainly by the Mohawk Joseph Brant, began negotiating instead to form a confederation to confine or even expel the whites. To prevent the carnage—to protect white Americans from the Indians and vice versa—Governor General Haldiman of Canada opted to disregard the treaty commitment and retain the posts. His successor as governor, Lord Dorchester, along with his lieutenant, John Graves Simcoe, went a step further, and had the backing of London in so doing: they treated the Ohio country as if it were still a part of the British empire, justifying the action on the ground that the United States was itself violating the treaty in several particulars.

Spanish policy in the Southwest was not dissimilar to British policy in the Northwest, except that the Spaniards were more vigorous and more surreptitious. They encouraged a confederacy of southern tribes (encouragement that the ablest southern chief, the half-breed Alexander McGillivray of the Creeks, did not need, for his hatred of the Americans was unbounded) and also set afoot various schemes by which whites would secede from the United States and come under Spanish protection. Among the westerners most consistently supporting such schemes was James Wilkinson of Kentucky, a veteran of the Continental Line and, for most of the next twenty years, commander of the American army in the Southwest and the recipient of regular bribes from Spain. Ironically, one of the by-products of Wilkinson's duplicity was that Spain opened New Orleans to American commodities sent downriver, subject to a moderate tax.

About the time of Washington's first inauguration, circumstances and policies began to change. For one thing, Dorchester and Simcoe, through Major George Beckwith, George Hammond, and other British agents and various adventurers, began to emulate the Spanish. That is, they intrigued to lure American frontiersmen to secede from the United States and come under British protection, thus hedging the United States on the north and west with Anglo-American provinces and providing a buffer between Indians, Spaniards, whites loyal to the United States, and Canada. Republican Congressman Thomas Scott of western Pennsylvania, among others, secretly conferred with Beckwith and agreed to such an arrangement (thereby lending substance to Republican fears of an English plot to dismember America, except that the effort was made through Republicans, not Federalists). Meanwhile the red men became unmanageable: partly in retaliation for attacks by Kentuckians, they took to the warpath, driving Ohio settlers to the protection of Marietta and Cincinnati, and later defeating United States army troops and militiamen under Generals Joseph Harmar and Arthur St. Clair. After St. Clair's defeat the British supported and encouraged the Indians. In the Southwest, the Creeks under McGillivray also began active warfare.

Almost simultaneously, Great Britain and Spain became involved in a controversy over Nootka Sound that threatened, for a time, to lead to war. Britain formally requested permission to march troops overland from Canada toward New Orleans. Hamilton, thinking it advisable to favor the British if doing so did not jeopardize the territorial integrity of the United States and apparently unaware of Dorchester's intrigues in the West, counseled Washington to honor the request. Washington, however, had been conditioned since his youth to be jealous of foreigners in the Ohio country, and besides, he owned huge tracts of land in the area himself; and so he heeded Jefferson's advice and refused permission. What was more, he took advantage of the controversy to alienate the Creeks from Spain. Negotiating directly with McGillivray, he obtained a treaty whereby the Creeks ceded to the United States all the lands between the Ogeechee and Oconee rivers in northeastern Georgia, in exchange for which McGillivray received a handsome bribe (in the form of a commission as brigadier general in the American army at $1,200 a year) and the Creeks received a perpetual guarantee to their remaining hunting grounds, including those claimed by the Yazoo companies. As a result of the arrangement there was peace in the area for the first time in years.

Peace did not last long. The Anglo-Spanish dispute was settled without incident, and afterward Spain reappraised its policy in the

Southwest. Deciding that all previous policies had been failures, and desperately afraid that the Americans would eventually overrun them in the area, Spain adopted a new policy that turned out to be even less successful than its others. It offered McGillivray a bribe $800 larger than what the Americans were paying and attempted to form offensive alliances with the Cherokees, Chickasaws, Choctaws, and Chickamaugas as well as the Creeks. McGillivray accepted the Spanish bribe while continuing to receive that of the United States, and the several tribes accepted Spanish guns and ammunition, but then the Indians went to war among themselves. Moreover, American militiamen, despite the treaty, started attacking the Indians. By the middle of 1792 the Spanish position in the Southwest was as precarious as the American position in the Northwest.[1]

So matters stood in the winter of 1792–1793, when the French Revolution began to interfere with everything. Northern Indians, backed by the British, were waging a successful offensive that threatened to remove white Americans from all lands north of the Ohio. Southern Indians, backed by Spain, were in retreat and were engaged in warfare among themselves. President Washington, within the limits imposed by other commitments and policies, was seeking to promote and protect the interests of American citizens in the West. American land speculators and western settlers were clamoring that the administration's efforts were not enough.

Enter Revolutionary France, at war with both Britain and Spain, declaring itself the champion of liberty against monarchy, claiming the legal sanction of an alliance with the United States, offering a license for plunder to all who would attack its enemies or their possessions. Small wonder that many Americans, most of them residing south of Philadelphia, rediscovered that their hearts lay with France.

As indicated, Genet landed in Charleston, South Carolina, on April 8, 1793. The Washington administration had known for some time that he was coming, and where and approximately when he would arrive. The president and his advisers, each from his own perspective, understood the broader implications of Genet's mission and knew what to do about him. What none of them anticipated was the enthusiasm of the welcome he would receive and the ex-

---

[1] As a by-product of these various activities and mainly as a counter to British policy, Vermont (1791) and Kentucky (1792) were hastily admitted as states and equal partners in the American Union.

travagant way he would behave. Indeed, Washington so underestimated Genet's impact that he left for a vacation in Mount Vernon just before the emissary arrived.

Charleston pointed the way for what was coming. A few local Federalists, fearing the worst, tried to induce Stephen Brindley, pilot for the port of Charleston, to run Genet's ship *L'Embuscade* aground, but to no avail. Most inhabitants of the city went virtually berserk in cheering, entertaining, and toasting the revolutionary diplomat. More ominously, conniving began at once. Planters such as William Clay Snipes (owner of eighty-seven slaves), Isaac Huger (upwards of two hundred slaves), and Alexander Moultrie (upwards of three hundred) quickly discovered their enthusiasm for French-style liberty, for they had plunged deeply into the Yazoo Land Company of South Carolina, and Genet was armed with commissions for raising an *Armée du Mississippi* and an *Armée des Florides*—which, if successful in "liberating" Louisiana and the Floridas, would yield untold wealth. The Charleston merchants-mechanics-adventurers James O'Fallon and Alexander Gillon, who were ardent Republicans and long-time friends of Thomas Paine, had likewise invested in Yazoo, and they were among the first to accept military commissions from Genet. Recruitment of volunteers for an attack on St. Augustine was begun, and soon a force of sixteen hundred had been raised. Similarly, Genet issued licenses for plunder by sea: commissions for American vessels to act as privateers, whereby they could attack unarmed British merchant vessels, haul them into American ports to be sold as prizes of war, and share the proceeds with the government of France, two-thirds going to the privateer. Genet issued four such commissions even before presenting his credentials in Charleston.

During the next month the Frenchman made a triumphal trip northward to Philadelphia, meeting with enthusiasm and making deals all the way. In Virginia he hired the services of the old hero of the West, George Rogers Clark, to lead the expeditions against Louisiana and the Floridas. At various places along the way he commissioned privateers and actively participated in financing, arming, and equipping them. Later, when he ventured into New York, Genet and the French consul contracted with two prominent Republican merchants, Ebenezer Stevens and Commodore James Nicholson, to provision the French fleet in New York, and he authorized the creation of an army to invade Canada. Some of these efforts were fiascoes: Clark proved to be a decrepit old alcoholic, the *Armée du Canada* attracted only a handful of French refugees and sixty-three Irish immigrants, and Genet found himself spending far more money than his government had provided. Nothing quelled the Frenchman's popularity or his enthusiasm, however; he blithely approached Alexander Hamilton for an advance against American loan repayments to France, and asked Secretary of War Henry Knox to provide him with cannon. With the covert approval of Jefferson, he dispatched undercover agents to the West and to Canada, one of whom was André Michaux, a well-known French botanist and friend of Jefferson's.

Genet's doings threw the Washington administration into a tizzy. Indeed, they necessitated a change in the president's well-established procedures for handling his duties, for a system based upon lengthy written reports, supplemented by relaxed conversation at the breakfast table, was too leisurely for the new circumstances. As it happened, Washington had been moving toward a supplementary method of seeking information and counsel. In the spring of 1791, while away on a southern tour, the president had authorized the three department heads to meet jointly if the need should arise and had delegated to them joint power to act in his name. They did meet on April 11 and settled a matter of foreign loans, and Washington later ratified their action. The following November 26 he convened them for a formal advisory meeting in his presence for the first time, and he did so four more times the next year. Now, in the crisis attending Genet's activities, such "cabinet meetings" became a frequently used (though not yet regularly scheduled) instrument of presidential administration.

The calling of the first cabinet meeting on the Genet affair was provoked more by exasperation than by a sense of emergency. Washington, hastily recalled from his vacation, had fired off to Jefferson instructions to prepare a written plan for preserving American neutrality; but when he arrived in Philadelphia on April 17, the secretary of state greeted him with a stack of routine correspondence and nothing on the subject of neutrality. Secretary Knox, to whose War Department the question of neutrality held some interest, was ready with a draft of instructions for some negotiations with western Indians, and nothing else. Secretary Hamilton, whose department nominally had no concern with foreign relations, had a detailed blueprint for announcing and following a course of neutrality, including the draft of a proclamation drawn up by Jay. The question of responsibility was clouded further by unilateral (and diametrically opposed) commitments that the secretaries of treasury and state had made with regard to France. Hamilton had withheld payments on the French debt on the ground that France, lacking as yet a "finally established and secured government," could not be diplomatically recognized as existing. Jefferson had, on March 12, 1793, instructed Gouverneur Morris, the American minister in Paris, to recognize the National Assembly as the legal government of France.

Angrily, the president dictated and sent to his department heads a list of thirteen questions, anti-French in tone, instructed the secretaries to prepare answers, and summoned a cabinet meeting for the next morning. In that and in a succession of subsequent meetings Hamilton (supported by Knox) and Jefferson (supported by Randolph) took predictable stands. Hamilton argued for neutrality, holding that the treaty of 1778 should be "temporarily and provisionally suspended" on the ground that, though treaties remained in force despite changes in the form of government of either signatory, France in fact had no permanent government. Even if this reasoning were not accepted, he added, the treaty required American aid only in a defensive war, and France had declared war upon Britain. As to Genet, Hamilton opposed his reception with the argument that to receive him would be to recognize the legitimacy of the French Republic and therefore to accept the binding force of the treaty. Jefferson took the position that treaties were between peoples, not governments; that it was not up to the United States to decide whether France's war was offensive or defensive; and that Genet must be received officially as the representative of a legitimate government.

There was also a constitutional question at issue, involving a definition of the powers of the presidential office and a related question of policy. Congress was out of session, not to be convened until December. Hamilton insisted that, in the absence of a declaration of war by Congress, the executive had full power to proclaim and enforce "the neutrality of the nation" and should forthwith do so; Jefferson argued that, since only Congress could declare war, only it could commit the country to neutrality. Jefferson also proposed to put a price on American neutrality, hoping that the belligerents would make commercial concessions to the United States to keep it neutral.

President Washington, for the moment, took a middle ground. He refused to declare the treaty suspended, and he decided to receive Genet (making the United States the first nation to receive an emissary from the Republic of France), but he accepted Hamilton's views regarding a proclamation of neutrality. To mollify Jefferson the word "neutrality" was not used, but the sense was there; and on

April 19 the cabinet unanimously recommended that such a document be issued in the name of the president of the United States. The proclamation, as published, declared to the world that the United States would follow "a conduct friendly and impartial toward the belligerent powers." To Americans, it prohibited "aiding or abetting hostilities" or engaging in any other unneutral acts within the jurisdiction of the United States.

In taking this action and attempting to enforce it, the Washington administration set a number of important legal and constitutional precedents. One was the very issuance of the proclamation, for it implicitly asserted the initiative of the executive branch in the conduct of foreign relations and, what was more important, laid the cornerstone for what became a crucial point in international law, namely, the law of neutrality. Another arose from efforts to restrain French agents and their American supporters. Since the navy did not exist and the small regular army was occupied on the western frontier, the administration had only treasury agents and state governments as its genuine executive arms; and since treasury men proved inadequate, governors were frequently requested to use their subordinate officials and state militias to enforce the federal "law."[2]

That was a shaky footing for the national authority, for it rested upon the voluntary cooperation of state judges and governors, by no means all of whom approved the administration's position. As things turned out, many state judges were uncooperative, but most governors solidly supported the president. In some instances that was no surprise: Governor Arnoldus Vanderhorst of South Carolina had, even before the neutrality proclamation was issued, banned the fitting of privateers and ordered the closing of all Charleston houses used as recruiting rendezvous for French-sponsored military volunteers, and thus his support was expected. But most Republican

---

[2] There was a recently passed act of Congress to justify this course. The Fugitive Slave Law, passed in March of 1793 mainly at the instance of southern Republicans, required state officials to enforce the return of slaves who fled into free states. Few people protested at the time, for the more ardent defenders of "states' rights," except those in New York, were southern slaveowners. Many years later (in 1826) Pennsylvania passed a law that made kidnapping a felony and defined the capture of runaway slaves as kidnapping. In 1842 the United States Supreme Court (in *Prigg* v. *Pennsylvania*, 16 Peters 539) upheld the Pennsylvania act and ruled that states could prohibit their officials from being required to enforce federal statutes. In time, the federal government did evolve something of a police authoriy in the form of federal marshals, but these were, significantly, officers of the courts rather than of the executive.

governors cooperated, too, even such enthusiastic Francophiles as George Clinton of New York and Richard Dobbs Spaight of North Carolina. Yet the weakness of the administration's authority was revealed in July, when a pair of American citizens named Gideon Henfield and John Singletary were arrested in Philadelphia for having signed on board a French privateer in Charleston. When they were tried in a federal court in Philadelphia, Attorney General Randolph found there was no federal law against recruiting (the presidential proclamation could not be construed as such) and had to resort to basing his case on the common-law offense of disturbing the peace. The jury acquitted the prisoners, and one of them promptly reenlisted on another French privateer. Altogether, despite the proclamation, at least twelve ships commissioned by Genet went to sea, and there they captured more than eighty British merchant vessels, some inside American territorial waters. These prizes were taken to American ports, tried, condemned, and sold by French consuls—who, according to Genet, had extraterritorial privileges by virtue of the Franco-American treaty.

Two more important precedents were established by the Supreme Court, both in matters arising from privateering. The first came in July, when Washington asked the Court for an advisory opinion in regard to a federal district court's refusal to take jurisdiction over French seizures of American vessels in American waters. The Supreme Court took a firm constitutional line (as Hamilton had hoped, contrary to Jefferson), and refused the president's request on the grounds that it had no authority to speak, even in an advisory capacity, except in actual cases brought under proper legal proceedings, and that it was a coequal branch with the executive department and was by no means a mere counsel to it. That action, or refusal to act, made the Court useless in the existing emergency; but in a case that reached the Court a year later, the judges resolved several matters and set still other precedents. In 1794 the Supreme Court held, in the case of *Glass* v. *Sloop Betsy*, that the French consular tribunes Genet had established in the United States were illegal and ruled that American federal courts must serve as admiralty courts to determine the legitimacy of prizes brought into American ports, district courts being required to take original jurisdiction, notwithstanding the earlier district-court ruling.

In the meantime, the Genet affair was running its course. In August 1793, after Genet had made himself thoroughly obnoxious to Washington by accepting the reception but wantonly defying the neutrality proclamation, the administration issued a set of Rules

Governing Belligerents. These rules permitted sale of French prizes in America—not as a matter of treaty right, but because the president saw nothing in international or national law that prohibited it —and thus set up *Glass* v. *Sloop Betsy*. But otherwise the rules were designed to crack down on Genet: they prohibited filibustering expeditions against Spanish and British territory and ordered ships commissioned by Genet as privateers to stay out of American ports on penalty of seizure. Genet, drunk with enthusiasm and popular support and at best not the soul of discretion, publicly threatened to defy the new rules by appealing "over Washington's head" to the people. That ruined him: it was such folly to expect the people to choose France over Washington that even Jefferson, Madison, and Burr recognized that Genet was harming American Republicanism far more than he was helping it. Moreover, both he and his country grew increasingly embarrassing to local Republicans as news of the Terror began to filter into the United States and alienate more and more erstwhile Francophiles. Jefferson therefore renounced Genet as "all imagination, no judgment, passionate, disrespectful & even indecent towards the President" and soon acquiesced in Hamilton's demand that Washington request his recall.

The request was in fact unnecessary, for the Jacobins in France had already sent Genet's replacement, Joseph Fauchet, with instructions that Genet be returned home to face trial for his "crimes" against the Revolution, namely, to face the guillotine as a Girondist. Washington magnanimously refused to extradite Genet, who shortly married George Clinton's daughter and settled into a life of quiet obscurity.

The matter by no means ended with Genet; indeed, by the time of his recall a number of "Democratic" or "Republican" societies, modeled in part after the Jacobin clubs in France, had sprung up in the United States. At least eleven such organizations were created in 1793, and at least twenty-four more were formed in 1794. Thereafter the movement faded, but not before the societies made an important contribution toward the nationalization of American politics. Before 1792, as has been indicated, national and state politics were two different games played in two different arenas. The activities of the Republicans in 1792 brought the two part of the way toward synchronization, and the French Revolution and Genet moved them much further in the same direction. What the Democratic-Republican Societies did was give cohesive, if temporary, organization to the trend, transforming it into a nationwide movement.

129

Philadelphia was the center of the movement. The first organization, the German Republican society, originated there before Genet arrived, and a second was formed in Norfolk-Portsmouth, Virginia, shortly afterward; but it was not until July 3, 1793, that the "parent" Democratic Society of Pennsylvania was founded. This society, created by Governor Mifflin's secretary, Alexander Dallas, and several of the Philadelphians who had sponsored Mifflin in 1790, published a circular letter calling for the creation of a network of societies and a constitution spelling out its purposes: to "cultivate a just knowledge of rational liberty," to enlighten the people in the responsibilities of representative government, to keep a vigil on public servants, and to defend the sovereignty of the people, including their right to alter the form of government. In sum, the Pennsylvania society urged the formation of societies the nation over that would engage in propaganda, discussion, and political activism—all of which were contrary to the tendencies of the Washington administration. Most of the eight other societies formed in 1793—three in Kentucky, two in South Carolina, and one each in New York, Connecticut, and Massachusetts—were organized in direct response to the Pennsylvania society's circular letter. The same is true of most of the societies organized the next year: five more in Pennsylvania, four in Vermont, three apiece in Virginia and New York, two each in New Jersey and both Carolinas, and one each in Maryland, Delaware, and the Province of Maine.[3]

The Democratic-Republican societies were not Jacobin clubs, despite what Federalists charged and believed. There were some such—notably the Societé Patriotique Française in Charleston and the Friends of Liberty and Equality in Philadelphia—which were not only pro-French but clearly subversive; but most Democratic-Republican societies, while sympathizing with France and looking to it for help for a time, were made up of patriotic Americans concerned with radical republicanism in America. Nor were the Democratic-Republicans the people who promoted separatist movements and filibustering expeditions. Some in New York and Vermont, to

[3] These data are from Eugene Perry Link, *Democratic-Republican Societies, 1790–1800* (New York: Columbia University Press, 1942), pp. 10–15. Link's study is biased and far from definitive, but it contains much useful information. In a seminar I conducted at Brown University in 1962, many errors and oversights were found in Link's work; and Messrs. John Worsley and Lee Verstandig found nearly a dozen societies in New England that Link had overlooked. Nonetheless, Link's findings on the relative geographical distribution of the societies apparently hold up, and for that reason are cited here.

be sure, were eager to attack Canada and participated in abortive efforts to raise volunteers for that purpose; and those in Kentucky found it difficult to distinguish republicanism and liberty from efforts to obtain free navigation of the Mississippi, even if that entailed seizing New Orleans by force. But, on the opposite hand, the Democratic-Republicans in Kentucky were distrustful of and generally opposed to the double agent James Wilkinson, and those in western Pennsylvania were rivals of Representative Thomas Scott.

Rather, the Democratic-Republicans were the militant left wing of the American Republican movement in general. Their character is indicated by their roots, five sets of which can be distinguished. One was old patriotic organizations, dating from the Sons of Liberty of the 1760s and 1770s, which themselves partially inspired the Jacobin clubs of France. A handful of former Sons of Liberty were still around, among them Sam Adams in Massachusetts and John Lamb in New York, and their presence as well as their earlier example inspired their emulators in the 1790s. This strain of the movement was urban, lower class, radical, and active. A second strain was intellectual. For some time, societies had been formed in the cities to promote science, rationalism, libraries, and the Enlightenment; and it was no coincidence that members of such organizations often joined Democratic-Republican societies, for the appeal of both groups—essentially the love of theoretical discussion and argument—was the same. Still another strain was cultural. Every city of any ethnic diversity had its Germania society, its Sons of St. Andrew, its Sons of France, its local equivalent of the United Irishmen; and each of these was likely, in 1793–1794, to transform itself into a "Democratic" society, whose real aim was to promote the identity and interests of the particular ethnic group. Fourth, there were organizations of artisans and mechanics in every major city, founded for benevolent and charitable purposes but acutely aware of the advantages of solidarity to any interest group seeking to obtain favorable legislation. When these groups turned wholly political, as several did in 1793–1794, they understandably blended in with Democratic-Republicans. Finally, there were the Tammany Societies, related to the societies of the artisans and mechanics but separate from them, partly benevolent but political from the outset, partly fraternal and secret like the Masonic Order but based on city working classes. The Society of St. Tammany had chapters in Rhode Island, Connecticut, New York, Pennsylvania, Virginia, and North Carolina.

It was the very diversity of the roots and aims of the Democratic-Republican societies, in fact, that made them a national force in 1793 and ultimately resulted in their undoing. In Philadelphia, for example, the guiding spirits of the mother society were the likes of Blair McClenachan, a wealthy merchant and speculator who had fought the Penns in the 1770s, had fought Robert Morris and the Constitution in the 1780s, and had opposed Hamilton's program but had profited from it by virtue of investments in public securities. In the Pennsylvania back country the radical Republicans were mainly of Scotch-Irish origins, grew corn for whisky as an occupation, opposed Hamilton's excise tax, and were rebellious to the verge of secession. Despite their social and economic differences the Philadelphia and Pittsburgh Democratic-Republicans found common cause in 1793 and thereby advanced the establishment of a national party system. Similarly, in other states, merchants forged temporary alliances with mechanics, Anglicans with Ulstermen, city dwellers with back-country men.

Accompanying the rise of the Democratic-Republican societies was a loosening of restraint in political discourse. For example, mass meetings began to be common in the larger cities, on a scale not seen in America since the turbulent times on the eve of independence. A few years later John Adams recalled that at the height of the "French frenzy, ten thousand people in the streets of Philadelphia, day after day, threatened to drag Washington out of his house, and effect a revolution in the government, or compel it to declare war in favor of the French Revolution and against England." Adams's statement was doubtless exaggerated, but mob violence was a fact, in New York and Boston as well as Philadelphia.

Even more distressing to the president and to other conservative members of society was the intensification of reckless and vitriolic newspaper partisanship. Indeed, Washington himself lost his immunity from attack. The following sarcasm, from Freneau's *National Gazette* of March 2, 1793, was typical of the first barrages: "The monarchical farce [of Washington's birthday celebration] was as usual kept. . . . The President has been pictured as spotless and infallible, as having no likes or dislikes. The glory and achievement of the late Revolution have been entirely imputed to him, and were he Virtue's self the strains of panegyric could not have been louder." That was only the beginning; the attacks steadily mounted in intensity and shrillness, and before the year's end Thomas Greenleaf's *New-York Journal* (on December 7) was emboldened to charge that "gambling, reveling, horseracing and horse whipping" had been the essentials of Washington's education, that he was "infamously niggardly" in private dealings and a "most horrid swearer and blasphemer" despite his pretended religious piety. Meanwhile, Jefferson, Randolph, Hamilton, and Knox—depending on the prejudices of the writer—were castigated as "rascals, liars, and jackals" who ought to be hanged. In public, Washington retained his decorum despite the attacks; but privately he suffered, in Jefferson's words, "more than any person I ever yet met with," and more than once he interrupted cabinet meetings to indulge himself in tirades against the press or in fits of self-pity.

The principal result of all this—the activities of the Democratic-Republican societies, the mass meetings, and the semihysterical partisan newspapers—was a large step toward the politicization of American life. Earlier, no more than a fourth of the eligible voters —propertied adult white males—had turned out for the most important election the nation had known, that on delegates to the conventions which ratified the Constitution, and no more than 10 percent normally showed. Henceforth, far higher proportions of the electorate would vote, even in the most trivial of elections.

And that, in the nature of things, fundamentally changed the game.

So far the narrative suggests a certain logic in events, albeit a complex logic. But then chance or mischance or the gods intervened. Toward the end of the summer of 1793, as Washington and his advisers squared off against Genet—as if to decide the fate of the world, though the combined populations of France and the United States were less than 4 percent of the world's population and contained an even smaller portion of the world's wisdom—a bug infinitely smaller and more numerous than man smote Philadelphia. Yellow fever came, infected and very nearly killed Alexander Hamilton, wiped out a tenth of the inhabitants of the city, and terrified the rest of the country.

Matching the bugs in predictability were the French and the British. In fact all three were entirely predictable, if one understood the premises on which they acted: shibboleths and slogans and mottoes to the contrary notwithstanding, the ruling principle among nations as well as among bugs was to take care of one's own immediate kind, disregarding the whole. The French, for example, chanting *liberté, égalité,* and *fraternité* all the while, as they guillotined twenty thousand of their *frères* toward those noble ends, nevertheless took care of France first and treated the republicans and revolutionaries of other nations as mere pawns when it suited

France's needs to do so. Thus the National Assembly, in February, flung open France's ports to American vessels; and come summer, American ships flocked to French harbors, filled with cargoes indispensable to the Revolution. Come fall, after perhaps a hundred American shipmasters had been allowed to sell their cargoes, the French decided it would be more profitable simply to steal the cargoes as well as the ships. Accordingly, by government fiat, nearly eighty American vessels were seized, charged with irregularities, and confiscated.

Britain likewise placed national self-aggrandizement ahead of ideology or consideration for its friends and allies, and if anything did so more ruthlessly than did France. The weakness in Britain's policy, and the element that most directly involved the United States, was that Britain acted shrewdly but not very intelligently. The Prime Minister, William Pitt the Younger, chose to follow a strategy like that employed by his father three and a half decades earlier—namely, while the Continental powers were fighting among themselves, to plunder their empires in America. Thus, when the coalition had opportunity to crush the French republicans by united effort, and even when a promising counterrevolution broke out in the Vendée and the locals appealed to the British for help, Britain sent no more than a token force to the Netherlands, with orders that they not be deployed even in Belgium. By late summer, however, seven thousand British troops and much of the Royal Navy had been dispatched to the West Indies, their targets being the conquest of Tobago, Martinique, St. Lucia, and Guadeloupe—rich French sugar colonies in the Lesser Antilles—and France's richest glory of all, Saint-Domingue, the western half of the island of Hispaniola in the Greater Antilles. Santo Domingo, a Spanish colony, occupied the eastern half of the island.[4]

The smaller islands fell readily enough, but in attempting to take Saint-Domingue the British were committing a major blunder and incidentally setting the stage for a fierce anti-British reaction in the southern United States. A revolt of Saint-Domingue mulattoes in 1791 had evolved into a sustained and bloody slave insurrection in 1792, and by the time the British began to arrive in 1793, the colony was in chaos. The Spanish, attacking the French from Santo Domingo, had made the colossal mistake of enlisting and arming the greatest of the black rebel leaders, Toussaint L'Ouverture. The

---

[4] Saint-Domingue is roughly the equivalent of modern Haiti; Santo Domingo, of modern Dominican Republic.

British, in a seizure of nonmindedness, continued to put arms in the hands of Toussaint's men. Thus they successfully captured the various port towns, beginning in September, and by the following June had taken Port au Prince; but the "conquest" was useless, for the countryside was dominated by rebellious blacks and scarcely a plantation was still operative.

Dispossessed French plantation masters poured into Charleston, Norfolk, Baltimore, Philadelphia, New York. There they constituted an important Frenchifying cultural influence, but more importantly they horrified the Americans with stories of plunder and burning and killing by the rebellious blacks, who were armed with machetes and British and Spanish guns. Southern whites, almost to a man, joined in a conspiracy to suppress the news of the slave insurrection, lest it infect their own slaves. Southern governors and legislatures even prohibited the interstate transportation or sale of slaves, sometimes on the pretext that they were concerned about the spread of yellow fever from Philadelphia; their real concern was fear of the "black fever" spreading from Saint-Domingue.

News from Saint-Domingue spread through the white South even as news arrived from the Ohio country of depredations by British-armed and British-incited Indians. It is therefore small wonder that many slave-owning, land-speculating southern Republicans, already disposed toward Francophilia and Anglophobia, looked upon the British as madmen who incited slaves and savages to butchery, to a blood bath that would make the guillotine of France's "Reign of Terror" seem polite by comparison. It is likewise not surprising that the southerners were suspicious of, and confused by, northern Federalists who continued to be pro-British and to declare that the exportation of French ideas and policies would lead to massive bloodshed.

Additional British policies were on the way, and these would try the patience and friendship even of northern Federalists. In June of 1793 Britain declared France under blockade, ordered the seizure of all neutral vessels carrying contraband to France, and drastically broadened the traditional limits of blockades by including wheat and other footstuffs on the list of contraband articles— thus showing an apparent intention of starving civilian populations, rather than merely inflicting economic and military damage, as a means of suppressing its enemy. About the same time, since the invasion of the French West Indies was in the offing and the Royal Navy was below strength (115 available ships of the line and twenty-five thousand men),[5] the raising of men through impressment gangs was authorized, and, as an adjunct to that operation, naval captains were ordered to stop neutral vessels on the high seas and search them for British deserters. For practical purpose that meant stopping American ships, for that was where most of the deserters were; and besides, a high-handed captain, short of men, could always take American citizens on the pretext that they were Englishmen, and many of them did so.

There was still more. For years, Portugal had been in a state of perpetual war with the pirates on the Barbary Coast of North Africa and, with the support of a British subsidy, had patrolled the Straits of Gibraltar, containing the pirates in the Mediterranean and often convoying American and other merchant ships through the most dangerous waters. In 1793 Britain, thinking to release the Portuguese navy to help against France, negotiated (and subsidized) a treaty that brought peace between Portugal and the Algerians. The pirates were thereby released into the Atlantic and freed to prey upon American shipping in the Mediterranean. American Republicans were convinced that the by-product was the main aim of Britain's policy: to unleash the barbaric pirates, even as the blacks and red men had been unleashed.

The most direct blow of all was held as a surprise. On November 6, 1793, the British government adopted Orders in Council instructing British warships to seize every neutral vessel they should meet, if the vessel was carrying supplies to, or produce from, French possessions in the West Indies. The orders were kept secret until late December, when virtually the whole American merchant fleet devoted to the trade was in the Caribbean; and then, in an enormously rich raid, no less than 250 American vessels were pounced upon and taken into British ports for condemnation. British admiralty courts held hearings and condemned more than half for sale as prizes under the "Rule of the War of 1756"—that is, that any trade illegal in peacetime was also illegal in wartime.

When Congress convened in December, all these developments save the last were well known in America, and the Republicans were

---

[5] In 1793 the French had 76 ships of the line (sailing's approximate equivalent of battleships) but were crippled by desertion, treason, and lack of discipline. Spain had 56 seaworthy ships of the line, Holland 49 mediocre vessels, Portugal 6, Naples 4. The normal complement of men for Britain's active ships was forty thousand.

prepared with a plan of retaliation. Jefferson, having long since informed Washington that he intended to retire after the president's first term, had delayed his retirement until year's end, partly because he could not retire while the Genet frenzy was at its peak, perhaps partly also because of the near death of Hamilton just after the Genet matter was settled, but no doubt mainly because he had authored and wanted to present to Congress a broad anti-British strategy as his valedictory.

Jefferson's plan was couched as a "Report of the Privileges and Restrictions on the Commerce of the United States in Foreign Countries." In a long, labored argument, crammed with statistical evidence, Jefferson attempted to prove that France's commercial policy was friendly toward the United States and that Britain's was designed to preserve an "unnatural" monopoly of American imports and exports. Jefferson held that the long-range goal toward which the United States should strive was free trade among all nations, but that in light of Britain's policies (and also in light of its monarchism and France's republicanism), the United States should now adopt a restrictive and protective program of regulations, patterned after those of Great Britain but aimed against Great Britain. By such means, Jefferson said, the Americans would strike a blow against tyranny, foster "the progress of household manufacturers," and create an impregnable line of defense in its merchant marine.

As Hamilton put it, Jefferson "threw this FIREBRAND of discord" into the laps of Congress "and instantly decamped to Monticello." Moreover, under Madison's leadership, the Republicans in the Third Congress had the votes to enact Jefferson's plan, and they had something else as well: proof, which they had lacked a year earlier, that Hamilton had reallocated certain government funds without an executive order, in direct violation of the law. Thus, in the interaction of chance, revolution, British bungling, and republican politicking, the masterful system engineered by Alexander Hamilton seemed about to be undone. To a great many people this meant that Washington's presidency and the constitutional experiment itself were about to be undone.

But the wheel of events was soon to take another turn, and this time Hamilton would regain the initiative.

7

★★★★★

1794

For a few weeks early in 1794 it appeared that Jefferson had left the government safely in the hands of his friends and allies. Madison was firmly in control of the House. Hamilton was under a cloud, and the cloud darkened when Hamilton asked Washington for a certificate verifying that he had verbally approved Hamilton's questioned transactions, for Washington refused. Moreover, Washington appointed Edmund Randolph, who was every bit as devoutly Republican and pro-French as Jefferson, to succeed Jefferson as secretary of state.

But Randolph was not nearly so able as Jefferson, was not trusted by his fellow Republicans, and soon lost what little influence he had upon the president. Hamilton, without Jefferson around to interfere and make accusations, rapidly rose in Washington's favor and came to exert far greater influence than ever before. Simultaneously, the president, without Jefferson's strong restraining hand in the cabinet, became much more of an activist and very nearly became, for practical purposes, a Hamiltonian Federalist.

Those developments in the executive branch, together with some bold diplomacy and a measure of luck, had vast consequences for the young nation. The United States was able to avoid both war and "entangling alliances" with Europe for the remainder of Washington's presidency, and by acting as neutral carrier and supplier to the belligerents, it underwent an economic boom of major proportions. The more nearly subversive political elements in the country abated in their fury and were brought under control. The likelihood of importing the extremism of the French Revolution disappeared. The frontier Indians were pacificated, and the diplomatic problems concerning the West were advantageously resolved, at least temporarily. In sum, beginning in 1794 Washington's second administration, while not as creative as the first, was nonetheless a whopping success.

This is not to suggest an absence of acrimony. A bitterly divided two-party system became reality, passions were aroused at the slightest provocation, and the partisan press plunged to the very depths of scurrilousness. By the end of his second term the president was sick of the whole business. For all that, however, the events of 1794 and their aftermath saved his presidency and possibly saved his country.

When the year began, Republicans seemed to be in control of the tide of events. On Friday, January 3, James Madison proposed a series of "Commercial Propositions," aimed at enacting Jefferson's strategy into law, which would have created an American mercantilist system opposed to Britain and favorable to France. Madison's speech appeared to be irrefutable, based as it was on the painstaking research that Jefferson had done or hired done for more than two years. But William L. Smith of South Carolina arose in rebuttal, casually affecting the posture of a man who just happened to know more about the subject than Madison did. Smith, like Madison, drew most of his data and arguments from someone who had worked out the arguments long in advance; and Hamilton, in preparing data for Smith, was far better versed in the matter than was his adversary, Jefferson, and he supplied his man in Congress with far the better ammunition.

The debates actually counted for little, for the Madison-Jefferson Republicans had the votes. But just as the issue reached its climax and a vote loomed near, news of the British seizures in the West Indies reached America. Of a sudden, Madison's position seemed both conservative and absurd: why adopt measures to build up the merchant marine when the Royal Navy was devouring it in large gulps? A great cry for retaliation, for a second War of Independence, swept the country, infecting members of all parties. Republican leaders, virtual pacifists and convinced that Britain could be moved only when its pocketbook was pinched, were thrown into confusion. Vainly and somewhat half-heartedly, they attempted to restrict retaliation to economic sanctions. Federalist leaders, generally pro-British and fully aware of the grave consequences of war with England, nonetheless had hot blood and an understanding that when force enters international relations, one had best be armed. Accordingly, they seized the initiative in Congress, proposing that an army of fifteen thousand be created, that the president be authorized to request the state governors to hold eighty thousand militiamen in readiness, that provisional war taxes be enacted, and that a navy be established.

No large army was forthcoming, but Federalist actions were vigorous. Congress authorized and the president proclaimed an embargo. Congress also, over the vehement opposition of Virginia Republicans, authorized the creation of a navy and appropriated money to build six frigates. (It was expected that the navy would be used against Algerians, and the law provided that the appropriation should be cut off if a treaty were negotiated with the dey —which happened a few months later. But secretaries Hamilton and Knox shrewdly saw to it that contracts were let early, thus assuring completion of the ships. Moreover, the contracts were with the Philadelphia shipbuilding genius Joshua Humphreys, who designed a ship that was fast, oversized, and equipped with an extra gun deck; and the Humphreys frigates became the best and most powerful ships of their class in the world. Thus was born the United States Navy, though it was administered as part of the army and did not become a separate branch of the armed forces until 1798.)

These steps having been taken, the next was to send a minister plenipotentiary to London to see what could be negotiated. In March of 1794 a group of Federalist senators, having conferred with Hamilton, called upon Washington and urged him to send someone, preferably Hamilton himself, to undertake the negotiations. The president agreed that a minister extraordinary should be sent, but shrewdly recognized that Hamilton was too controversial for the assignment, inasmuch as political opposition to him might jeopardize ratification of any treaty he might bring back. Instead, Washington selected Chief Justice Jay, over the protests of Republicans that to do so was an improper mixing of the executive and judicial branches. Then the president placated the Republicans and hedged his diplomatic bets by recalling the arch-Federalist minister to France, Gouverneur Morris, and replacing him with the arch-Republican James Monroe.

In keeping with his usual practice, Washington asked each of his department heads to prepare drafts of proposed instructions for Jay, and that proved to be the beginning of the end for Randolph

141

and the occasion for the virtually total ascendency of Hamilton. Randolph had grown lukewarm toward the mission and devoted much of his attention to trying to force Jay to resign his chief justiceship before accepting the diplomatic assignment. Hamilton was vigorous, urgent, and fluent in his defense of the mission. Washington was swayed and gave Hamilton the principal responsibility for preparing Jay's instructions, even though the instructions were issued over Randolph's signature.

The instructions formally gave Jay wide latitude, but Hamilton privately amplified them with a detailed letter that amounted to instructions from the Federalist party. Carefully warning Jay not to be excessively adamant ("We are still in the path of negotiation: let us not plant it with thorns"), Hamilton spelled out what Jay was to try to obtain. Four items were to take priority—compensation for the recent seizures, evacuation of the British posts in the Northwest Territory, compensation for the slaves that the British army had freed during the War of Independence or carried away at the end of the war, and a commercial treaty with Great Britain.

In dealing with the matter Hamilton was being less than candid, either with Jay or with the president. As early as 1789 he had engaged in private discussions with George Beckwith, the informal British emissary, and subsequently he had talked on several occasions with the British minister George Hammond; to both men he had made clear the terms on which he would support an Anglo-American treaty. Every term save one ran directly counter to the hopes of the southern Republicans, and some were at variance with the instructions to Jay. First came favorable trade relations—an object that was almost frustrated from the outset, for, on the eve of Jay's departure, Madison pushed through the House a bill cutting off all commercial intercourse with Britain, though the bill was defeated in the Senate by the tie-breaking vote of Vice-President Adams. Next, Hamilton believed, was the matter of the northwestern posts, which he insisted must be evacuated. So far, nothing special; but on two other points his position was at odds not only with southern feelings but with most popular opinion in America as well. As a devout enemy of the institution of slavery, he had suggested to the British representatives that none of the liberated or confiscated slaves be returned, that no compensation be paid their former owners, and that indeed the question never enter the negotiations. On the other hand, he suggested that the question of private prewar debts—amounting, with accrued interest, to some £3 million, owed mainly by Virginia and Maryland tobacco planters to London merchants, and sequestered, canceled, or avoided since 1776—should enter the negotiations and that some means of collecting the debts should be incorporated into a treaty in return for commercial favors from Britain. This matter, too, was almost stifled by legislation: Congressman Jonathan Dayton proposed that current as well as older private debts, amounting in all to about £4 million, be sequestered by the United States government and held as "hostage" until Britain compensated Americans in full and with damages for the recent seizures. Dayton's bill was also defeated just before Jay embarked.

There was one other bit of under-the-table dealing. Denmark and Sweden had recently formed a League of Armed Neutrality, with a view toward protecting their rights as neutral carriers and, what was more to the point, extracting trade concessions from the belligerents. There was talk that the United States might profitably join the league, and several people, mostly Republicans, thought that Jay might successfully use the threat of joining the league as a weapon in his negotiations. There was, in fact, no likelihood that the United States would join; and it is probable that Jay could have gained nothing, and perhaps might have lost a great deal, by raising the threat. In any event, he had no chance to do so, for Hamilton assured Hammond that the administration would have no part of the league, and Hammond so advised his government.

Jay sailed in the spring and landed in England in June. Even before he departed he learned that the most immediate bone of contention had been removed. On January 8, 1794, the Orders in Council of November 6, 1793, had been repealed, and new orders had been issued, allowing direct trade between the United States and the French West Indies. Inasmuch as American trade with France was already permitted, American vessels could now carry goods between France and her possessions merely by stopping at an American port on the way, under the doctrine of the "continuous voyage." Russian, Danish, Swedish, and other northern European vessels were not accorded similar privileges; indeed, they were cut out of the trade entirely. As a result of this privilege, the American merchant marine would grow and prosper in the next few years in proportions that the most euphoric Jeffersonians had not dared predict would be the result of their own system. Had Jay brought home that concession alone as the fruit of his labors, he might legitimately have been hailed as a hero. As things turned out, he brought home more—and was castigated.

The greatest difficulty in negotiating from Jay's position was neither the weakness of the United States nor the rigidity of the British. It was, rather, that the broad international context, in the absence of a single dominating power, was continually and erratically shifting. During the course of Jay's mission, relevant events took place in four broad areas: the courts and battlefields of Europe, the halls of Congress, the mountains of Pennsylvania, and the plains of the Ohio country.

On the European continent the most important developments were that the extreme radicalism of the French Revolution came to an end, bringing veritable collapse inside France, and yet the French armies continued to win in the field. The Reign of Terror spent itself by the early summer of 1794, and the Thermidorian Reaction, presaging a stabilization of power in the hands of the bourgeoisie and the army, took place in July. One immediate consequence was the end of rigid government control over the economy, which in turn resulted in devastating inflation. The inflation, coupled with widespread crop failures, made the nation's economy a shambles by fall. Meanwhile, however, the Revolutionary armies continued to succeed: They overran Holland, established France's "natural boundary" at the Rhine as a defense perimeter, and, in the south, defeated Spanish armies on Spanish soil.

In Congress two actions were directly related to Anglo-American relations, one being the work of Republicans, the other of Federalists. In cases decided in its February terms of 1793 and 1794, the Supreme Court had ruled that the state of Georgia could be sued by British creditors for private debts which the state had sequestered during the Revolution and that the sequestration law did not operate to confiscate or vest title to the debt in the state. In reaction to these decisions, on the eve of Jay's departure Republicans pushed through Congress a constitutional amendment that prevented states from being sued by foreigners or citizens of another state.[1] That amendment, if ratified, would obviously limit the effectiveness of any settlement of the debt question that Jay might make. The other congressional action, this one sponsored by Federalists, was the passage on June 5 of the Neutrality Act, which confirmed the president's neutrality proclamation, forbade American citizens to

---

[1] The cases were *Chisholm* v. *Georgia* (2 Dallas 419, 1793) and *Georgia* v. *Brailsford* (2 Dallas 402, 3 Dallas 1, 1794). The amendment was ratified in 1798 as the Eleventh Amendment.

enlist in the service of a foreign power, and banned the fitting of foreign armed vessels in American ports.

The event in western Pennsylvania was the so-called Whisky Rebellion. Superficially, what happened can be told briefly. In back-country Pennsylvania, where perhaps a quarter of the nation's whisky stills were located and where, indeed, whisky was so important as to constitute a medium of exchange, the inhabitants had resisted and had avoided paying the federal excise tax on spiritous liquors since it had first been levied in 1791. In the summer of 1794 resistance turned into mass defiance of the law, stimulated at least in part by a Democratic-Republican society in the vicinity, the Mingo Creek Society. On August 7 President Washington, alarmed and outraged by the challenge to federal authority, issued a proclamation declaring that the resistance amounted to an insurrection and ordering the "rebels" to return to their homes. Almost simultaneously, after satisfying the law by securing from Supreme Court justice James Wilson a certification that the situation was beyond the control of federal marshals or judicial proceedings, Washington requested the governors of Pennsylvania, New Jersey, Maryland, and Virginia to supply a militia army to put down the rebellion. The militiamen, 12,950 strong, assembled in Harrisburg in September; Washington accompanied them for a few weeks, and Hamilton stayed with them throughout the march, though General Henry Lee was in command. The "rebellion," such as it was, disappeared; and only twenty rebels were found. These were subsequently paraded as captives in Philadelphia and were charged with treason. Two were convicted, but Washington pardoned them, inasmuch as one was "insane" and the other a retardate.

Underneath the surface, the episode was far more complex. Though it is true that the larger and more respectable distillers had all begun to comply with the law, that several radical Republican societies had recently sprung up in the area, and that resistance to the excise among smaller distillers increased sharply in the spring of 1794, it is not to be inferred that the "democracy" of the distillers provoked the uprising, either for political or economic motives. Rather, it seems entirely probable that the provocation came from Alexander Hamilton, and that his motive was to discredit and crush his political enemies by identifying them with treason.

In March 1794 Hamilton seemingly bowed to appeals for reason and justice and urged Congress to revise the excise law. Western Pennsylvanians had complained repeatedly against the feature of the original law that required accused violators to be arrested and taken all the way across the state to Philadelphia, to be held there until a federal court convened and they could be tried. On April 4, at Hamilton's suggestion, a bill was introduced into Congress that would make such cases cognizable in state courts when they arose more than fifty miles from the nearest seat of a federal district court. But then, having raised the hopes of the back-country men, Hamilton carefully and deliberately dashed them. On May 31, with the bill only a few hours away from passage, treasury agents secured from the federal district court in Philadelphia processes against seventy-five distillers who had not registered and paid taxes in June 1793; and at least sixty-one of the writs, ordering appearances in Philadelphia, were against distillers in the radical "Fourth Survey" district of western Pennsylvania. Moreover, though the writs were entered on the docket on May 31, they were not served until July, weeks after the new law had been passed and published in the West.

The provocation proved to be effective. On June 22 federal marshal David Lenox left Philadelphia with the writs. He met no difficulty in serving writs in Cumberland, Bedford, and Fayette counties in the central part of the state. On July 15 he and the excise inspector, General John Neville, set out westward from Pittsburgh for the Mingo Creek area to serve the remaining writs, which ordered various small distillers to "set aside all manner of business and excuses" and appear on August 12, in person, at the federal district court in Philadelphia, where ruinous fines of $250 could be expected. Rumors spread around the area that "the Federal Sheriff was taking away people to Philadelphia." At daybreak on July 16 a party of about forty men, some of them armed, made an abortive attack on Neville's private mansion at Bower Hill, where Neville had gone and Lenox was mistakenly assumed to have gone; one of the attackers was killed and several were wounded before the rest withdrew. By late afternoon the attackers, fearing they would be indicted for attempted murder and angry over the killing of one of their number, had roused about five hundred militiamen among their neighbors and returned to Bowers Hill to "negotiate" and demand Neville's resignation. Neville, for his part, had induced seventeen regular soldiers to defend his house while he discreetly absented himself. Some shooting ensued, the insurgent leader was killed, the soldiers capitulated, and the insurgent militiamen destroyed Neville's residence. Neville and Lenox fled the area, and in the next two weeks it teemed with impassioned meetings, radical oratory, threats to take Pittsburgh by force and oust all federal authority, and occasional acts of violence. The climax came on August 1, when about seven thousand men gathered at Braddock's Field, and most of them marched on Pittsburgh. They did no especial damage to the town; excisemen and their sympathizers, however, were terrorized, and a general reign of lawlessness prevailed for about two more weeks. That was the rebellion.

Washington and his advisers knew nothing of this when the cabinet met and determined to declare an insurrection and then suppress it by a massive display of force. The cabinet meeting took place on August 2, at which time all that was known was the news of the attack on Bowers Hill. In short, Washington and Hamilton had already made up their minds. Vainly, Governor Mifflin insisted that Pennsylvania authority was adequate to cope with the lawlessness. Frantically, but by no means inaccurately, Madison charged that the insurrection was being used to "establish the principle that a standing army was necessary for *enforcing the laws.*" And so the army was assembled and marched, with the anticlimactic results already noted. Said Jefferson: "An insurrection was announced and proclaimed and armed against, but could never be found."

In November, Washington delivered before Congress an angry address that was well calculated to extract maximum political mileage from the episode—and also to wreak personal vengeance upon those who, in the president's eyes, were responsible for the calumny to which he had been subjected. He insisted that the insurrection was real, that it was treason, that it involved a movement in the entire West to renounce federal authority; and he laid blame squarely on "self-created societies," meaning the Democratic-Republican societies. The Whisky Rebellion, he charged, was but "the first formidable fruit" of the societies, and he declared that if they were not suppressed "or did not fall into detestation from the knowledge of their (Jacobin) origin . . . they would shake the government to its foundation." The president did not see fit to mention, if he was aware, that members of Democratic societies in Philadelphia and Baltimore had turned out in large numbers as part of the federal force against the insurrection.

Hamilton's part in the affair, on the other hand, was neither angry nor even emotional, but shrewdly calculated. And the "counter-insurrection" was effective: the spread of Democratic-Republican societies was arrested, and after one more episode in 1795 they rapidly faded. More immediately to the point, Federalists regained full control of Congress in the 1794 elections.

One more event of the summer had a direct bearing on the

subject matter of Jay's negotiations. In February, Lord Dorchester and Simcoe had convened a meeting of Indian chiefs. These militant, aggressive British officials, avid to oust the Americans from the Ohio country and oblivious to the needs or wishes of their superiors in London, roused the Indians to make a massive, decisive attack, completing the work that had begun with the defeat of St. Clair in 1791. Dorchester told the red men that war between the United States and Great Britain was imminent and inevitable, and he assured them that when war came, British and Indians would fight side by side to restore the Indians to control of their hunting grounds forever. To show his good faith, and also for sound tactical reasons, Dorchester ordered Simcoe to construct a new post, Fort Miami, on the Maumee just south of what later became Toledo. In response, the chiefs sped war belts through the forest to summon warriors, and by mid June two thousand of them had gathered at the new fort.

Meanwhile, General "Mad Anthony" Wayne had been sent to replace St. Clair and defend the area. Wayne arrived in the summer of 1793 and, directly disobeying President Washington's explicit but ill-considered orders to attack immediately, set out to organize, provision, and discipline his troops. Using the small "regular" army as a core and steadily adding carefully screened frontier riflemen, Wayne had a force of two thousand tough, disciplined men ready by the spring of 1794. Then he began to move slowly northward from Fort Greenville, stopping at the site of St. Clair's defeat to build Fort Recovery. There, late in June, he beat off a strong Indian attack, inflicting considerable losses and suffering few.

In July, Wayne resumed his movement northward along the Au Glaize river, and on August 8 he reached the Maumee and threw up a rough fortification. Then, showing an understanding of his enemy that few American generals or statesmen have ever shown, Wayne began to implement a clever stratagem. The Indians had a custom of fasting before a battle. Wayne sent word through the forest that on August 17 he would march against the position that the Indians had chosen for making their defense, an area near Fort Miami where a maze of fallen trees would afford them excellent protection. At the appointed time Wayne marched toward the area but, instead of attacking, encamped ten miles away. The Indian party of thirteen hundred men, mystified, maintained an impatient vigil and also continued their fasting. For three days and nights Wayne made not a move, and the Indians grew progressively hungrier. Finally, on August 20, more than five hundred hungry warriors decided to break their fast and went back to Fort Miami to get food. As soon as they had gone, Wayne attacked, moving forward in two tight columns. One column hit the Indians frontally, the other poured a withering rifle fire into their left flank. No British troops came to the Indians' aid; the betrayed and hungry red men stood their ground only briefly, then fled. The entire Battle of Fallen Timbers, climaxing a decade of British-Indian-American relations, was over in two hours.

The battle was decisive, not because of the magnitude of Wayne's victory but because the British commander at Fort Miami (for all Dorchester's inflammatory and irresponsible promises) did not dare risk war with a neutral by sending his men into the battle. The dispirited Indians went back to their villages; disorganized, they fell easy prey to Wayne's raids. Wayne destroyed village after village, built a fort named after himself at the head of the Maumee, and, in less than a year, was able to command the chiefs of twelve tribes to attend a conclave—at which he dictated a treaty removing the Indians from the entire area of what was to become the state of Ohio.

And thus, no matter what arrangements Jay was able to work out in London concerning the Northwest Territory, the power of the British on American soil was broken.

These events were happening while Jay was in London, and though they would markedly influence the reaction to his negotiations, news of them did not reach England in time to affect the negotiations themselves. Acting on the basis of the way things were when he left in May, but also employing shrewd common sense, Jay proceeded slowly, carefully, and in a firm but friendly manner.

It was well that he did so, for had he taken a hard line—had he threatened to go to war or even to join the League of Armed Neutrality—Lord Grenville, the British Secretary of State for Foreign Affairs, would have sent him packing for home in a fortnight. For the British were in a peculiar position vis-à-vis the United States. Politically and militarily they had no cause to fear the Americans; a dozen of His Majesty's ships of the line could have rendered the United States impotent with a blockade and made a profit in the doing. Economically, however, war with the United States could be a serious irritant. The most obvious drawback, in short-range terms, was that British merchants in the American trade would lose the considerable sums owed them by American debtors, though Grenville could and did resist the merchants' pressures on that score. One British minister maintained that the Americans were "so much in debt to this country that we scarcely dare quarrel with them"; but Lord Hawkesbury, chairman of the Board of Trade, insisted that the merchants had always recognized the risks of extending credit to Americans and marked up their prices accordingly, so that if they were ever paid in full, they would gain "more than they had any Reason to expect."

Far more important was the broader economic situation of Great Britain, should the European war go on as long as was generally expected. In the first year of war, tightened credit bankrupted thousands of Englishmen and brought the collapse of a hundred banks, the aggregate tonnage of British ports declined 17 percent, and exports fell from £24 million to £19 million. The Bank of England held firm, and trade was restored to its normal levels by 1794; but in that year and again in the next, French privateers swept six hundred British ships from the seas, and the portion of Britain's international trade carried by foreigners rose from 10 percent to 25 percent. Meanwhile, government finance was likewise strained: revenues fell from £14.3 million in 1792 to £13.6 million in 1795, while naval expenditures rose from £1.9 million to £6.3 million and those of the army from £1.8 million to £11.6 million. To top it all off, grain crops in Britain failed calamitously in 1794, as they did again the next year.

In the circumstances the British thought it prudent to get the best possible deal with Jay—but by all means to deal, to keep the United States neutral, and to keep Anglo-American trade open. The revocation in January of the harsh Orders in Council of the preceding November was a step toward those ends. So was the treatment afforded Jay personally: in diplomatic circles it was felt that his most vulnerable spot was vanity, so he was received and warmly welcomed by VIPs ranging from the celebrated scientific farmer Sir John Sinclair (who made Jay an honorary member of the Board of Agriculture) all the way up to King George himself. In the first informal substantive discussions, late in June, it suddenly appeared that things might not go as well as the reception suggested; for when Jay mentioned compensation for the recent spoliations of American commerce, Grenville replied that no instance of that kind had come to his attention. But when Jay presented, at the end of July, a formal complaint and request for compensation, Grenville was all conciliation, assuring Jay that "*justice* should, at *all events*, be done" and that forthwith they would enter discussions "of the *measures* to be adopted, and the principles to be established, for that purpose." He also promised satisfaction on the matter of impressments. A few days later the king said to Jay, "Well, sir, I imagine you begin to see that your mission will probably be successful." Hard-nosed bargaining began on August 5. The discussions got off to a bad start, for the question immediately arose, Who was responsible for the first violations of the treaty? Jay scored a point, maintaining that the British, by carrying off slaves at the end of the war, obviously were guilty of the first violation. Grenville responded that when the slaves went behind British lines, they either became free or British property; and Jay, who was as strongly opposed to slavery as Hamilton was, did not press the matter. After five fruitless hours it was settled that neither party would admit responsibility for the infractions. Jay suggested that past differences be forgotten and that they concentrate on finding reciprocal concessions that would be mutually beneficial. Grenville agreed and, less magnanimously than it seemed, asked Jay to prepare a draft of a treaty.

Jay submitted a draft the next day, containing only provisions that he thought important and advantageous to the United States. It provided for compensation for the recent maritime seizures, evacuation of the western posts by June 1, 1795, a guarantee of American boundaries as fixed by the treaty of 1783, admittance of American vessels of up to one hundred tons to the British West Indies, and mutual trading concessions to be agreed upon. The two matters dearest to the hearts of southerners—compensation for confiscated slaves and the question of prewar debts—were not mentioned. In his reply on August 30 Grenville likewise omitted reference to the slaves, and the subject did not come up in the negotiations again, but he did ask for a guarantee that in case of war in the future, there would be no confiscation or sequestration of debts. As to commerce, he argued that there should be no tariff discriminations between the two countries, proposed that Britons be compensated for losses from privateers that had been outfitted in American ports, insisted on maintaining the Rule of 1756, and offered admittance to the British West Indies of American ships only up to seventy tons. (The last was consistent with British policy as contained in the January Orders in Council. Vessels under seventy tons could not safely engage in transatlantic trade, and the British reckoned that if Americans had to transship West Indies goods through their home ports, they could offer a secondary source of freightage but could not be competitive with British carriers.) Finally, in regard to the West, Grenville was willing to evacuate all British posts on American soil, but not before June 1, 1796; and he insisted that British traders be allowed the privilege of trading with Indians in American territory and that British Canada be ensured free access to the Mississippi. (Neither Grenville nor Jay knew just where the headwaters of the Mississippi were, but Jay did understand that this concession would involve ceding some territory to Great Britain and estimated the total at 35,500 square miles.)

Different as the two sets of proposals were, they were close enough to be negotiable; and Jay, encumbered with no other duties, prepared now to do some earnest dealing, aimed especially at ensuring freedom of the seas. But Grenville suddenly hardened, for news from a variety of sources made a tougher approach both possible and necessary. The possibility arose with the arrival in September of Hammond's dispatch containing Hamilton's assurances that the United States would have nothing to do with the League of Armed Neutrality. Probably Jay would not have used that threat, but Grenville feared it far more than Jay suspected, and now the fear was gone. At almost the same time, from Paris came news that infuriated Grenville. As has been indicated, President Washington had sent the Republican James Monroe to Paris just after he had sent Jay to London. Now news arrived in London that Monroe had been accorded an enthusiastic reception, had exchanged fraternal kisses with the president of the national Convention, and had behaved himself generally as if the United States and France were ardent friends and allies. Upon learning this, Grenville coldly informed Jay that if Monroe represented the attitude of his government, His Majesty's ministers would find it difficult to treat the United States as a neutral.

More important yet was news from the Caribbean and from the European continent, which together doomed the strategy that Britain had hoped to follow in the War of the First Coalition. On the one hand, adventuring in the French West Indies was now certain to fail; for France had abolished slavery in February, and in response Toussaint L'Ouverture and the other black leaders had broken with the Spanish and had joined forces with the French general Étienne Lavaux. On the other hand, the Continental Coalition itself was disintegrating. The French, hoping to divide the members of the coalition through separate negotiations, had made overtures to Spain and Prussia, and both those powers agreed to meet with French diplomats in Basel, Switzerland, in November. England feared that both would agree to withdraw from the war—which they did in fact the following spring.

In these circumstances Grenville was in a mood not to dicker but to dictate. Had Jay been foolhardy, he might, at that juncture, have reasoned that Britain's back was to the wall and that the time had arrived for the United States to take a hard line; Republicans later criticized him for not doing so. But the Americans, sorely divided, had neither navy nor army to speak of, and in the event of war they would have had virtually no revenues, either. Moreover, the purpose of Jay's mission was to make peace, not war. Accordingly, he could only concilate, backtrack, and take whatever he could get. The result, as incorporated in a treaty signed on November 19, was an agreement about halfway between what Hamilton wanted and what the Foreign Secretary's office had secretly agreed upon as desirable even when the negotiations began.

Jay's Treaty may be fruitfully analyzed on three different levels: in terms of its significance to the conduct of international relations as such, its immediate effects upon the two signatory nations, and its effects upon domestic political arrangements in the United States. In the long range the treaty was of considerable importance in two respects. One was that it introduced (at the instance of Grenville) a major innovation into the art of diplomacy. Three vexing questions—those concerning pre-Revolutionary debts, compensation for illegal maritime seizures, and settlement of the boundaries between New England and Canada—were not settled in the treaty but were referred to arbitration commissions. The commissions—which were to consist of two members appointed by the king, two by the president, and a fifth to be agreed upon by the first four—would conduct hearings and examine all relevant documents, and their rulings would be binding on both governments. In regard to debts and spoliations, each government would be responsible for compensating citizens or subjects of the other, if the commission so ruled. In regard to the debts specifically, the United States agreed to compensate in full all British creditors who were unable to collect lawful debts because of legal impediments erected either by states or by the national government. Thus the Eleventh Amendment was circumvented: British creditors were secured in their rights, and American debtors—because the United States government could sue for recovery and, being responsible for their debts, was likely to do so—were jeopardized.[2]

² The commissions were duly appointed and, after several years of investigations, made their findings, though it was not until 1802 that all three issues were finally resolved. As an experiment in diplomatic techniques the arbitration commissions were successful on two of the issues, less so on the third. The

Another long-range implication of the treaty was that in it the United States effectively renounced its claim to freedom of the seas. Jay's defense of this position was realistic. Under its present circumstances, he wrote in forwarding the treaty to Washington, Britain could scarcely be expected to "admit principles, which would impeach the propriety of her conduct in seizing provisions bound to France, and enemy's property in neutral ships"; and no such admission was forthcoming. The principles that the United States had bound itself to in treaties with other foreign powers—that free ships make free goods, that neutrals have the right to trade freely in noncontraband goods with belligerents, and that contraband lists must be limited to war materials—were abandoned in Jay's Treaty. Instead, Britain's conception of the rights of belligerents was incorporated into it: the Rule of 1756 was confirmed, naval stores were defined as contraband, and under certain unclearly defined conditions (which is to say when it suited Britain's convenience) even provisions could be treated as contraband. Impressment of seamen was not mentioned in the treaty and was thereby tacitly accepted.

The immediate effects upon Britain and the United States amounted to a fair bargain for both. Apart from compensation for the seizures, the greatest gain to the Americans, ironically, was no gain at all; Britain agreed to evacuate the Northwest posts by June of 1796, whereas, though neither Grenville nor Jay yet knew it, the British position in territory of the United States had already been destroyed by Anthony Wayne. Of mutual advantage was that war was avoided and each nation placed the other, in terms of tariffs, on a most-favored-nation basis. Of some advantage to the United States were cracks allowed into Britain's wall of mercantilism. The British East Indies were opened to Americans, and that trade brought Americans many millions in profits in the next few years; but the British West Indies were opened to American vessels only

boundary dispute was settled amicably; and American shippers were awarded nearly one and one-third million pounds (about $6 million); but Americans succeeded in thwarting the efforts of the debt commission. Finally, President Jefferson's government offered Britain £600,000 as payment in full, though the debts were actually ten times that amount, including accrued interest. Knowing that this was all they could get and being promised (in defiance of the Eleventh Amendment) that federal courts would be opened to British creditors in the future, Britain accepted. For a good running account of the work of the commissions, see Bradford Perkins, *The First Rapprochement: England and the United States, 1795–1805* (Berkeley: University of California Press, 1967), chapters 10–12.

up to seventy tons burden. Even that, of course, was a concession by the British, for the islands had been closed since 1784 to American vessels larger than forty tons. Besides, Jamaica and the smaller British islands were far less important than the Spanish and French islands, and American trade with the French islands had been protected by the January Orders in Council. But one feature of Article XII of the treaty, that covering trade with the British West Indies, was likely to rankle some Americans: it stipulated that molasses, sugar, coffee, cocoa, and cotton would not be carried in American ships to any part of the world except the United States. It was apparently intended that this restriction would apply only to such of those products as were imported from the British West Indies, but the wording was ambiguous; strictly read, the article prevented Americans from carrying the commodities to Europe even if they were imported from French or Spanish colonies or, for that matter, if they were produced in the United States.[3] Still, all things considered, Admiral Mahan was not entirely off the mark when he concluded that Britain's signature of any treaty with the United States was of "epochal significance," a far more definite recognition of American independence than the treaty that had been forced upon Great Britain in 1783. Indeed, critics of the Pitt ministry charged that Grenville had conceded too much in the face of American complaints, while equally valid complaints from other nations were being ignored.

Because public opinion counted in the United States far more than in Britain or most other places, the treaty's effect on international relations was less immediately significant than its effect upon domestic politics. In the latter arena, reactions were entirely predictable. Since the revised Orders in Council were known in America before Jay's negotiations began, and since the greatest gain registered in the treaty was the hollow one concerning the Northwest posts, few Americans were likely to be excited by it. North and

[3] The only one of the enumerated commodities actually being produced in the United States was cotton, and that was as yet of small consequence. Before 1793, when the cotton gin was invented, the only profitable form of cotton was the long-staple variety, which could be grown in America only on sea islands. The gin made it profitable to grow short-staple cotton, which could be raised in abundance on American uplands. The spread of cotton culture thereafter was extremely rapid: exports increased from less than a million pounds in 1793 to more than eighteen million in 1800. But in 1794 cotton exports amounted to only two million pounds, and in 1795 to six million—only a tiny fraction of the total amount of American exports.

east of Philadelphia, few were likely to be especially offended by it, either, except for the ambiguous twelfth article; and most people who were not ardently Francophile were likely to be grateful, if lukewarmly so, for the peace it confirmed and the general and specific advantages it brought. South and west of Philadelphia was another story. The treaty was deafening by its silence in regard to confiscated slaves, which southerners reckoned as a loss of about $10 million; and what was more, the southerners stood in jeopardy of having to repay private debts of long standing, which, with accrued interest, ranged between £2 million and £5 million sterling. Francophilia alone was enough to ensure that southern Republicans would oppose the treaty. With $20 million in out-of-pocket costs added to the bargain, their opposition was certain to be fierce.

Yet the Hamiltonian Federalists expected the resistance to be moderate. Continuing to believe, inaccurately, that in a popular government it is enough merely to govern well, they counted their achievements and then counted themselves secure. The Whisky Rebellion had been scuttled, and in its wake the dangerous Democratic-Republican societies had apparently been sunk. The Indians and the British had been beaten in the Ohio country, and Jay's Treaty confirmed the victory. The treaty itself, though it left some things to be desired, insured neutrality and protected the fiscal and governmental superstructure that Hamilton had erected upon the Constitution.

And there was one more thing, a turn of events and a move by the administration that could scarcely fail to win the hearts of southerners and westerners—and it was in part a by-product of Jay's negotiations. Spain, after twenty years of hostility and conspiracy against the United States in the Southwest, suddenly reversed itself and informed Washington that if he would send a diplomat of more stature than the present American commissioners in Madrid, William Short and William Carmichael, Spain would discuss the navigation of the Mississippi and all other matters at issue between the two nations.

Moreover, the prospects of an advantageous outcome of such talks were favorable—not because of Spain's interests in America but because of her concerns in Europe. Spain had entered the coalition as a matter of principle, but had become disgusted with the opportunistic behavior of its allies, mainly Britain. Scarcely less galling was that most of Spain's fighting against the French Revolution was taking place not in France but in Spain and was a losing proposition. For those reasons Manuel de Godoy, the most powerful man in the Spanish government (thanks to his being the queen's lover and thanks to the weakness and effeminacy of the king, Charles IV), began late in the summer of 1794 to move toward abandoning the coalition. He was confident that doing so would ultimately lead to war with Britain, and Jay's warm treatment in England convinced him that the United States would be allied with England in such a confrontation. Accordingly, Godoy (who styled himself Prince of Peace) set out to appease the Americans and thereby neutralize them.

No one in the United States imagined how far Godoy was willing to go—he was in fact prepared to dispose of Louisiana entirely—but President Washington immediately recognized that here was an opportunity to settle some vexing problems and to win political favor into the bargain. Thus he responded to Spain's overture by appointing Thomas Pinckney, the regular American minister in London, to go to Madrid as minister extraordinary and sole plenipotentiary to the court of Spain.

In the face of all these favorable developments, Alexander Hamilton thought it safe to resign as secretary of the treasury and attend to long-neglected private business. His resignation was effective January 31, 1795, exactly thirteen months after Jefferson's. His confidence was almost precisely as justified as Jefferson's had been, which is to say not at all; for 1795 would be the most turbulent of all Washington's years in office.

8

★★★★★

TREATIES AND INTRIGUE
1795–1796

The Democratic-Republican societies, under a cloud after Washington branded them with involvement in the Whisky Rebellion, nonetheless had one more inning before they disappeared: they organized a vociferous public opposition to the ratification of Jay's Treaty. To be sure, not much organization was necessary in the South; no treaty negotiated by John Jay was likely to be satisfactory to southerners, for his Federalism, his opposition to slavery, and his willingness to bargain away southern claims for northern commercial advantage (as revealed in the abortive Jay-Gardoqui negotiations of 1786) were legend south of the Potomac. But to the north a friendly treaty with Britain would be acceptable, if it were not totally disgraceful; and against this possibility, in the winter of 1794–1795, the Democratic-Republican societies prepared to mobilize all the opposition they could muster.

Moreover, neither France nor its supporters in America remained idle in regard to the treaty. France did, however, begin a fundamental shift in style and tactics. Earlier, in Genet's time, it had relied on enthusiasm for liberty, sweetened by the prospect of profit from participation in the "liberation" of Spanish lands and British prizes, as a means of winning American supporters; and its methods were generally open. By early 1795 much of the American enthusiasm for French-style *liberté* had vanished under the horror of the Terror, and the sweeteners had gone sour. Simultaneously, the stabilization of government under the corrupt Directory and the breakup of the First Coalition enabled France to play a different game in America, one based on intrigue and bribery and aimed at the restoration of the French empire that was lost to the British in 1763. Several influential Americans—including, quite possibly, Secretary of State Edmund Randolph, Senator Aaron Burr of New York, and Ira Allen of Vermont—sought or received French favors and, in repayment, supported the French cause in the struggle over Jay's Treaty.

Among American historians who have written on the subject, the consensus has been that the storm over Jay's Treaty crystallized the movement toward the creation of a two-party system in the United States. Careful attention to the behavior of the treaty's opponents makes it seem more likely that things were the other way around: that a preexisting polarization—based upon differences of personalities, ideologies, subcultures, and economic interests and influenced by French money and intrigue and by Republican organizational skill—capitalized on Jay's Treaty as a point of disputation over which a two-party system could be nationalized and hardened. In a sense, Jay's Treaty thus became the first national partisan "issue" in the history of American politics.

The American constitutional system contemplated a leisurely approach to government. The Second Congress, elected late in 1790, first met a year later and did not end its final session until March 3, 1793; the Third Congress, elected in 1792, was not scheduled to go out of business until March 3, 1795, though its successor had been elected five months earlier. President Washington and his advisers, running the executive branch on a different timetable and not being entirely sure of the partisan make-up of the Congress elected in 1794, devoutly hoped that a copy of Jay's Treaty would arrive before the Third Congress adjourned. News that a treaty had been signed reached Philadelphia late in January, and Jay had dispatched three separate copies of the treaty in the hope that one would make it in time. By chance, only one copy reached Philadelphia, and it arrived on March 7.

Forthwith, Washington called the new Senate into a special session to convene on June 8. The delay was advantageous to supporters of the treaty, for it enabled some new and friendly senators to take their seats, but the issue was still sure to be close. Most of the senators from New England and the Middle States were Federalists and would vote for ratification if the president himself approved the treaty, but all but three or four from the South were Republicans, and a two-thirds majority—twenty Senators—was necessary for approval.

Serious debate began on June 11, and two important decisions were made at the outset. The first, that the debates and the treaty itself would remain a secret until after ratifications were exchanged, was honored as much in the breach as in the observation. Pierce Butler of South Carolina sent a copy of the treaty to Madison, one page at a time, with the request that it be shown to Jefferson and no one else; and during the next two weeks several senators leaked copies to trusted friends. The other decision was more complex. Federalist leaders (including Hamilton, who was officially out of the government but unofficially still the most influential man in it, save Washington himself) decided that Article XII was dangerously ambiguous and should be rejected. The article, it will be recalled, was intended to prohibit the reexport to Europe of commodities imported from the British West Indies, but was so worded that it possibly prevented the reexport of products of the French and Spanish West Indies as well. On June 17, at Hamilton's suggestion and probably on motion of Rufus King, Federalists proposed that the Senate approve all the treaty except Article XII and that the Senate recommend further negotiation in regard to trade with the British West Indies.

That maneuver deprived the Republicans of their best weapon against the treaty, for decorum and the socio-political code of the times prevented senators from admitting that they opposed merely out of a bias against Britain and in favor of France. Under the leadership of Burr they obtained a four-day recess, after which Burr delivered a powerful speech pointing out flaws in the treaty—a speech given more for the record and for future elections than in the hope of changing votes—and proposed that the treaty be postponed in favor of "further friendly negotiations with His Britannic Majesty, in order to effect alterations in the Treaty." The vote against Burr's motion, twenty to ten, demonstrated that the Federalists had the necessary votes; but on the very next day it appeared that perhaps they did not have them, after all. Jacob Read, a Federalist newcomer from South Carolina, proposed to amend the motion for ratification by demanding compensation for slaves confiscated at the end of the Revolution. Read was persuaded to withdraw the motion, but southern Republicans introduced it again, only to have it beaten, fifteen to thirteen. Afterward the southern Federalists came back into line, and on June 24, by the precise constitutional margin, the Senate ratified the treaty.

Five days later Benjamin Franklin Bache, editor of the least restrained of the Republican newspapers, the Philadelphia *Aurora*, publicly broke the silence on the treaty, publishing an abstract taken from a full copy supplied him by Senator Stevens Thomson Mason of Virginia. After three more days Bache had printed up, in pamphlet form, a huge quantity of full copies of the treaty (including the rejected Article XII) and had set out for New York and New England to reap a tidy sum from their sale. By mid July, copies were spread all over New England; by the twenty-fifth the treaty had also been published in Charleston and Savannah.

A wave of protest meetings followed—and, significantly, in several places even preceded—the revelation of the terms of the treaty. In Boston, mass meetings, organized by the mechanic-turned-Republican-politician Benjamin Austin, condemned Jay and his treaty before the terms of the treaty were known, and impressive numbers of signatures were gathered for antitreaty petitions. The town was already ablaze with emotion, a mob having burned the privateer *Betsy*; but the skill with which the frenzy was redirected against Jay's Treaty attests to long planning and careful organizing by Austin and his allies. A similar pattern was repeated in port towns all over New England. In New York, ironically, Jay had just been elected governor, without any activity on his part, and on July 1, the day he was inaugurated, the first abstract was published in the city. On the fourth, the Independence Day celebrations were turned into denunciations of the new governor and his treaty. On the nineteenth a massive "Town Meeting," attended by nearly five thousand people—mainly workers off for the dinner hour at noon, in accordance with the plans of the meeting's organizers—was almost riotous in its disapproval of the treaty. Hamilton attempted to address the crowd, but his voice was drowned in a sea of "hissings, coughings, and humphing," and (according to some reports) stones were thrown that drew blood. Before the afternoon was over, Hamilton had challenged an officer of the New York Democratic Society to a duel (which was never fought), and a resolutions committee had been appointed to draw up a list of objections to the treaty. Several other meetings followed, and twenty-eight specific objections were presented and approved. In Philadelphia the story was almost identical. It was reported that Jay could walk from one end of the country to the other in the dead of night, finding his way with the light from dummies of himself burning in effigy.

The thoroughness of the Republicans' organization against the treaty caught the Federalists unprepared. For once, Hamilton, who did not especially like the treaty but recognized that any treaty was better than none, was not alert to the schemes of his adversaries. Few Northern Federalist politicians, in fact, were armed with anything to say in defense of the treaty; for they naively assumed, without thinking much about it, that any treaty of "Amity and Commerce" with Great Britain would be popularly acceptable because it was in the interest of the United States. Had they been ready with a defense of the treaty, the public reaction north of Baltimore would doubtless have been different, for they won great popular support when they finally began to organize their campaign in August. But the Republicans were better prepared and shrewder, and they carried the first round.

South of Baltimore was another story. Southern reaction to the treaty was overwhelming and spontaneous. Epitomizing part of the reaction was the conduct of John Rutledge of South Carolina, a civilian hero of the Revolution, a principal architect of the Constitution, an arch-Federalist, and Washington's nominee for the Chief Justiceship vacated by Jay. Rutledge was said to have been a bit demented as a result of the recent death of his wife; for whatever reason, he ranted and raved on the streets of Charleston in denunciation of the treaty—on the logical but peculiar ground that the arbitration commissions established by the treaty removed jurisdiction of suits for debt from the American courts and thereby subverted the Constitution. In time, his antitreaty speeches and rumors of his insanity would cost Rutledge senatorial confirmation of his appointment, though he actually heard and ruled upon a few cases in his interim capacity. But the vehemence of his reaction to the treaty was typical of the reaction of the entire South. Underlying the vehemence, throughout the region, were three considerations: fear of signing any treaty with a power that actively engaged in the arming of Indians and rebel slaves, anger at not not being compensated for slaves that were taken off at the end of the Revolution, and fear of being held responsible for debts that were overdue to British subjects.

Protests against the treaty, of both the organized and the spontaneous variety, came too late to affect the Senate's vote, but they had a political aim nonetheless. President Washington had yet to

163

sign the treaty, and if he could be convinced that the American people were overwhelmingly opposed to it, he might never sign it.

At just that point the British government—which was far less concerned about American opinion than the French were—did something that came perilously close to preventing Washington from signing. Unfavorable weather in Britain had ruined the winter wheat crop, and by spring the country faced a severe shortage of food. France and the rest of western Europe were short as well, and American exporters of wheat and rice sent out their cargoes in the expectation of making handsome profits. But on April 24 the British issued a new Order in Council, instructing the commanders of all naval vessels to seize every ship they encountered, of whatever nation, that was carrying grain to France or French-occupied areas. The commanders were told not to be "over nice or scrupulous respecting the nature of the papers of those ships" and to haul them straightway to England. There the cargoes would be sold at a "fair price"; it was just that the Royal Navy was to prevent Americans or anybody else from selling grain to France when Englishmen were hungry. For months after the issuance of the order, the British regularly seized American vessels and hauled them in, sometimes as many as nine at a time. The first reports of such seizures reached Philadelphia at the end of June, just after the Senate had ratified the treaty.

Washington was furious. Randolph, who was preparing an analysis of the treaty for the president, told his chief that the switch in British policy was "too irreconcilable with a state of harmony, for the treaty to be put in motion during its existence." Every member of the cabinet except Hamilton's replacement, Oliver Wolcott, concurred; and Hamilton himself concurred. Accordingly, Washington instructed Randolph to inform Hammond, the British minister, that if the reports of the Order in Council and the seizures proved to be accurate, the president would require "farther time to determine on the Course of Proceeding which . . . it may be expedient for him to adopt." Hamilton urged an even stronger protest, suggesting that an exchange of ratifications be withheld "till the order is rescinded; since the U. States cannot ever give an implied sanction to the principle."

But then, just as the Republicans seemed to have rejection of the treaty within reach, a totally unexpected development took place. Some months earlier H.M.S. *Cerberus* had captured the French ship *Jean Bart*, which happened to be carrying secret dispatches from Joseph Fauchet to his superiors in France. Among the dispatches was one in which Fauchet reported, in ambiguous language, that Randolph had sought a French bribe to induce certain unnamed Americans to put down the Whisky Rebellion, which Randolph represented as British-inspired. "Thus," concluded Fauchet, "the pretended patriots of America have already their scale of prices!" The captured document found its way to Lord Grenville, who forwarded it to Hammond with instructions to place it in the hands of "well disposed Persons in America" when the opportune moment should arise.[1]

The moment arose in July of 1795. Washington had returned to Mount Vernon, taking the unsigned treaty with him; Hammond showed Fauchet's letter to Wolcott. Wolcott took the original and showed it to Attorney General William Bradford and to Timothy Pickering, who had succeeded Knox as secretary of war, and Pickering immediately wrote Washington, requesting his return on an urgent, confidential matter. The president hastened to Philadelphia and, upon reading the dispatches, concluded instantly that Randolph had been trying to enrich himself and various Republican friends by trifling with national security. At a full meeting of the cabinet he required Randolph to read the dispatches, then asked him for an explanation of his conduct. Neither then nor later was Randolph able to offer a satisfactory explanation, and he was forced to resign. Before he did so, Washington subjected him to the humiliation of preparing and presenting to Hammond an announcement that Washington was signing Jay's Treaty, together with an explanation of the decision "and a confession of the Secretary's failure." Thus, in a fit of rage, or outrage, President Washington signed the treaty against his own best judgment and against the advice of his most trusted intimates.

Meanwhile, on another front, the administration was almost unconsciously scoring a diplomatic triumph. For a variety of reasons Thomas Pinckney had delayed several months before leaving from London, his regular diplomatic post, for Madrid, where Washington

---

[1] Historians have generally assumed that Randolph was guilty of soliciting a French bribe. Irving Brant, in "Edmund Randolph, Not Guilty!" *William and Mary Quarterly*, 7 (1950):180–189, argues strongly that Randolph was misunderstood and that the case against him hinged on certain key mistranslations. The present writer is not convinced of Randolph's innocence, but whether he was or was not guilty is of secondary importance. What is important is that Washington believed him guilty and acted accordingly.

had sent him as minister extraordinary on invitation of Godoy. The delay was both fortuitous and fortunate, for by the time Pinckney left London in May of 1795, Godoy had deeply committed himself and his country in some elaborate dealings. The French, having soundly trounced the Spanish in their military encounters so far, were demanding concessions from Spain as the price of a negotiated peace and were particularly interested in the reacquisition of Louisiana. Godoy was, in fact, not especially interested in retaining Louisiana; it was traditionally French anyway, it was not militarily defensible against attacks by either British or Americans from the north, and efforts to unify the southwestern Indians against the Americans had been expensive failures. But before dumping Louisiana, Godoy proposed to put it to good use. In the Treaty of Basel (June 22, 1795), Spain retained Louisiana and bought its way out of the First Coalition by ceding Santo Domingo to France. That manuever effectively destroyed British designs on the island and had the incidental advantage of saddling the French with an insupportable "blessing," for the black rebels under Toussaint had gone too far to be controlled by any white peoples.

Then, before passing along another indefensible gem to the French, in the form of Louisiana—which Godoy fully intended to do—the wily Spaniard proposed to insure its indefensibility. Enter Thomas Pinckney, hoping to capitalize upon what appeared to be Spanish weakness and to secure rights to navigation of the Mississippi. To Pinckney's surprise, Godoy greeted him with a proposal that Spain and the United States enter a military alliance, ultimately to include France, with mutual guarantees of territory in America. Pinckney replied that the United States wanted no part of European alliances and could not offer any guarantees of Spanish territory. Instead, he said, the talks should concentrate upon the right of Americans to free navigation of the river and upon the establishment of a port, preferably New Orleans, where Americans would have the privilege of "deposit" for the transshipment of goods from river boats to ocean-going ships. For good measure, Pinckney insisted that Spain recognize the thirty-first parallel as the southern boundary of the United States (which Spain had never done, despite the Anglo-American treaty of 1783) and renounce Indian agitation as a means of protecting Spanish interests in the area.

Pinckney was actually in no position to demand anything; like Jay before him, he could reasonably expect only what the European power found it advantageous to concede. Godoy found it advantageous to grant the United States the privilege (though not to admit the right) of navigation of the Mississippi through Spanish territory, along with the privilege of deposit at New Orleans for three years—renewable afterwards there or at some other place on the river—and to accept the thirty-first parallel and to pledge not to incite any Indians against citizens or settlements of the United States. In addition, since it cost him nothing, Godoy agreed to incorporate into the treaty a full statement of American doctrines about the freedom of the seas. All this was included in the Treaty of San Lorenzo, signed by Godoy and Pinckney in Madrid on October 27, 1795.

American historians have generally treated Godoy as a fop and a fool and have regarded Pinckney as something of a hero, as Americans did at the time. But Godoy knew what he was about. The British had failed Spain in the First Coalition, and in the treaties of Basel and San Lorenzo, Godoy exacted revenge upon them by frustrating their plans for territorial aggrandizement in the New World. The Americans were a threat to the Spanish empire in America, and by sacrificing a part of it that was not truly Spanish—Louisiana—he fended off the expansionist and land-hungry Americans for a quarter of a century. As to the French, Spanish alliance with them was unavoidable after the First Coalition failed, but Godoy fed their unrealistic dreams of restoring their American empire (meanwhile declining to honor the Treaty of San Lorenzo until, in a second treaty of the same name, he had retroceded Louisiana to France) and, by so doing, sapped French fighting forces and the French treasury into the bargain. And in the course of time it was the Spaniards who humbled the proud heir of the French Revolution, Napoleon Bonaparte, and brought him to his knees.

Jay's Treaty and Pinckney's Treaty, taken together, brought enormous advantages to the United States, three sets of gains that partisans in America generally had regarded as mutually exclusive: neutrality, commercial prosperity, and territorial expansion. The most euphoric American in 1793 might have regarded any two of these as worth the sacrifice of the third. So far, a maelstrom in Europe that might have engulfed the United States had been turned to the favor of the new republic, and if the achievement was due as much to luck as to American diplomatic skill, it nonetheless was a large achievement for the Washington administration.

But it was almost erased in the next few months by an interplay between American enthusiasm, greed, and politics. Enthusiasm was mainly responsible for a diplomatic tangle that arose in the Northwest. General Anthony Wayne followed up his victories in the area by convening various Indian chieftans at Fort Greenville in the spring of 1795. There and then he dictated a treaty whereby the Indians agreed, among other things, that all traders who entered their territory without licenses from the United States would be captured and turned over to American authorities. Wayne was merely acting on the principle that when an enemy is defeated, one extracts every possible concession from him; he disregarded the fact that his Treaty of Greenville contravened Jay's Treaty, which explicitly guaranteed Indian trading rights to Englishmen as well as to Americans. London, upon hearing the news of Greenville, instructed Dorchester not to surrender or dismantle any British posts in American territory until the matter had been straightened out, and it appeared briefly that the whole cycle of troubles in the West might start all over again. Time and chance worked things out, but Anglo-American relations were unnecessarily strained for several more months.

Greed was most vigorously at work in the Southwest. William Blount, sometimes member of the Philadelphia Constitutional Convention and congressman from North Carolina, now territorial governor of Tennessee, had become deeply involved in investments in vacant lands. He had hoped that the United States would join France in war against Spain and thus clear his lands for him by fighting against Spain's erstwhile ally, the Creek Indians. He had also hoped that a host of European immigrants would flock to America, avid to buy his lands. The events of 1794–1795 frustrated both sets of hopes and left him owning more than a million acres of land and tottering on bankruptcy. Late in 1795 Blount talked with his friend and associate John Chisholm, sometime British soldier and Indian agent, and laid plans for a filibustering attack upon Spanish possessions, to be manned by frontiersmen and financed by Great Britain. In the ensuing carnage, Blount and Chisholm hoped, both Indians and Spaniards might be ousted from the area. Negotiations with Robert Liston, successor to George Hammond as British minister to the United States, were set in train. They would fail, but they would also keep America's international relations unsettled for some time.

Domestic politics proved to be the most unsettling influence of all, as would be the norm in the future. President Washington—like Adams, Jefferson, Lincoln, both Roosevelts, Truman, and Nixon after him—attempted to direct America's foreign relations from the perspective of the executive branch, with a view toward advancing the interests and ideals of the United States. The interests and aspirations of other powers constituted a second ingredient in the equation, and perhaps chance or coincidence needed to be reckoned as a third; but in America there was still a fourth ingredient, public opinion as expressed through pressure groups and partisan politics. To its great credit, perhaps ranking as its greatest achievement except for the Hamiltonian fiscal system, the Washington administration understood all these complex ingredients and managed them with consummate skill.

First among the orders of business, in regard to domestic politics, was the defusing of popular antagonism toward Jay's Treaty. Hamilton took up his pen in the cause, authoring (with some assistance from King and Jay) a series of articles under the pseudonym Camillus. So heavy-handed were these articles that the Republican *Independent Chronicle* of Boston could dismiss them as "proverbial for prolixity and verbosity," and Jefferson, when the series started, bought copies and circulated them among his friends and neighbors in Virginia as illustrations of the absurdity of the pro-British Federalist position. But Hamilton hammered on, and his arguments began to take on the proportions and persuasiveness of the monumental Federalist essays of 1788; and soon Jefferson was pronouncing Hamilton a "colossus" to the cause of the Federalists and frantically urging Madison to find someone who could do battle with him. Instead, other Federalists penned powerful defenses of the treaty, until there were no arguments left against it.

Equally to the point, perhaps more so, was a hard grass-roots counterattack by the Federalists. In Boston and the outports of Massachusetts, Federalists staged public meetings that resulted in rousing endorsements of Jay's Treaty; and by fall, petition drives in the back country had brought more than twice as many signatures in favor of the treaty as Republicans had been able to gather against it. In Connecticut, Rhode Island, and New Hampshire such efforts were equally effective; by October the only vocal opponents of the treaty were merchants with vested interests in trade with France or the French West Indies, speculators in lands on the Canadian border or in Canada, members of the Tammany Society and the fragmented Democratic-Republican societies, and scattered ideologues. In New York and Pennsylvania the "merchant-republicans," supported by interested adventurers and adherents of the factions of former Governor Clinton and incumbent Governor Mifflin, were able to keep the urban working classes divided more or less equally in regard to the treaty, but the back-country men overwhelmingly committed themselves to it by petitions or instructions to their state legislative representatives. In Baltimore the leading merchants—sympathetic toward France, still, because of the great influx of refugees from Saint-Domingue—drifted the other way, the powerful cliques headed by Samuel and Robert Smith shifting from Federalist allegiance to solid Republicanism. Elsewhere in the South, however, Federalists made decided gains. Frontiersmen, as frontiersmen, were persuaded that the efforts of Washington's administration, of Anthony Wayne in tandem with John Jay, had removed the British-Indian menace; and as Scotsmen and Ulstermen the Bible-quoting, staunchly Baptist and Presbyterian back-country men came to favor Britain over France almost to a man. Calvinists, whether of the New England or southern Scots variety, had no stomach for French papists, even though (and, perversely, because) the French had desecrated the Church.

And thus, by the time the Fourth Congress assembled for its first full session in December of 1795, the Republican enemies of Jay's Treaty had entirely lost the momentum. The treaty, in the best of possible worlds, left much to be desired; but the most reliable index of popular opinion, signatures on petitions, indicated that it was acceptable to a clear majority of the vocal portion of the electorate. Jay's Treaty was also paired with Pinckney's, about which there was no question of acceptability. Moreover, both treaties were constitutionally accomplished facts—negotiated by ministers approved by the president and the Senate, ratified by the Senate, signed by the president. But there was a catch, just one: Jay's Treaty, calling for the establishment of arbitration commissions, could not be carried into effect without congressional appropriations, and "money bills," as the Constitution clearly specified, could originate only in the House of Representatives. Whether the House, by virtue of its power over appropriations, thereby shared the Senate's power in regard to foreign affairs had not yet been settled. Settlement of the question was the last great constitutional issue of the presidency of George Washington.

James Madison and his friends in the House of Representatives had no doubts in the matter, but they proceeded with the utmost of caution. Though Congress convened in its first regular session on December 7, 1795, nearly three months elapsed before the treaty was mentioned in any way. Then on March 2 Congressman Edward Livingston of New York—speculator, dandy, erstwhile Federalist, and, since 1793, Francophile and Republican convert—brashly and against the wishes of the "older members" proposed a resolution requesting that the president provide the House with copies of all papers relevant to the negotiation of Jay's Treaty. Madison, Albert Gallatin of Pennsylvania, and several other Republican leaders saw the dangers implicit in that approach and tried to soften it, but in vain. Uriah Tracy, a Connecticut Federalist, sarcastically asked Livingston whether he sought the information for the purpose of impeaching Washington or Jay. Livingston rashly responded that the documents themselves would settle the point.

For the most part, however, Republicans and Federalists alike steered clear of that ticklish point and stuck to the main constitutional issue. The debate raged from March 7 to March 27. Republicans defended a loose, common-sense interpretation of the Constitution, reversing the narrow position they had taken when opposing the charter of the Bank of the United States five years earlier. For example, John Swanwick of Pennsylvania—a merchant, speculator, and sometime partner of Robert Morris before becoming a militant Republican—focused on the "supreme law" clause of the Constitution. The gradations in what was supreme law, he pointed out, were (1) the Constitution itself, (2) laws made in pursuance of the Constitution and approved by all three branches, and (3) treaties. It was absurd, he said, to suppose that the third could repeal the first two; and yet if the House were required to act as a mere rubber stamp in carrying out treaties, as Federalists were insisting, that is what would be happening. Livingston himself, arguing that this was "the most important question that has ever been agitated within these walls," held that if a treaty were paramount to statutory law, foreign influence could in effect supersede the elective branch of Congress. Madison outlined five possible interpretations of treaties as supreme law, dismissed as preposterous the idea that treaties could annul the Constitution itself, and concluded that the treaty-making power was cooperative with congressional power, meaning that the House had independent authority to consider treaties and decide whether it chose to implement them. Gallatin went to great lengths to show that the British House of Commons had a concurrent power with the House of Lords in determining whether to validate treaties.

All of which was interesting but, as Madison himself noted, rather beside the point. The question before the House was whether it should (and could) demand of the president the confidential or secret papers attending a particular diplomatic mission. Underlying the position of Livingston and the more daring Republicans were convictions that secrecy in government was inherently dangerous in a republic and that the papers would doubtless reveal some politically juicy information. In part, attitudes turned upon who was in and who was out of power: everybody was for full disclosure of public documents when the other fellow was in power, and only then. But there was a deeper issue involved, one that Americans had not resolved a century and three quarters later, namely, how much information should properly be withheld from the public in the interest of national security. Underlying that one, in turn, was a more mundane consideration. Nothing in the papers of the Jay mission in any way compromised national security or jeopardized relations with Great Britain; but while there were no state secrets, there were some tidbits that would be politically embarrassing to Federalists, such as Hamilton's letter covering Jay's instructions and Jay's delight at his reception by George III. The chief executive office under the Constitution is an elective office, albeit through the intermediary of the electoral college, and as an elective office it is by definition a political office. Even George Washington was bound by the stricture, if one fails to be politic one fails to be president.

There was one final consideration. For a century and more, the Western world had moved away from ideological and religious conflict between nations and toward the naked pursuit of power and plunder. But as it so moved, the codes of proper behavior became ever more strict. Diplomacy, like war, became limited by international law, which is to say by rules of the game as inviolable as the rules governing a jousting match between knights, a duel, or an athletic contest. Republicans generally took the position that where liberty and republican ideology were at stake, it was unthinkable to conduct international relations as a mere game, replete with secrecy, diplomatic formalities, and other pretentious niceties. Federalists generally held that such niceties—irrational though they might be —were essential, that unless diplomacy was treated as a game with rules, the barbarism of uncompromising religious or ideological warfare would once again plague the earth.

The House passed Livingston's resolution on March 24, after softening it with the significant qualification "excepting such of said papers as any existing negotiation may render improper to be disclosed." The grounds on which the resolution was based were that this particular treaty, Jay's, involved both appropriations and the regulation of commerce, which were properly within the purview of the House, and thus that papers of the mission contained information essential to suitable action.

172

President Washington replied with a thundering refusal. Laying his damaged but still great prestige on the line, he informed the members of the House that the papers were none of their business, that the papers were not "relative to any purpose under the cognizance of the House of Representatives, except that of an impeachment; which the resolution has not expressed." Moreover, he lectured the congressmen on the Constitution. Secrecy was sometimes necessary in the conduct of foreign relations, he said, and though that could be dangerous, the Constitution checked the danger by making the Senate, not the House, privy to such matters. The purpose of that arrangement was to protect the rights of states: senators represented states as states, and for that reason the Senate was vested with certain powers not shared with the House. As to the supposed right of the House to withhold approval of treaties, Washington made two telling points. One was that the House had been carrying treaties into effect without question for seven years, and none of its members had once asserted a right to do otherwise; so it was a bit late in the day to claim the right on the present occasion. The second was that, as the official journal showed, it had been explicitly proposed in the Constitutional Convention that "no Treaty should be binding on the United States which was not ratified by a law," and that proposal was overwhelmingly rejected. Among those who had opposed the proposal, the president could have added, had been James Madison.

A total constitutional impasse had been reached. Angrily, the House went on record as insisting that it did have the right see the papers, but it was clear that there was no way to pry them from George Washington. There followed a tedious debate, consuming the entire month of April, on the substantive question of whether the House would appropriate the funds (about $90,000) necessary to carry the treaty into effect. Madison gave a speech lasting several hours and refuting the president's position, point by point, and various Republicans made desultory objections to the commercial provisions of the treaty, but it became unmistakably clear that the weight of the objections fell on two things: that there would be no compensation for confiscated slaves and that private debts to British merchants would be paid. And underlying the objections was a political aim. As it was put by John Beckley, clerk of the House and ex-officio national chairman of the Republican party, the goal was to defeat the treaty and thereby pave the way for "a Republican president to succeed Mr. Washington."

While the House debated, Federalists went to work out of

doors in the most intensive campaign of pressure politics the nation had yet known. Hamilton influenced banks to restrict loans to merchants until the House executed the treaty and, even more effectively, induced the leading insurance brokers in New York and Philadelphia to stop writing policies on all shipping. Thus inspired, merchants supported door-to-door petition drives, which in New York City alone resulted in thirty-two hundred protreaty signatures. Since that was, as Hamilton noted, "within about 300 of the highest poll we ever had in this city on *both sides* at the most controverted election," New York congressmen could ignore the petitions only on peril of their public careers. Meanwhile, in the back country everywhere, desire for evacuation of the British posts on the treaty's schedule (June 1, 1796) was great, and the desire was fanned by rumors that rejection of the treaty would result in renewed Indian wars. To put more direct pressure on the House, Federalist senators threatened to reject Pinckney's Treaty if the House thwarted Jay's. By such means, opposition in the House was chipped away.

The climax of Federalist efforts came on April 28, when Fisher Ames delivered a brilliant speech, one of the most famous in the history of the House. Beginning with a profound statement of the skeptical Federalist view of man and society, then moving through the great advantages the treaty would bring the nation and the dishonor that would result from rejection, he closed with a vivid description of the risks of renewed Indian war. By rejecting the treaty and thereby the posts, he said, "we light the savage fires, we bind the victims. . . . You are a father—the blood of your sons shall fatten your corn-field: you are a mother—the war whoop shall wake the sleep of the cradle."

It was said that when Ames sat down, there was scarcely a dry eye in the House. In any event, when the vote on implementing the treaty was taken in committee of the whole the next day, the result was a tie, and Speaker of the House Frederick Muhlenberg, a Republican, cast the deciding vote in favor. A day later the full House voted to support the treaty, 51 to 48.

Thus the Republicans' grand political strategy—to transform the first blush of hostility against Jay's Treaty into the central campaign issue of 1796—more or less fizzled. The organization created for the purpose survived, however, even though the issue failed, and the organization was far better suited for a nationwide campaign than the predecessor Democratic-Republican societies had been. Two other developments—one unrelated to the treaty fight and the other a by-product of it—unfolded while the House was locked in debate, and each had an important bearing on the election as well as on the future course of American politics. The first was a decision of the United States Supreme Court, reached without a chief justice, since Rutledge had been rejected by the Senate and his successor, Oliver Ellsworth, did not take his seat until after the arguments had been heard. On March 8, 1796, in the case of *Hylton* v. *United States*, the court held that a carriage tax levied in 1794 at the suggestion of Hamilton was not a direct tax but an excise. The constitutional significance of the case was that in it the Court ruled for the first time on the constitutionality of an act of Congress. The political significance was that in upholding the tax, which fell mainly upon Virginia and South Carolina aristocrats to whom elegant carriages were a way of life, the Supreme Court convinced southern Republicans that it was futile to appeal to the federal courts to support their constitutional theories. The lesson was the more painful because Alexander Hamilton, as a private attorney, was brought in by the Attorney General's office as special counsel to argue the case. Thenceforth the Republicans would seek to circumvent the Court (as they tried to do in the Virginia and Kentucky resolutions of 1798–1799) or to destroy it (as they tried to do under the presidency of Thomas Jefferson).

The other development was an election. In April of 1796, with the treaty fight still pending in the House, the state legislative elections were held in New York. The legislature elected then would choose presidential electors in the fall; and for the first time a state election turned almost exclusively on a national issue, for Jay's Treaty was what the election was all about. Federalists swept the elections, running especially strong in New York City and in Ulster and Dutchess counties, where Republicans had mounted their most intensive campaigns against the treaty in 1795, and in the frontier counties. Jay and his treaty had been vindicated at the polls. Moreover, the Federalists had twelve electoral votes sewed up even before the presidential campaign of 1796 properly began.

9

★★★★★

THE TRANSFER OF POWER,
AND AN EPILOGUE

One of Washington's apprehensions, when he first assumed the presidency, had been that his countrymen expected too much from him. "I fear," he said, that "if the issue of public measures should not correspond with their sanguine expectations, they will turn the extravagant (and I may say undue) praises which they are heaping upon me at this moment, into equally extravagant (though I will fondly hope, unmerited) censures." Now, after the fight over Jay's Treaty had subsided, it was a great comfort to him just to know that he could safely retire and, as he put it, have dinner alone with his wife for the first time in twenty years. Not that his reputation was untarnished; indeed, he had been villified beyond his most horrid nightmares of seven years earlier, "in such exaggerated and indecent terms as could scarcely be applied to a Nero, a notorious defaulter, or even a common pickpocket." But the time was ripe for him to get out before things grew worse. In truth, his presidency had been vindicated, the policies of his administration had been creative and successful, and his country was prosperous and at peace with the outside world, if not with itself. But the political part of his office and the vulgarization of politics that had taken place during his presidency were such as to dissolve his immunity from personal attack, and that was more than he was willing to endure for his country. He was determined to escape, and the only compromise he was willing to make with that determination was to delay the announcement of his retirement until a month or two before the electoral college met in December, so as to keep Republicans off balance as long as possible.

Hamilton and other Federalist leaders knew that Washington must step down, but it was no easy matter to choose a successor. If ability had counted more than popularity and that elusive presidential requirement of "availability," Hamilton himself would have been the logical man; but any illusions that Hamilton might have held were dashed when James T. Callender, a wild-eyed Republican journalist, obtained information from Beckley and published a lurid version of Hamilton's affair with Maria Reynolds, together with insinuations that Hamilton had been guilty of stealing from the treasury. When Hamilton published an astonishingly frank account of the affair, his vindication as secretary was complete, his reputation as a man and husband was thoroughly tarnished, and his availability as a presidential candidate was nonexistent. Among non-Republicans in the South, only Patrick Henry had sufficient national stature; and though he had long since abandoned anti-Federalism for the ideal of the Union he truly loved, he was too old and feeble to be seriously considered as a candidate. The Pinckneys of South Carolina—Charles Cotesworth (currently minister to Paris) and his brother Thomas (hero of the treaty of San Lorenzo)—were acceptable but were nonentities north of Philadelphia. Only Jay in the Middle States had the stature, and he was now too controversial; Chief Justice Oliver Ellsworth of Cincinnati had the ability, but was virtually unknown south of Philadelphia. By process of elimination, that left Vice-President John Adams, who could hold New England and whose reputation as a defender of aristocracy might win votes in the Middle States, while his older reputation as an architect of Independence might win the support of some Republicans in the South. In informal caucus, the Federalist "party" leaders agreed to support Adams for president and Thomas Pinckney for vice-president.

But the nomination was quite unofficial: Washington had no part in it, and Hamilton, though willing to give it nominal support, actually viewed Adams as scarcely less dangerous than Jefferson and Madison. Accordingly, Hamilton publicly supported Adams but privately (and not especially quietly) schemed along different lines: he would reverse the roles, making Pinckney president and Adams vice-president again. Under the rules of the electoral college before they were changed by the Twelfth Amendment in 1804, presidential electors did not vote separately for president and vice-president. Instead, they voted for two candidates; the one receiving the most votes became president, and the one receiving the second most became vice-president. To avoid ties it had to be prearranged that one or two electors would "waste" their second votes. If enough Federalists electors were chosen, if Federalist electors in every state except one voted equally, or nearly so, for Adams and Pinckney, and if South Carolina, the exception, should cast its eight votes for Pinckney and for either the Republican candidate or an also-ran, Hamilton's plan would work. Pinckney would be the front-runner, Adams second.

The Republicans had the advantage that differences among Federalists gave them, and a few more besides. For one thing, Republicans now had a nationwide political organization, or something approaching it, and the Federalists had none. True, the Federalists had on their side the reputation of Washington, along with reverence for the Constitution, a popular record, the patronage machinery built by Hamilton, and, above all, inertia—the tendency of voters to stick with whoever is in and whatever is, so long as things are going reasonably well and neither disruptive issues nor disruptive candidates upset them. But the Republicans were far better equipped in two of the essentials of popular politics, namely, rhetoric and organization. As to the first, all the sloganeering for thirty years and more, during the conscious lifetimes of two-thirds of the population, worked in the Republicans' favor. As to the second, political organizations—formed in advocacy of state sovereignty during the Confederation period, augmented by alliances against the Constitution and against Hamilton's financial program, strengthened by the personal politics and interests of Virginia Republicans and by the local interests of Middle-States Republicans, intensified by the Francophile Democratic-Republican societies, and finally crystallized by the campaign against Jay's Treaty—were Republican almost exclusively. The Federalists were merely "friends of the government," held together by strong bonds of interest, culture, prejudice, and principle, but essentially unorganized. The Republicans were a genuine political party, and though they had few adherents east of the Hudson, they were otherwise national in scope.

The one thing the Republicans were lacking, or nearly lacking, was a candidate for president. Their obvious choice was Jefferson; but Jefferson was not merely being coy or paying insincere homage to an eighteenth-century convention that required candidates to appear reluctant to stand for office when he urged that Madison

179

or some other more deserving person should be the candidate. Jefferson had his flaws, but ambition was not one of them: he loved Monticello at least as devoutly as Washington loved Mount Vernon and had even less stomach for the vileness, the scurrility, the personal abuse, and the intrigue that had come to surround the presidential office. He also happened to be far more gifted than Washington in playing the game that those conditions imposed, but he was as yet neither aware nor willing to admit that such was true. He therefore declined the "nomination," made by a caucus of Republican congressmen much in the same way that Federalists had chosen Adams, until the very eve of the election. Indeed, it was early October before John Beckley, managing Jefferson's campaign in Pennsylvania, could assure supporters that Jefferson would serve if elected. Anticlimactically, but not without its portents for the future, Aaron Burr was agreed upon as the Republicans' vice-presidential candidate.

The conditions of the contest were complex and diverse. The most crucial factor was that it was not a popular election, at least by modern standards. Though Republicans depicted the rivalry as being between aristocrats (Federalists) and the people (themselves), the decision was almost entirely in the hands of aristocrats—at least in the narrow political sense of the term, meaning a governing few. The candidates did not campaign in their own behalf, neither through speeches, personal appearances, platforms, and promises nor through written propaganda, though all these methods were customarily used in state and congressional elections. Moreover, the presidential electors who made the actual choice were not bound by custom, law, or party discipline to support anyone, they were free agents; though most were pledged to vote for one pair of candidates or the other, all had the privilege of voting as they pleased, and quite a number exercised that privilege. More important yet, a large percentage of the electors were chosen not by the voters but by the members of the state legislatures, whom the voters had chosen for reasons other than their attitudes toward the presidency. The forty-seven electors for the states of Rhode Island, Connecticut, New York, New Jersey, Delaware, South Carolina, and Vermont were chosen by the legislatures; and so were nine of the sixteen for Massachusetts and, through a complex process, the three from Tennessee—all told, 59 of the total of 138. The legislatures in all those states but New Jersey and Delaware had been elected before Washington announced that he was not a candidate and thus before anyone knew who the candidates would be; and in only two of them, New York and Rhode Island, was there a functioning state-level two-party system. Only in Pennsylvania, Georgia, and New Hampshire, with twenty-five electoral votes among them, were the electors chosen by the voters at large. The forty-seven electors for Maryland, Virginia, North Carolina, and Kentucky were chosen by the voters in districts, as were seven of the electors for Massachusetts. It is to be observed that where the two parties were more or less evenly balanced, the district system worked in effect to reduce a state's net electoral votes or even to deprive it of any.

Of all the persons who attempted, in the framework of this intricate system, to appraise and direct the course of the presidential election as it shaped up during the summer and early fall of 1796, none was better informed than Alexander Hamilton. As Hamilton saw things, practically all of New England's thirty-nine votes were safely Federalist. There were scatterings of anti-administration forces in the area, to be sure, but none was strong enough to constitute a serious threat. In New Hampshire the popular senator and former governor John Langdon had left the ranks of the Federalists largely because their foreign policies were not favorable to his extensive trade as a private merchant with France and the French West Indies, and he was supported by a number of merchants and lumber exporters with similar interests and sentiments; but the indolent, religiously oriented hill folk of the interior—by far a majority of the state's population—viewed Jefferson and his friends as atheists and Jacobins whom only the depraved could support. A similar attitude prevailed in Vermont, despite the continued connivings of Ira Allen and the organizing of a Republican faction under Matthew Lyon, a radical land speculator and newspaper editor. Eastern Massachusetts still had an assortment of old republican ideologues and disgruntled merchants who opposed Federalist policies, but they did not even dominate their section of the state. The interior was conservatively Calvinist (in opposition to the religious liberalism which had sprung up around Boston), even more conservative politically, and solidly Federalist. In any event, the state would go Federalist in 1796, because Adams was on the ticket. The same was true of Connecticut; and besides, Connecticut was destined to remain staunchly Federalist long after Federalism disappeared elsewhere—because of satisfaction with Washington's and Hamilton's policies, fear of radicalism, a solidly entrenched and Federalist-oriented Congregational church, and an electoral system that virtually guaranteed the reelection of incumbents. In Rhode Island the slave-trading DeWolfs of Bristol, the French traders and speculators

181

Clark and Nightingale of Providence, and the mechanic-dominated Tammany Society of Newport constituted a base for a Republican party, but as yet they had been unable to transform either of the old factions of the state into an organization geared to national politics. Elsewhere matters were more diverse and complex but scarcely less predictable. Virginia and the Scotch-Irish-dominated southwestern states—Georgia, Tennessee, and Kentucky—were multifactional but solidly preferred Jefferson. The Federalists' only hope there was that Pinckney would also pick up a few votes. In North Carolina the Federalists were a little better off: they were greatly outnumbered but concentrated in a few areas, and they had succeeded in pushing through the legislature, in the name of democratization, a district election law that might salvage them three or four of the state's twelve electoral votes. The district system in Maryland insured a divided vote, though Federalists had a slight edge despite the apostasy to Republicanism of Samuel Smith, a powerful and wily Baltimore merchant. The nonslaveholding farmers of New Jersey and Delaware, like their counterparts in New England, were generally satisfied with Federalist government (it had, among other things, greatly reduced their burden of taxes and public debts) and could be expected to cast all their electoral votes for the Federalists. New York was already assured for the Federalists.

So far in the analysis, things were close, but the Federalists had a definite edge. The remaining and pivotal state was Pennsylvania, which had a highly developed and closely balanced two-party system. Federalists there, confident of their voting supremacy in the state as a whole, fought to have the electors chosen by the voters at large. Republicans, sharing that appraisal of voting strength, fought for a district system that would assure them a goodly share of the electoral votes. The Federalists had their way; and that, ironically, nearly cost them the presidency.

The campaign was marked by unrestrained journalism and endless intrigue, all aimed at the few dozen or few hundred persons in critical areas who could alter the outcome. Republican editors Benjamin Bache and J. T. Callender descended into the depths of scurrility, where they were met and matched by the Federalist William Cobbett and his *Porcupine's Gazette*. Possibly the most influential piece of propaganda published during the campaign was Washington's Farewell Address, dated September 17, which was moderate in tone and designed as a sober valedictory and a justification of his presidency but was also aimed at winning votes. The Frenchman Pierre Adét, recently recalled as minister to the United

States in protest against ratification of Jay's Treaty, remained in the country to invest French money and his talents as a propagandist in behalf of Jefferson, but the campaign backfired and probably cost Jefferson votes. The shrewdest operator of all was John Beckley, who engineered a campaign for Republican electors in Pennsylvania, employed an assortment of tricks, and succeeded in giving Jefferson a slim majority in the state.

The loss in Pennsylvania was one of two things that went wrong with Hamilton's scheme, for it made the election hair's-breadth close. The other was that the electors refused to behave as partisan automatons and spewed their votes around. No fewer than thirteen persons received votes; even Washington got votes from two die-hards. Virginia's electors, not trusting Burr, gave most of their second votes to the aged governor of Massachusetts, Samuel Adams. New Englanders, not trusting Pinckney, scattered their second votes among Ellsworth, Jay, John Henry, and Samuel Johnston. South Carolinians voted equally for the Federalist Pinckney and the Republican Jefferson. As a result, John Adams received seventy-one votes and became president, but Thomas Jefferson was second with sixty-eight against Pinckney's fifty-nine, and thus became vice-president.

Perhaps the election of 1796 was a fitting conclusion to Washington's presidency, for in it, despite the intensity of passion and rhetoric that had prevailed for some time, neither party clearly won, nobody rebelled, and nobody seceded. Historians have frequently remarked upon the "peaceable transfer" that took place four years later, when Jefferson and the Republicans succeeded Adams and the Federalists into power, but the way things went in 1796–1797 was possibly of greater significance. The preservation of the political union of American states had, by that time, been ensured, even though the Americans would continue to be possessed of diverse and often antagonistic cultures and economic interests.

On the occasion of his inauguration as president, John Adams was able to say, fairly, that the operation of the Constitution had "equaled the most sanguine expectations of its friends." It was also fair to say in retrospect that Hamilton's view of it as a "frail fabric" had been justified—for, as a set of rules governing the exercise of power, it had been woefully incomplete. Washington, Madison, Hamilton, and Ellsworth had filled in many of the details, by law and by example, and had breathed life into it. To that extent the grand experiment was already a proven success when Washington handed down the mantle of power.

To be sure, in two important respects, or sets of respects, unanticipated weaknesses had appeared. One set was described in Washington's farewell address. The spirits of party or faction, of sectional loyalty and animosity, and of partiality toward one foreign nation as opposed to another had manifested themselves repeatedly during Washington's presidency; and despite his sober warning against them, they would continue to beset the nation and all but tear it asunder.

The other weakness was that service to the nation had proved to be a frightful consumer of reputations. Even Washington himself, once regarded as holier than holy, had been subjected to personal abuse. On lower levels, no holds were barred. Adams had been and would continue to be denounced in the press as unfit, weak, perverse, a drunk, and a semimaniac, "liable to gusts of passion little short of frenzy, which drive him beyond the control of any rational reflection." Hamilton had been revealed as an adulterer and branded as a thief. Randolph's reputation had been destroyed as a traitor and solicitor of bribes, and James Monroe was recalled from Paris in 1796 under the cloud of charges that bordered on treason. Jefferson was castigated as an atheist, a bloodthirsty revolutionary, a leveler, a demagogue, and a fop. John Jay, in 1795, had been subjected to as much abuse, perhaps, as all the others put together. Under these circumstances, few persons of quality were anxious, or even willing, to serve their country again.

It is not easy to appraise what had been accomplished, or to assign credit and blame. Washington had conducted himself according to firm rules. He scrupulously avoided interfering in the affairs of Congress; he explored and then defined the ambiguous lines separating the executive branch from, and connecting it with, the Senate and the judiciary; and he established regular procedures for seeing to it that the president was personally responsible for the actions of department heads, except when they were acting directly in response to instructions or requests from Congress. He also ensured that the written records of the executive department would be full and clear, by insisting that lengthy reports in writing be submitted by department heads before conversations could begin.

The precedents that Washington established in these various respects were not, however, especially durable. Under his immediate successor, John Adams, members of the cabinet assumed independent executive responsibility. Under Adams's successor, Jefferson, the presidential practice of refusing to interfere in legislative proceedings was dropped. Under Andrew Jackson the idea that the presidential veto power properly extended only to constitutional questions and not to policy questions was abandoned. And so on: each of Washington's successors talked about the infallible example that Washington had set, then departed from it.

Moreover, the harsh reality of Washington's presidency is that the Father of his Country was not, except in a symbolic sense, particularly efficacious in establishing the permanence of his country, or even of the executive branch of his country's government. His administration was responsible for four monumental achievements: Hamilton's financial program, neutrality in a belligerent world, the opening of the Mississippi River, and the removal of the threat of red men and redcoats in the Northwest Territory. A brief review of each of these will clarify Washington's role.

Hamilton's financial system bound the nation with economic ties that ensured the perdurance of the national government, no matter how powerful the centrifugal forces in the country as a whole. The strength of the system lay not so much (as historians have been wont to suggest) in binding the interests of the wealthy and more influential members of society to the fate of the national government as it did in making energetic national government *convenient* to the society it served and the absence of such government indescribably inconvenient. A uniform and elastic currency, based upon a monetized public debt and a national bank, facilitated the ordinary activities of everyone, from the lowliest farmer to the greatest international merchant, and to dismantle the system would have occasioned dislocations of nightmarish complexity. That was the system. President Washington's role in creating it, apart from giving his implied blessing, was nothing at all—except when he very nearly prevented its creation by proposing to veto the charter of the bank.

The second great achievement—steering a course of neutrality —began with the Neutrality Proclamation of 1793 and culminated in Jay's Treaty, which precluded war with Britain despite the Franco-American alliance of 1778. Washington was indecisive in regard to the Neutrality Proclamation: he watered it down (lest he offend Jefferson) by excluding the word neutrality, and he followed Hamilton's advice to rebuff Genet only when Genet outrageously challenged Washington's own popularity. As to the Jay Treaty—which, despite its flaws, was a crucial part of the policy of peace—Washington originally opposed the mission, and he signed the treaty only in a fit of rage against Randolph, who quite possibly had been unjustly accused.

The opening of the Mississippi through Pinckney's Treaty was a significant step toward the future territorial expansion of the United States, and it also defused a set of conditions that might soon have led to war. Large as the achievement was, no American could take any special credit for it: It was simply dumped in the lap of the Washington administration by the ministry of Manuel Godoy of Spain.

As significant, toward the same end, was the removal of the threat posed by the British and the Indians in the Northwest Territory. Jay's Treaty formally brought an end to British activity in that area, but the end really came as a result of the brilliant military campaign waged by General Anthony Wayne. Washington appointed Wayne to the command, but only after previously appointing Arthur St. Clair, whose command was a disaster; and Wayne succeeded in 1794 only because he totally ignored Washington's explicit instructions to attack immediately.

We end, then, where we began. George Washington was indispensable, but only for what he was, not for what he did. He was the symbol of the presidency, the epitome of propriety in government, the means by which Americans accommodated the change from monarchy to republicanism, and the instrument by which an inconsequential people took its first steps toward becoming a great nation.

No one who followed Washington in the presidency could escape the legends that surrounded his tenure in the office, but the more perceptive among them shared a secret: Washington had done little in his own right, had often opposed the best measures of his subordinates, and had taken credit for achievements that he had no share in bringing about.

They kept the secret to themselves. After all, other people had to be president, too.

A Note on the Sources

Certain works and collections of documents, along with extensive files of contemporary newspapers, were used in the writing of virtually every chapter of this book. One was the best recent survey of the period, John C. Miller's *The Federalist Era, 1789–1801* (New York: Harper & Brothers, 1960). Extremely valuable, rich in detail as well as in understanding, is volume 4 of a much older work, Richard Hildreth's *The History of the United States of America*, 6 vols. (New York: Harper & Brothers, 1849–1856). Also rich in detail, though far less so in interpretive value, are volume 6 of Douglas Southall Freeman's *George Washington* (New York: Charles Scribner's Sons, 1956) and the seventh and final volume in that monumental work, written from Freeman's notes by John Alexander Carroll and Mary Wells Ashworth and published in 1957. A crucial work is Leonard D. White, *The Federalists: A Study in Administrative History* (New York: Macmillan Co., 1948). Three sets of published writings of Founding Fathers are also indispensable to any student of the period: *The Papers of Thomas Jefferson*, ed. Julian P. Boyd, 21 vols. to date, extending to 1791 (Princeton, N.J.: Princeton University Press, 1950–); *The Papers of Alexander Hamilton*, ed. Harold C. Syrett and Jacob E. Cooke, 15 vols. to date, extending to 1794 (New York: Columbia University Press, 1961–); and *The Writings of George Washington*, ed. John C. Fitzpatrick, 39 vols. (Washington, D.C.: Government Printing Office, 1931–1944). Finally, of considerable value on a variety of aspects of the subject is U.S. Bureau of the Census, *Historical Statistics of the United States, Colonial Times to 1957* (Washington, D.C.: Government Printing Office, 1960).

The following citations comprehend the principal additional works and sources that were used in the writing of each chapter individually. Asterisks indicate the sources of direct quotations. A fuller exposition of source materials follows in the Historiographical and Bibliographical Essay.

CHAPTER 1

This survey chapter is based largely upon the author's years of research in primary sources—correspondence, newspapers, pamphlets, tax records, travel accounts, and so on—and upon study of countless works, most of them antiquarian, of local history. Other materials used include U.S. Bureau of the Census, *Heads of Families at the First Census of the United States, Taken in the Year 1790*, 12 vols. (Washington, D.C.: Government Printing Office, 1907–1908); American Council of Learned Societies, "Report of Committee on Linguistic and National Stocks in the Population of the United States [in 1790]," in *Annual Report of the American Historical Association for the Year 1931*, 1:103–441 (Washington, D.C.: Government Printing Office, 1932); J. H. Plumb, *England in the Eighteenth Century** (Baltimore, Md.: Penguin Books, 1950); J. R. Pole, *Political Representation in England and the Origins of the American Republic* (Berkeley, Calif.: University of California Press, 1971); James G. Leyburn, *The Scotch-Irish: A Social History* (Chapel Hill, N.C.: University of North Carolina Press, 1962); Henry Adams, *The United States in 1800** (Ithaca, N.Y.: Cornell University Press, 1955); J. Hector St. John Crèvecoeur, *Letters from an American Farmer** (New York: Dolphin Books, 1961). The Washington quotations are from the *Washington Papers*, ed. Fitzpatrick.

CHAPTER 2

Freeman, *Washington*, vol. 6; James Thomas Flexner, *George Washington and the New Nation, 1783–1793** (Boston, Mass.: Little, Brown & Co., 1969); William Maclay, *Journal of William Maclay*,* ed. Edgard S. Maclay (New York: D. Appleton & Co., 1890); *Abridgment of the Debates of Congress, from 1789 to 1856*, vol. 1 (New York: D. Appleton & Co., 1857); Page Smith, *John Adams*, 2 vols. (Garden City, N.Y.: Doubleday, 1962); Irving Brant, *James Madison*, 6 vols. (Indianapolis, Ind.: Bobbs-Merrill, 1941–1961); Ralph L. Ketcham, *James Madison: A Biography* (New York: Macmillan Co., 1971); Edward Dumbauld, *The Bill of Rights and What It Means Today* (Norman, Okla.: University of Oklahoma Press, 1957); Robert Allen Rutland, *The Birth of the Bill of Rights, 1776–1791* (Chapel Hill, N.C.: University of North Carolina Press, 1955); Julius Goebel, Jr., *History of the Supreme Court of the United States: Volume I, Antecedents and Beginnings to 1801* (New York: Macmillan Co., 1971); Charles Warren, *The Supreme Court in United States History*, 2 vols. (Boston, Mass.: Little, Brown & Co., 1923).

CHAPTER 3

Hamilton Papers,* ed. Syrett and Cooke, especially vols. 6 and

7; John C. Miller, *Alexander Hamilton: Portrait in Paradox* (New York: Harper & Brothers, 1959); Broaddus Mitchell, *Alexander Hamilton*, 2 vols. (New York: Macmillan Co., 1957, 1962); E. James Ferguson, *The Power of the Purse: A History of American Public Finance, 1776–1790* (Chapel Hill, N.C.: University of North Carolina Press, 1961); Records of the Loan of 1790, manuscripts in the Fiscal Section of the National Archives, Washington, D.C., and the related records, bearing various titles, in the Massachusetts Archives, Boston, and the Rhode Island Archives, Providence; Bray Hammond, *Banks and Politics in America, from the Revolution to the Civil War* (Princeton, N.J.: Princeton University Press, 1957); *Abridgment of Debates of Congress;* P. G. M. Dickson, *The Financial Revolution in England: A Study in the Development of Public Credit, 1688–1756* (London, Macmillan, 1967); Isaac Kramnick, *Bolingbroke and His Circle* (Cambridge, Mass.: Harvard University Press, 1968).

CHAPTER 4

All the materials cited for chapter three, together with Brant, *Madison*, vol. 4; Ketcham, *Madison*; Lewis C. Gray, *History of Agriculture in the Southern United States to 1860*, 2 vols. (Washington, D.C.: Carnegie Institution, 1933); Winfred E. A. Bernhard, *Fisher Ames, Federalist and Statesman, 1758–1808* (Chapel Hill, N.C.: University of North Carolina Press, 1965); Kenneth R. Bowling, "The Bank Bill, the Capital City, and President Washington," in *Capitol Studies*, 1,1 (Spring 1972):59–71; Jacob E. Cooke, "The Compromise of 1790," *William and Mary Quarterly*, 3d ser., 27,4 (Oct. 1970):523–545; Kenneth R. Bowling, "Dinner at Jefferson's: A Note on Jacob E. Cooke's 'The Compromise of 1790,'" ibid., 28,4 (Oct. 1971):629–640; Henry Adams, *John Randolph** (Greenwich, Conn.: Fawcett Publications, 1961); Burton Alva Konkle, *Thomas Willing and the First American Financial System** (Philadelphia, Pa.: University of Pennsylvania Press, 1937); Miller, *Alexander Hamilton;* Jefferson Papers*, ed. Boyd; Edward Dumbauld, *Thomas Jefferson, American Tourist* (Norman, Okla.: University of Oklahoma Press, 1946); Alfred F. Young, *The Democratic Republicans of New York: The Origins, 1763–1797* (Chapel Hill, N.C.: University of North Carolina Press, 1967); Joseph S. Davis, *Essays in the Earlier History of American Corporations*, 2 vols. (Cambridge, Mass.: Harvard University Press, 1916, 1917).

CHAPTER 5

Young, *Democratic Republicans of New York;** Merrill D. Peterson, *Thomas Jefferson and the New Nation* (New York: Oxford University Press, 1970); Dumas Malone, *Jefferson and the Rights of Man* (Boston, Mass.: Little, Brown & Co., 1951); Ketcham, *Madison;* Noble E. Cunningham, Jr., *The Jeffersonian Republicans: The Formation of Party Organization, 1789–1801* (Chapel Hill, N.C.: University of North Carolina Press, 1957); Herbert S. Parmet and Marie B. Hecht, *Aaron Burr: Portrait of an Ambitious Man* (New York: Macmillan Co., 1967); the newspapers mentioned in the text; Clarence S. Brigham, *History and Bibliography of American Newspapers, 1690–1820,* 2 vols. (Worcester, Mass.: American Antiquarian Society, 1947); Lewis Leary, *That Rascal Freneau* (New Brunswick, N.J.: Rutgers University Press, 1941); Miller, *Federalist Era;** Miller, *Hamilton;* C. Peter Magrath, *Yazoo: Law and Politics in the New Republic, The Case of Fletcher v. Peck* (Providence, R.I.: Brown University Press, 1966); Harry M. Tinkcom, *The Republicans and Federalists in Pennsylvania, 1790–1801* (Harrisburg, Pa.: Pennsylvania Historical and Museum Commission, 1950); John H. Wolfe, *Jeffersonian Democracy in South Carolina* (Chapel Hill, N.C.: University of North Carolina Press, 1940); Delbert H. Gilpatrick, *Jeffersonian Democracy in North Carolina, 1789–1816* (New York: Columbia University Press, 1931); Carl E. Prince, *New Jersey's Jeffersonian Republicans: The Genesis of an Early Party Machine, 1789–1817* (Chapel Hill, N.C.: University of North Carolina Press, 1967); Paul Goodman, *The Democratic-Republicans of Massachusetts* (Cambridge, Mass.: Harvard University Press, 1964); Lee Lovely Verstandig, "The Emergence of the Two-Party System in Maryland, 1787–1796" (Ph.D. diss., Brown University, 1970).

CHAPTER 6

Georges Lefebvre, *The French Revolution,* 2 vols. (New York: Columbia University Press, 1962, 1964); Ray Allen Billington, *Westward Expansion: A History of the American Frontier* (New York: Macmillan Co., 1960); Alfred L. Burt, *The United States, Great Britain and British North America from the Revolution to the Establishment of Peace after the War of 1812* (New Haven, Conn.: Yale University Press, 1940); Arthur P. Whitaker, *The Spanish-American Frontier, 1783–1795* (Boston, Mass: Houghton-Mifflin, 1927); John W. Caughey, *McGillivray of the Creeks* (Norman,

Okla.: University of Oklahoma Press, 1938); Young, *Democratic Republicans of New York*; Miller, *Hamilton*;* Goebel, *Supreme Court*; Warren, *Supreme Court*; Eugene Perry Link, *Democratic-Republican Societies, 1790–1800* (New York: Columbia University Press, 1942); C. L. R. James, *The Black Jacobins* (2d ed., rev., New York: Vintage Books, 1963). In addition, the material in this and the next two chapters has been enriched by lengthy study of contemporary newspapers in all parts of the country and by seminar papers, done under my direction at Brown University in the early 1960s, by Barry Statham, Anthony Thompson, Lee L. Verstandig, John A. Worsley, and Franklin Coyle.

CHAPTER 7

Alexander De Conde, *Entangling Alliance: Politics & Diplomacy under George Washington* (Durham, N.C.: Duke University Press, 1958); Samuel Flagg Bemis, *Jay's Treaty* (New York: Macmillan Co., 1923) and *Pinckney's Treaty* (Baltimore, Md.: Johns Hopkins Press, 1926); Frank Monaghan, *John Jay** (New York and Indianapolis, Ind.: Bobbs-Merrill, 1935); Bradford Perkins, *The First Rapprochement: England and the United States, 1795–1805* (Berkeley: University of California Press, 1967; first printing by University of Pennsylvania Press, 1955); *Abridgment of Debates of Congress*; Lefebvre, *French Revolution*; Warren, *Supreme Court*; Leland D. Baldwin, *Whisky Rebels: The Story of a Frontier Uprising* (Pittsburgh, Pa.: University of Pittsburgh Press, 1939); Billington, *Westward Expansion*; James, *Black Jacobins*; Arthur P. Whitaker, *The Mississippi Question, 1795–1803: A Study in Trade, Politics, and Diplomacy* (New York: D. Appleton-Century, 1934) and *The Spanish American Frontier*; Burt, *U.S., Great Britain and British North America.*

CHAPTER 8

The principal sources used for chapter 8 are the same as those for chapter 7, plus *Abridgment of Debates*;* Young, *Democratic Republicans of New York*;* Miller, *Hamilton* and *Federalist Era*;* Parmet and Hecht, *Aaron Burr*; Joseph Charles, *The Origins of the American Party System: Three Essays* (New York: Harper & Brothers, 1961); Verstandig, "Two-Party System in Maryland"; Tinkcom, *Republicans and Federalists in Pennsylvania*; Warren, *Supreme Court*; Bernhard, *Fisher Ames.*

191

CHAPTER 9

A *Compilation of the Messages and Papers of the Presidents, 1789-1817,* ed. James D. Richardson, vol. 1 (Washington, D.C.: Government Printing Office, 1896); Miller, *Hamilton*; Peterson, *Jefferson*; Cunningham, *Jeffersonian Republicans*; Manning J. Dauer, *The Adams Federalists* (Baltimore, Md.: Johns Hopkins Press, 1953); Chilton Williamson, *American Suffrage: From Property to Democracy, 1760-1860* (Princeton, N.J.: Princeton University Press, 1960); and the monographic studies of state politics cited for the earlier chapters.

Historiographical and Bibliographical Note

Being essentially a nonideological people, the Americans of Washington's time rarely behaved in accordance with the dictates of dogma in the way that, say, the Girondists or Jacobins did in France. But they were not entirely comfortable about this characteristic: somehow it did not seem proper for the free citizens of a republic. One way they compensated or apologized for the supposed shortcoming was to dress their political rhetoric in ideological garb. More importantly, after each of their great political battles they vied anew in a different arena, each side trying to establish that it (and not the other) had been governed by the purest ideology. In that manner, mythology replaced ideology as a motivating principle in American life: he who controlled history—in the sense of what people believed had happened rather than what had actually happened—delimited (if he did not control) what could happen in the future.

Federalists got the jump on Republicans in this historiographical warfare, and as a consequence exercised an influence upon American life and values that far outlasted the period of their political supremacy. Already in 1799, a relatively obscure New England Federalist named Timothy Pitkin published his *Statistical Annals of the United States*, justifying his party's achievements in quantitative as well as philosophical terms. The next year came Parson Mason L. Weems's famous moralistic life of Washington. Shortly afterward appeared the first major interpretive work: Chief Justice John Marshall's *Life of Washington* (5 vols., 1804–1807). Volume 5, covering the years after 1789, so enraged President Jefferson that he hindered its circulation and, with the aid of Madison, tried long and diligently, though in vain, to have a Republican history of the 1790s written and circulated.

Washington became and remained the father figure: strong, pure, incorruptible, symbol of the nation but not of the people, object of idolization but not of love, a demigod not a mere man. Beneath him, as rivals for Fame or for ranking in the hagiology, were Adams, Madison, Jefferson, and Hamilton. Neither Adams nor

Madison had a strong enough or clear enough image, in their own time or afterward, to remain in contention. Jefferson and Hamilton, on the other hand, became the central figures of the American mythology. They came to personify two opposed views of government, of American destiny, of life, and of mankind—the one representing democracy, agrarianism, and states' rights, the other representing conservatism, capitalism, and nationalism. In political rhetoric Jefferson had the better of it much of the time; in written history and as history was used to indoctrinate children in schools, however, things were the other way around.

In the wave of nationalism that swept the country after the war of 1812, the Republican version of what had happened during the founding years was virtually submerged. A large number of American-history textbooks were published during the next generation, most of them written by New Englanders and based upon the Reverend Abiel Holmes's *American Annals* (2 vols., 1805), a survey of the history of all the colonies/states from their inception until 1800. The textbooks taught the young their duties as citizens and patriots, extolled New England ways as opposed to southern, denounced rebellions (except the Puritan Revolution and the War for Independence) and all resistance to established authority as the work of lawless rabble, and generally gave Federalist leaders and positions favorable treatment while slighting the Republicans. Biographies followed the same pattern. All Founding Fathers who were written about were exalted; but most biographies were about Federalists. John Sanderson's *Biography of the Signers to the Declaration of Independence* (9 vols., 1820–1827) praised the signers irrespective of their later politics; more typical and far more widely read were the biographical portions of the *McGuffey Readers*, which lauded Hamilton and omitted all reference to Jefferson. Jefferson finally found his first biographer (Henry S. Randall, 3 vols., 1858) on the eve of the Civil War, as did Madison (William Rives, 3 vols., 1859–1868) and John Adams (his grandson Charles Francis Adams, 1856).

As sectional tensions mounted in the late 1840s and the 1850s, two new major works on the early republic appeared, one written from the point of view of the South and the Republicans, the other from that of the North and the Federalists. In *The Southern-Republican* (4 vols., 1856–1857), George Tucker made Jefferson the patron saint of the southern cause on the eve of the Civil War; even in the South, the work was neither widely read at the time nor influential later. Richard Hildreth's *History of the United States of America* (to 1820) (6 vols., 1849–1856) was persuasive, carefully researched, and pro-Federalist; and it set a general interpretive pattern that all subsequent writers followed until well into the twentieth century.

In the wake of the Civil War, Jefferson was all but erased from the pages of respectable history, for he was stigmatized by identification with the defeated South; and thereafter (except in the South) Hamilton surpassed him even in the arena of political rhetoric, for Jefferson was now identified with slavery, states' rights, and radical agrarian opposition to industrial progress. Moreover, though the tradition and the mythology had wandered far from the past they supposedly described, neither the first generation of professionally trained academic historians (the "Scientific Historians," ca. 1880–1910, who tended to be pro-Federalist) nor the second (the "New Historians," ca. 1910–1940, who were generally pro-Republican) seriously challenged the Jefferson-Hamilton legend.

The most influential of the New Historians was Charles A. Beard, who accepted the traditional interpretive framework but gave it new meaning with an economic analysis. In his *Economic Origins of Jeffersonian Democracy* (1915), Beard picked up where his *An Economic Interpretation of the Constitution of the United States* (1913) had left off. Beard maintained that, with few exceptions, the alignments he had seen in the contest over the Constitution —merchants, shippers, speculators in public securities and lands, and other "personalty" interest groups (Federalists) against small farming and debtor groups (anti-Federalists)—continued to prevail into the 1790s. The Hamiltonian system, Beard argued, was designed for and supported by the first group and deleterious to and opposed by the second. But many wealthy southern planters who had supported the Constitution responded to Hamilton's program by crossing over and joining the anti-Federalists, who, under Jefferson's leadership, were beginning to call themselves Republicans. Jay's Treaty, which aligned the administration with Britain against Revolutionary France, intensified the "agrarian" resistance; and the lines hardened even more during Adams's administration. Finally in 1800 the nation's small farmers—united under the leadership of aristocratic planters, supported by urban working classes, and pursuing their own economic interests as avidly as the personalty interests under Hamilton had pursued theirs—succeeded in gaining control of the national government.

Beard's interpretation became the Revised Standard Version, so to speak, and went virtually unchallenged for more than four decades. Only in regard to one particular was there disagreement, and that concerned the specific time and issues that had brought about the hardening of the two-party system; no one questioned that a two-party system had emerged, that Jefferson and Hamilton had been the party organizers, and that their economic class bases had been as Beard depicted them. But, contrary to Beard's suggestion that parties were continuous from 1787–1788 onward (or from the 1760s or 1770s onward, as claimed in the work of Carl Becker and other New Historians), three other schools of thought developed. John S. Bassett, in *The Federalist System* (1906), maintained that the divisions of 1787–1788 collapsed and that permanent divisions arose only in response to Hamilton's financial program, especially the Bank of the United States. Orin G. Libby, whose work on the Constitution had provided much of the factual foundation for Beard's book on that subject, had also analyzed voting patterns in Congress and had concluded that there was no continuity of parties at any time before the beginning of the quasi war with France in 1798. Much later, in *The Origins of the American Party System* (1956), Joseph Charles maintained that parties developed and hardened in 1795 or thereabouts, over the issue of Jay's Treaty.

Meanwhile, the balance of popular sentiment and political rhetoric was once again tipping to Jefferson. President Theodore Roosevelt (1901–1909) was a thoroughgoing Hamiltonian, as he understood the term, and Herbert Croly's *The Promise of American Life* (1909) justified Roosevelt's presidency on a Hamiltonian (and strongly anti-Jeffersonian and anti-Jacksonian) basis; but Woodrow Wilson (1913–1921) was a thoroughgoing Jeffersonian, as he understood that term. Then, though the Republican party of the 1920s attempted to canonize Hamilton, the Democratic "scholar-statesman" Claude G. Bowers, in *Jefferson and Hamilton: The Struggle for Democracy in America* (1925) and *Jefferson in Power* (1936), reincarnated Jefferson as the champion of all good men (the poor, the oppressed, the farmers and workers, and twentieth-century Democrats) against the wicked (the rich, northern and eastern aristocrats, and modern Republicans). In 1932 the Democratic presidential candidate closed the debate, and it has not been re-opened by politicians: in his celebrated Commonwealth Club speech, Franklin Roosevelt declared that there were two traditions in America, that of the "haves," or Hamiltonians, and that of the "have nots," or Jeffersonians, and he pledged the New Deal and the Democratic party in support of the Jeffersonian way.

Even in our own irreverent times, the historian tampers with the legend of the Founding Fathers only with a caution not unmixed with trepidation, for neither the scholar nor the common man can readily accept challenges to his nation's sacred myths. In 1958 I published a large and arid tome called *We The People: The Economic Origins of the Constitution,* whose aim was to demonstrate that Beard's interpretation of the Constitution was quite inaccurate and a gross oversimplification of what had happened. The work was widely praised, in no small measure because many reviewers erroneously read it as an effort to restore the sainted Founding Fathers to the holy niches from which Beard had removed them. When, in 1965, I published *E Pluribus Unum: The Formation of the American Republic, 1776–1790,* my work was greeted with a considerably cooler reception, at least in some measure because I now attempted to show that the Founders were not only preoccupied with getting rich, but also drank intoxicants and not infrequently violated the Seventh Commandment. Between these dates Professor Leonard Levy published *Jefferson & Civil Liberties: The Darker Side* (1963), and though this was a work of thorough scholarship, it won its author a great deal of severe criticism even in the historical profession, for it abundantly documented what its title implied. In June of 1972 *American Heritage* published Professor Fawn Brodie's veritably irrefutable article showing that Jefferson sired several children by a slave concubine. The publication of it was an act of considerable courage on the parts of both the author and the editors; and the editors found it prudent, for the first time in the history of the magazine, to support an article with a full regalia of documentary notes.

Despite that atmosphere, a great many sound, scholarly monographs and articles on the founding years have been published, especially since World War II. The interpretation presented in the present work is an effort to create a new synthesis, respectful but not mythological, that will accommodate the best of the older works, the findings of the modern specialists, and my own researches in the primary sources. The materials I found most useful have been cited in the Note on the Sources. Other important and valuable works are cited below.

Abernethy, Thomas Perkins. *From Frontier to Plantation in Tennessee: A Study in Frontier Democracy.* Chapel Hill, N.C.: University of North Carolina Press, 1932.

Adams, John. *Diary and Autobiography.* Edited by Lyman H. Butterfield. 4 vols. Cambridge, Mass.: Harvard University Press, 1961.

Ammon, Harry. *The Genet Mission.* New York: W. W. Norton, 1973.

Borden, Morton. *Parties and Politics in the Early Republic, 1789–1815.* New York: Crowell, 1967.
———. *The Federalism of James A. Bayard.* New York: Columbia University Press, 1955.

Chambers, William N. *Political Parties in a New Nation: The American Experience, 1776–1809.* New York: Oxford University Press, 1963.

Chapelle, Howard I. *The History of the American Sailing Navy.* New York: W. W. Norton, 1949.

Clark, Victor S. *History of Manufactures in the United States.* 3 vols. Washington, D.C.: Carnegie Institution, 1916–1928.

Clauder, Anna C. *American Commerce As Affected by the Wars of the French Revolution and Napoleon, 1793–1812.* Philadelphia, Pa.: University of Pennsylvania Press, 1932.

Cresson, W. P. *James Monroe.* Chapel Hill, N.C.: University of North Carolina Press, 1946.

Crosskey, William W. *Politics and the Constitution in the History of the United States.* Chicago: University of Chicago Press, 1952.

Dangerfield, George. *Chancellor Robert R. Livingston of New York, 1746–1813.* New York: Harcourt, Brace, 1960.

Echeverria, Durand, tr. "General Collot's Plan for a Reconnaissance of the Ohio and Mississippi Valleys, 1796." *William and Mary Quarterly,* 9 (1952):512–520.

Fischer, David H. *The Revolution of American Conservatism: The Federalist Party in the Era of Jefferson Democracy.* New York: Harper & Row, 1965.

Graham, Gerald S. *Sea Power and British North America, 1783–1820.* Cambridge, Mass.: Harvard University Press, 1941.

Haskins, Charles Homer. *The Yazoo Land Companies.* New York: The Knickerbocker Press, 1891.

Jacobs, James R. *The Beginning of the U.S. Army, 1783–1812.*

Princeton, N.J.: Princeton University Press, 1947.

Kelly, Alfred H., and Harbison, Winfred A. *The American Constitution.* 4th ed. New York: W. W. Norton, 1970.

Koch, Adrienne. *Jefferson and Madison: The Great Collaboration.* New York: Knopf, 1950.

Kurtz, Stephen G. *The Presidency of John Adams: The Collapse of Federalism, 1795–1800.* Philadelphia, Pa.: University of Pennsylvania Press, 1957.

Kyte, George W. "A Spy on the Western Waters: The Military Intelligence Mission of General Collot in 1796." *Mississippi Valley Historical Review,* 34 (1947): 427–442.

Logan, Rayford W. *The Diplomatic Relations of the United States with Haiti, 1776–1891.* Chapel Hill, N.C.: University of North Carolina Press, 1941.

Lyon, E. W. *Louisiana in French Diplomacy, 1759–1804.* Norman, Okla.: University of Oklahoma Press, 1934.

Mahan, Alfred T. *The Influence of Sea Power upon the French Revolution and Empire, 1793–1812.* 2 vols. Boston, Mass.: Little, Brown & Co., copyright 1892.

Munroe, John A. *Federalist Delaware, 1775–1815.* New Brunswick, N.J.: Rutgers University Press, 1954.

Nettels, Curtis P. *The Emergence of a National Economy, 1775–1815.* New York: Holt, Rinehart & Winston, 1962.

North, Douglass C. *The Economic Growth of the United States, 1790–1860.* Englewood Cliffs, N.J.: Prentice-Hall, 1961.

Ostrogorski, M. I. *Democracy and the Organization of Political Parties.* 2 vols. New York: The Macmillan Co., 1902.

Pratt, Fletcher. *The Compact History of the United States Navy.* New York: Hawthorn Books, 1957.

Purcell, Richard J. *Connecticut in*

Transition, *1775–1818.* Washington, D.C.: American Historical Association, 1918.

Rogers, George C. *Evolution of a Federalist: William Loughton Smith of Charleston, 1758–1812.* Columbia, S.C.: University of South Carolina Press, 1962.

Rossiter, Clinton. *Seedtime of the Republic.* New York: Harcourt, Brace, 1953.

Rossman, Kenneth R. *Thomas Mifflin and the Politics of the American Revolution.* Chapel Hill, N.C.: University of North Carolina Press, 1952.

Simms, H. H. *Life of John Taylor.* Richmond, Va.: William Byrd Press, 1932.

Turner, Frederick J. "The Policy of France toward the Mississippi Valley in the Period of Washington and Adams." *American His-* *torical Review,* 10,2 (Jan. 1905): 249–279.

Turner, Kathryn B. "Federalist Policy and the Judiciary Act of 1801." *William and Mary Quarterly,* 22 (1965):3–32.

Varg, Paul A. *Foreign Policies of the Founding Fathers.* East Lansing, Mich.: Michigan State University Press, 1963.

Walters, Raymond, Jr. *Alexander James Dallas.* Philadelphia, Pa.: University of Pennsylvania Press, 1943.

————. *Albert Gallatin.* New York: The Macmillan Co., 1957.

Wandell, Samuel H., and Minnigerode, Meade. *Aaron Burr.* 2 vols. New York: G. P. Putnam's Sons, 1925.

Welch, Richard E. *Theodore Sedgwick, Federalist: A Political Portrait.* Middletown, Conn.: Wesleyan University Press, 1965.

Index